John D. Duncan

Under the Old Oak Tree

Holy Fire, Faith, and Fables in the Stories of Life

Under the Old Oak Tree
Holy Fire, Faith, and Fables in the Stories of Life

John D. Duncan

Published by Austin Brothers Publishing, Fort Worth, Texas
www.abpbooks.com

Copyright 2022 by John D. Duncan

The copyright supports and encourages the right to free expression. The purpose is to encourage writers and artists to continue producing work that enriches our culture.

Scanning, uploading, and distribution of this book without permission by the publisher is theft of the author's intellectual property. To obtain permission to use material from the book (other than for review purposes) contact terry@abpbooks.com.

ISBN: 978-1-7375807-7-5
Photo by Alexander Andrews on Unsplash

Printed in the United States of America
2022 -- First Edition

Austin Brothers
— PUBLISHING —
www.abpbooks.com

THE FAMILY

Martha Duncan
Judy, Amy and Scott, Jenifer and Tyler, Melanie and Patrick
Abigail, Ethan, Luke, Brooke, Barrett, Savannah,
And in memory of George D. Duncan, Sr.

Table of Contents

Spring

Bluebonnets	3
Her Name was Easter	5
Laughter Does a Family Good	7
Faith and a Flying Cat	10
Waiting for Green	14
Bluebonnet Blossoms and Randall Purvis	17
Glorious Spring	21
Words and Deeds	23
There is no "I" in Team	26
Running Wild	29
The House	31
God's Message Board	35
The Days After Easter	41
Pastors and Mavericks	45
Snowflakes Falling	49
The Quality God Blesses	54
Simple Things	57
Dad's Old Glove	60
Bonnie, a Flower in the Desert	62
King Jesus	65
God's Fingerprints	67
Life as a Pastor	69
Grace Reigns	72
Ascension Gifts	75
Sweet, Sweet Pie	79
Awaiting Spring	84
Where Would We Be Without Easter?	88

Summer

Rome and God's Love	95
Life is a Race	98
Motorcycle Man Carl Knows Peace — Don't Blink...	101
Pride Goes Before a Fall	104
Glory and Reality	107
Grass and Weeds, Wheat and Tares	109
A Trip Down the River	111
Where was God When the 'Twisting Wind' Came?	114
Roses, Thorns, and Silken Twine	117
Mowing and Praying	120
From a Rock House	123
I Dress for Success	127
The Swarm of Bees	130
The One that Got Away	132
Of Marathons and Truth	135
The Presence of Christ	137
A World of Contrasts	140
Dreams	142
Twenty Years in One Place	146
Hope Radiates	151
Above, Where Christ Is	157
Forgiveness	162

Autumn

A Garden of Good Cheer	169
Pillars of Granite and Crystal	172
'Just Right' Thanksgiving	176
Holy Fire	178
In Our Town	181
The Great Separation	185
Tumbling Turtles	188

Daniel in the Lion's Den	191
Goings-On at Church	195
The Bridge	198
Good News	201
Rain Must Fall	206
Blessed Rest	209
Seasons of Change	212
The Light of the World	215
Life of a Pastor	218
Thinking of Carolina	221
Thanksgiving List	225
Thinking Baseball	230
A Sea of Change	235

Winter

Under the Old Oak Tree	241
Christmas Reminds Us of What's Really Important	243
We Live in a Fantasy World	246
Letting Go of Great Treasure	250
Life Passes Quickly	253
Of Caves and Christmas	259
The Kingdom of Heaven	262
Prospects for the New Year	265
God and Fishermen	267
Hope Abounds	269
Tears Tell Tale of Love	271
A Priority on Service	273
Reflection on Tears	276
Grandmother's Simple Faith	279
Unpacking Memory, Nostalgia, and Emotion	284
Merry Christmas, Ross Wolfe	288

FOREWORD

As I write, I sit in my office. Books surround me. Sometimes, I feel, they talk to me, often inform me, and, occasionally, motivate me. As I sit at my desk, located behind me, lay my favorite authors: Annie Dillard, Frederick Buechner, and C. S. Lewis. Nearby filling the bookshelves are poetry anthologies, Milton and his Paradise Lost, Coleridge and his Mariner, Keats and his odes, Wordsworth and his nature poems as the master of Romantic poetry, George Herbert, Gerard Manley Hopkins, and a shelf full of just about every famous poet you can imagine. Hovering near the poets, you will find Greco-Roman stuff from my Ph. D. days, including books from Cambridge, England.

Moving to my right and along the path, you will find books on preaching, pastoring, devotional books, and a vintage multi-volume collection of the old British preacher Charles Haddon Spurgeon. In front of me and in front of my desk, you will find two chairs for guests and a globe of the world. My grandchildren love to spin the globe. I like to put a finger on places I have lived and have journeyed to, places like Hong Kong, Beijing, Paris, London, New York, Seattle, Los Angeles, and Austin, Texas. I also like to look at the map of the world and imagine where I wish to travel. The English poet and priest Gerard Manley Hopkins once penned, "The world is charged with the grandeur of God," and it is.

To my left again, you will find bookshelves, the classics in greens and reds, friends like Aristotle, Plato, Philo, and my good friend Cicero. The Roman lawyer, statesman, politician, and exiled rebel once quipped, "A room without books is like a body without a soul." To the immediate left of my desk, you will find file cabinets of sermons, stories, and New Testament Greek translations and notes.

It sounds boring, but this library ignites a fire of memory, joy, pain, agony, happiness, and writing in my soul. Also, in this office, you will find a picture of the house my grandfather built in the Blue Ridge Mountains of North Carolina. You will observe pictures of Cambridge, England, and pictures and treasures galore of churches, old clocks, and other stuff. Maybe I should write a book about this library.

I have written articles, stories, saved quotes and imagined worlds beyond for years. The articles and stories reveal places I have loved, people I have known, and living voices that have spoken to me from these surrounding books. In this library, you will find every kind of Bible imaginable, highlighted in yellow, marked in ink, and red-letter addition in English, Hebrew, and Greek.

Anyway, on one of the shelves near Cicero and Aristotle, a thick book manuscript sat for years. It contained mostly stuff I had written years ago. I mean, YEARS ago. One day, in a flash of "maybe I should publish this manuscript for posterity"- for family, a few friends, and anyone who wishes to read Under the Old Oak Tree: Holy Fire, faith, and Fables in the Stories of Life. It's really just stuff out of my heart and out of this library. So enjoy and catch a glimpse of holy fire, faith, and fables, stories that shape the fabric of life.

Dr. John D. Duncan
Cambridge, England 2022

Spring

John D. Duncan

*Nothing is so beautiful as Spring –
When weeds, in wheels, shoot long and lovely
and lush:
Thrush's eggs look little low heavens, and thrush
Through the echoing timber does so rinse and wring
The ear, it strikes like lightnings to hear him sing;
The glassy pear tree leaves and blooms, they brush
The descending blue; that blue is all in a rush
With richness, the racing lambs too have fair their fling.*

*What is all this juice and all this joy?
A strain of the earth's sweet being in the beginning
In Eden garden, - Have, get, before it cloys,*

*Before it clouds, Christ, lord, and sour with sinning,
Innocent mind and Mayday in girl and boy,
Most, O maid's child, they choice and worthy the
Winning.*

Gerard Manley Hopkins

Bluebonnets

I'm sitting here under the old oak tree, awaiting the beautiful flowers of spring. It won't be long until the Texas hillsides sprout a sea of blue, our infamous bluebonnets dotting landscapes with an array of beauty.

Had Jesus lived in Texas, his Sermon on the Mount might have included, "Consider the bluebonnets, how they grow; they neither toil nor spin; yet I say to you that even Solomon in all his glory did not clothe himself like one of these." Beholding the beauty of flowers reminds me of a visit I once made to Switzerland.

While at Lake Lucerne, my family and I rode a railcar and then an incline to reach the breathtaking scenery of Switzerland, overlooking the lake and valley below. The beauty of God's creation shouted glory to God. As we stepped off the incline, we noticed a short yet steep trail leading up to the peak. We followed the trail, breathing heavily to reach the scenic view. We paused to catch our breath and behold the view as we walked. We even took pictures. While descending from the peak of Mount Pilatus on the trail, several people from our tour group picked flowers.

Our family became friends with five Christian girls from Los Angeles. Each, to my knowledge, was a long-time California native. These girls, enjoying themselves in the splendor of Switzerland, picked the colorful flowers along the trail.

A lady walked up to them, a serious, furrowed brow above her eyes, and scolded them in German, *Verboten*!

Thinking the lady was saying, "Beautiful! " The girls politely said, "Thank you," and continued to pick the flowers. Melanie, my daughter, picked her share of flowers too.

We descended from the peak of the mountain. Since our children were "dying of thirst," if you understand kids, we decided to stop for a soft drink. We entered the line for concessions, only to be scolded by the cashier with the same powerful word. She pointed to Melanie and the flowers she proudly displayed with her glowing smile and announced, *Verboten*. I turned to look at Melanie, who stood behind me. My eye caught a sign on the wall: "Picking the mountain flowers is forbidden." I know a little German, so I matched the English "forbidden" with the German *verboten*.

"Oh my," I said to myself as my brain connected English and German, "picking the flowers is forbidden." "OOPS!"

Melanie discarded her flowers, and we shared with our friends that *verboten* is "forbidden" and that flowers are to stay on the mountain. And so we learned a new word, an unforgettable one, and we all had a good laugh.

"Forbidden" is a biblical word: "Take heed to yourselves, lest you forget the covenant of the Lord your God which he made with you, and make for yourselves a carved image in the form of anything which the Lord your God has forbidden you (Deuteronomy 4:23).

God warns us. He tells us to refuse, even to flee that which he forbids. Isn't this a replay of God's instruction in the Garden of Eden? Wasn't Adam and Eve's sin eating from the tree that God had forbidden? And isn't that why we now refer to it as the forbidden fruit? Isn't temptation the desire to pick that which is forbidden even after we're warned?

God clearly warns us. Hear him. Heed his warnings. If you walk with Jesus, stay away from what he forbids. Take time to behold the beauty of his creation. And so, I'll say, take heed, read the signs; it might keep you out of a lot of trouble. And don't pick the flowers in Switzerland, nor the bluebonnets in Texas. It's *verboten*.

Her Name was Easter

I'm sitting here under the old oak tree awaiting the wondrous glory of Easter. Easter reminds me of two things—the resurrection of Christ, that all-glorious joy of eternal life, and my precious grandmother.

The year was 1904. Easter arrived on April 12 that year. Allen and Ibbie Wilson, residents of the Blue Ridge Mountains, gave birth to a daughter. They named her Ruth, an obvious reference to that elegant woman of faith by the same name in the Bible. Since Ruth was born on Easter Sunday, her parents joyously added a middle name—Easter. Ruth Easter Duncan grew and married. She moved to a small town called Spruce Pine, North Carolina. She and her husband suffered through the depression, learned the art of hanging onto faith in the tough times, and enjoyed the happiness of their three children. One child was a son named George. He graduated from high school, joined the Army, and married. Later, George moved to Texas with his wife and two sons.

One of those sons was me. Each summer, we visited my grandmother. What joy! I remember those long car rides to the mountains. We took Jeep rides. We played in the creek behind my grandmother's house. We toured the Blue Ridge Parkway. I sat in the porch swing as a gentle breeze blew. I caught fireflies, which I kept in a jar on the nightstand. Life was simple.

Grandmother always did two things when our family visited—bake chocolate pies and pray. Her tasty pies dropped down to the tummy with scrumptious delight. Her prayers filled the ears with a sweet-sounding melody. She would slip into my room just as I lay my head on the pillow. Her words seemed an echo in my ear as she always began, "Now I lay me down to sleep, I pray the Lord my soul to keep ... " The cool mountain air chilled the room, but her prayers warmed my heart. Oh, how she prayed to Jesus! Ruth Easter Duncan passed away July 7, 1997, a little over eight months shy of Easter, 1998, it too, on April 12. And so, as Easter fast approaches, I cherish the faith of my grandmother, faith in the risen Jesus. And I recall Jesus' words to Martha, words that my grandmother knew all too well, words passed down from generation to generation, words that celebrate Easter's hope in the midst of grief, words that shine light in the shadows of life, words that literally raise the dead: Jesus said to her, "I am the resurrection and the life. He who believes in Me, though he may die, he shall live. And whoever lives and believes in Me shall never die. Do you believe this?" (John 11:25-26).

Maybe, just maybe, I was destined to be a preacher with a grandmother whose middle name was Easter. Better yet, you're destined to live forever if only you'll call upon the name of Jesus this Easter. After all, Jesus raises the dead. Do you believe this?

Laughter Does a Family Good

I'm sitting here under the old oak tree pondering the ways of the world. News of an early morning raid sweeps across our continent. Drought dehydrates portions of Africa. Devastation and poverty plague Eastern Europe. And here in Granbury, I hear worrisome talk on the square about the volatile stock market. We live in a world where pain shouts, and laughter stills the night with silence. Here under the old oak tree, as the fresh wind blows, I'm hopeful of a world where we hear the rattle of laughter.

I'm pondering the world but remembering the rattle of laughter in our home not too long ago.

"Laugh, and the world laughs with you; Weep, and you weep alone." I am not sure what Ella Wheeler Wilcox thought when she wrote her poem "Solitude" in her *Collected Poems* in 1917. Was she envisioning a dinner table discussion that brought barrels of laughter?

Saturday afternoon came in grand style. The lazy sun started its daily downward plunge. Long shadows fell across the back porch. Three Duncan girls bounced and giggled on the trampoline.

"Daddy, will you jump?" came a voice from a body hang-gliding in midair.

"No, not right now. I am grilling the chicken." I stood by the gas grill, dividing my time between flipping the chicken and watching the bouncers take flight on the trampoline.

My Martha Stewart impersonation completed; I called to the girls, "Time to come in and eat."

"Just a few more minutes on the trampoline, please, Daddy, pleeeease!!!" I know that's not how you spell "please," but that's what it sounds like when parents bark orders and children try to buy a few more minutes to do something they enjoy.

After a short time, everyone in our family arrived at the dinner table and sat in their chairs. One of our girls spoke a prayer: "I thank you, God, for our family. Thank you for the pretty day. Help Jenifer's basketball team to win a game. Thank you for the chicken and other stuff. Amen. Dig in." She probably picked up that last phrase at a youth pizza function at the church.

The meal went nicely. The conversation about school, work, friends, baby dolls, and the like flowed freely. I finished my glass of ice water and decided I would go to the sink for more. I began to scoot my chair back when an unusual thing happened.

I sat in an antique chair with a flowery-patterned-cloth seat. The chair had been hammered, glued, refinished, and who knows what else, or how many times. As I scooted my chair back, the chair popped, the wood cracked, and dumped me seat first right into the floor! The chair lay in six pieces while I sprawled on the floor. I was reminded of the Psalmist (11:5) who said, "If the foundations be destroyed, what can the righteous do?"

I saw no faces, nor could mine be seen, but I heard barrels of laughter. This laughter was not the hee-hee kind, but the hee-haw, snorting, side-splitting kind you get when spontaneity grabs your laugher and turns up the volume. Finally, an "Are you all right?" entered my ears between the laughter.

I laughed, too. And for some reason, the laughter got louder when I slowly rose from the pile of wood. Laugh, and the world laughs with you. I recovered from my mini-free-fall, tossed the chair in the fireplace, and determined that the Bible is right, "A merry heart does good, like medicine, but a broken spirit dries the bones" (Proverbs 17:22). Laughter does a family good.

But weep, and you weep alone. I could not help but think that we live in a world where people's lives shatter, sending them on painful falls, a world where foundations are destroyed daily. It's a world where homes splinter, relationships crash, and sin takes its victims kicking and screaming on a downward plunge. It's a world where broken spirits dry weary bones. What can the righteous do?

For one thing, we can learn to laugh at ourselves once in a while. Bring laughter to the world. Why not?

For another, we might offer to pick up those who fall. Isn't this what the gospel is about? Restoring one's fallen nature, replacing it with the power of God? Isn't this what the Apostle Paul encouraged the Galatians to do? To bear one another's burdens and thus fulfill the law of Christ? To pick others up?

For another, we might weep with the hurting, so they do not have to weep alone.

And always, should I say again, always, check your chair before you sit down or scoot back. If you do fall, though, remember the experience: Pick yourself up, and get a glass of ice water. Or, as the gospels say, give a cup of cold water in Jesus' name. There's happiness in laughter, joy in rising to walk again, and glory in helping others.

Does anybody have a chair for sale?

John D. Duncan

Faith and a Flying Cat

I'm sitting here under the old oak tree reflecting on faith. "What is faith?" is a question zooming around my brain like children circling a roller-skating rink.

What is faith? The writer of Hebrews says faith is the substance of things hoped for, the conviction of things not seen (Hebrews 11:1). Scholars remind us faith has a foundation connected to more than a wish and proof that you cannot see. The ancient Greeks noted conviction as being legal proof in court in the circumstance of an accusation.

So, let me get this right, faith has an invisible foundation and proof that you cannot get your eyes on. I think that's why I struggle with faith because I don't crave the invisible. I like to see proof.

Long before the book of Hebrews was written, Jesus said faith is like a tiny mustard seed. Plant it deep in the soil of the soul, and it grows.

Jesus also commended the faith of a man who wanted his son healed. The man told Jesus he did not even need to go see his son. All Jesus needed to do, begged the man, was make his son well in that present moment. Whatever faith is, Jesus and the man together hint that faith covers a lot of distance in a short period of time.

And, of course, my favorite is Jesus calling the little children to him. The disciples tried to shoo the nasty, snotty-nosed kids away. But Jesus welcomed them into his lap and said that the kingdom of God requires the wide-eyed wonder and faith of a child.

What is faith?

When I cannot understand something, a story often helps. Not so long ago, a church member passed me the story of a little girl. The story may be one of those e-mail stories that makes its way into your computer or a story whose details have changed with the telling. You know how that goes. The girl, though, does not have a name. And a pastor shows up in the story—it could be yours, it could be mine.

What is faith?

A pastor and his family, a wife and daughters, had a kitten, once upon a time, that climbed up in a tree in the family's backyard. The girls loved the kitty, and the pastor watched the kitty cat as it would not come down out of the tree. The pastor did everything he could to force the cat out of the tree. He offered milk. He chanted, "Here, kitty, kitty." He reached high with his hand, hoping that the kitty would take hold.

The pastor thought of climbing the tree. The tree, one of those young, budding trees with green wood, was not strong enough to climb. The pastor, ingenious as a pastor can be, came up with a great plan to rescue the beloved kitty cat from the tree.

The pastor decided that he would tie a rope to the tree, tie the other end of the rope to his car, then slowly ease the car forward while bending the tree down just far enough to reach up and secure the little cat.

Anxiously, the pastor tied the rope to the tree, the other end of the rope to the car just like he planned. He sat down in the seat of the car, fired up the car engine, and slowly eased the car forward—until the rope broke. Now, I do not have to tell you pastors and their ideas can sometimes get them in trouble. But I will tell you that when the rope broke, the cat was removed from the tree, catapulted into mid-air like a rocket launch that sends the space shuttle into orbit. If I may wax poetic, the cat took flight out of sight!

The pastor, as pastors are prone to feel sometimes, felt horrible. He felt bad for himself, his daughters, and, yes, the cat. What is faith?

Immediately, the pastor turned off the car engine and began to look all over the neighborhood for the cat. The pastor went door to door, never explaining the details of his predicament, but simply asking, "Have you seen a little kitty cat?" As the pastor walked, he prayed until finally he gave up the search. Only pastors do this kind of thing, so he prayed one final prayer for the cat, "Lord, I commit this cat to your care." The pastor went home and returned to life as normal.

Two days later, the pastor shopped at the grocery store. He met a lady, one of his church members, and a neighbor, while cruising the aisles and loading his shopping cart. They chatted, and he looked into her shopping cart and noticed cat food.

The pastor's mind now raced. After all, this church member and neighbor, he knew, and the whole world knew, was a cat hater. He looked, thought, and asked, "Why are you buying cat food when you don't like cats?"

She smiled and responded with her story. "Pastor, you will not believe this," she began as she shared the news about her little girl who had been begging for a cat. "Every time my daughter begged for a cat, I told her no, repeatedly, until finally, I had it up to here with her begging for a cat. So, I just told her, 'If the Lord gives you a cat, I'll let you keep it.'

"Pastor, you won't believe this. I told you this is unbelievable, but I saw it with my own eyes. As soon as I said, 'If the Lord gives you a cat ...,' my little girl marched right out the front door and into the front yard and got down on her knees and asked the Lord for a cat. And, then, with my own eyes watching out the kitchen window, a kitten came flying right out of the big, blue sky, paws spread out, its fur standing on edge, and landed right in front of my little girl."

What is faith?

Faith is the substance of things hoped for, the conviction of things not seen, and the courage to seek God. Faith is a little girl kneeling in the front yard asking God for a cat, followed by the laughter of God.

John D. Duncan

Waiting for Green

I'm sitting here under the old oak tree, contemplating green.

I wait in haste for the coming of spring, that season in Texas when winter's yellow colors the world in fields of green. It will soon happen on my front lawn. But already green stains the glorious fields in England. While riding the train recently from London to Cambridge, I noticed sheep grazing in lush green pastures. Beauty indeed!

One day in Cambridge. I found myself standing in the square at the Trinity College campus. In the center, a neatly patterned square patch of green decorated the plaza. My mind drifts back to the poet Gerard Manley Hopkins, "The whole world is charged with the grandeur of God!" God's grandeur blossoms in green!

A leaflet at Trinity College in Cambridge leads you on a tour. Face east, and you will see a marble statue of the college's founder, King Henry VIII. Face south, and you will see a statue of Queen Elizabeth I over the archway. Face west, and you will see the towering great hall with a statue of King James I, infamous for ordering the compilation of the King James Version of the Bible in 1611. Face north and look up, and you will see a clock with gold letters. Even if you have never been to Cambridge, this clock may look familiar. It is the clock used in the movie Chariots of Fire in the race between Harold Abrahams and Lord Burghley. The boys raced around the courtyard in the time it took the clock to strike noon. I love the statement near the middle of the movie made by Eric Liddel, "If I win, I win for God." "Winning for God" might be a good title for a sermon.

Tour guides will point a finger over the green patch in the middle of the courtyard to a window. Then they will tell you

W.M. Thackeray (1811-1863) lived there and wrote Vanity Fair. They will mention the names of people who walked the libraries and great halls, including Sir Isaac Newton and the poet Lord Tennyson. The library houses two-valued manuscripts: the original manuscript by AA Milne on Winnie-the-Pooh and an eighth-century copy of the epistles of the Apostle Paul. During World War I, curtains blocked off the halls, and a makeshift hospital treated wounded soldiers in pain.

I learned all of this while standing on the edge of green. And now I am thinking. We live in a world where people try to find direction; a world of vanity; a world where time presses us in the race of life; a world of mathematics, like balancing the checkbook, or a world of poetry with words flying into our ears in this information age. We live in a world of spiritual warfare, where God and Satan war and aim to penetrate the soul; a world where Winnie-the-Pooh plays and the Apostle Paul seeks to freshen the heart like a child; a world of pain where, in words of C.S. Lewis, "God shouts in our pleasures, but whispers in our pain."

And so here I am under the old oak tree, saying that if your soul will grow green, follow Jesus, yet know that it takes God's rain sprinkling the soul with grace in a world where so much stuff keeps coming at us. Life is certainly no picnic but a place fully alive when you drink in the grandeur of all God offers.

Jesus, the shepherd. invites you. "He wants to lead you to green pastures" (Psalm 23). If you walk with Jesus, you, his "righteous," will "thrive like a green leaf." The person who trusts and hopes in God will be blessed:

> *For he shall be like a tree planted by the waters,*
> *Which spreads out its roots by the river,*
> *And will not fear when the heat comes;*
> *But its leaf will be green,*
> *And will not be anxious in the year of drought,*

Nor will it cease from yielding fruit. (Jeremiah 17:7-8).

Even Jesus invited people to the green. "Then Jesus directed them (the disciples) to have all the people to sit down on the green grass" (Mark 6:39). And here's what he told them: Bear fruit!

I am under the tree, waiting for green and wishing for you a heart of green. Yes, I wanted to sit down on the grass at Trinity College, but a sign said, "Keep off the grass." Now here's my sign, "Keep on bearing fruit."

Bluebonnet Blossoms and Randall Purvis

I'm sitting here under the old oak tree, watching the bluebonnets usher in the glory of spring. My mind travels to Strawn.

A lone wildflower pushed up from the earth in Strawn, near Pedigo Street and Highway 108, not far from a gas station there. The Strawn Lady Greyhounds ended basketball season, and the high school band decided not to meet for the rest of the year. You see, family and friends and students gathered not long ago to lay to rest the band and music teacher, Randall.

Randall entered mother earth near Cross Plains in the community of Atwell. I never heard Randall talk about it much, maybe because he did not remember the occasion or, more likely, because his father was a preacher—and preachers don't stay in one spot too long. Randall made way to Tyler, where he went to high school, played basketball, and began singing in churches. He then attended Howard Payne College, played basketball there, and cheered for the fighting Yellow Jackets.

Randall received the call from God and served the Lord as a youth minister and minister of music. He served in churches in Devine, Haltom City (Birdville Baptist), Dumas (First Baptist), Pampa (First Baptist), Hurst (First Baptist), in Phoenix, Ariz. (North Phoenix Baptist), and numerous other churches in Granbury, Gordon, and Strawn.

Friends who knew his booming voice called him "Leather Lungs." Few folks called him by his first name, Marlin. Many called him friend. Six hundred friends gathered in the high school gymnasium for the memorial service.

I, too, called Randall friend. He forever quipped homespun proverbs like "We're just sittin' here like a bar of soap," or "Don't get your dauber down" or, his favorite, "A blind hog finds an acorn ever once in awhile."

As a sophomore at L.D. Bell High School in Hurst, I had the opportunity to shoot two game-ending free throws to win the game for our basketball team. I missed both free throws. After the game, I rushed to the locker room. I sat on the bench in front of the locker. I buried my hands in my face as tears watered my eyes.

Randall arrived, put his arm around me, and uttered unforgettable words: "Hey, don't get your dauber down. At least you hit the rim—both times." That was Randall, boiling life down to its basics, putting life in perspective. In the locker room, Randall reminded me that your best is all you can give.

How amazing that for all the things we do in our lives, life boils down to the simple things—a locker-room hug; time shared digging together on a farm; instruction on a baseball field; a meal shared with laughter after a revival; skinning a raccoon in the middle of the night; a choir trip; changing a flat tire in the desert on a mission trip; a coaching tip on how to shoot a basketball ("Point your elbow toward the basket, and keep your eyes on the goal," as he would often say); small talk driving down the road in a van; a phone conversation about old times. Life climaxes not in the big moments of accomplishment but in the small slices of life shared.

Randall and I shared slices of life together.

Once, we served together at Lakeside Baptist Church when Randall, as he was prone to do, arrived before the worship service and gave instruction to the organist as to the song he would sing during the worship service. He went about the business of preparing for the worship service without rehearsing the song. The climactic time arrived for Randall to sing the special music. He sang one song while the organist played another. He never skipped a beat as he improvised, sputtering created musical notes and words, old Leather Lungs bellowing melodious sound against the dissonance of wandering organ music. Randall, not wanting to embarrass the organist, kept plugging along.

Try preaching after the song service goes flat. At the end of that worship service, Randall asked the organist to play the original song he had selected, stating with a chuckle, "Let's try that again and see if we can make it sound better this time." That was Randall, making the best of an awkward situation. We shared side-splitting laughter over that story, which we discussed several times.

The stories rolled off tongues, one by one, after the memorial service. The stories filled in the gaps from Atwell to Strawn, from 1935 to 2001, stories of the agony and ecstasy of Randall's life. Stories filtered down, signaling the numerous lives quietly touched in churches and his days as the band and music teacher at Strawn High School.

It was my job to do the impossible—to summarize Randall's 65 years and point people beyond death to life; beyond the musical scores of earth to the music of heaven that echoes in the shadows; beyond Randall to Jesus, who guided him and called him home. Randall, like Peter stepping out of the boat on the water in Galilee, responded to Jesus' call, "Come." Like Peter, Randall knew the grandeur of high moments and the angst of sinking on life's journey. Along life's path, he aimed to keep his eyes on Jesus. As a child, as a servant, and as a teacher quoting homespun proverbs, he both believed himself and invited others to hear the cry of Peter, "Lord, save me!"

It was also my job to do the unbelievable--to offer words of comfort to his widow, Glenda, to his sons, Randy and Ritchie, and their families, to his mother, Rebecca Faye, and a host of family and friends. I watched as teenagers wept, as family members grieved, and how, in death, Randall's faith lived on. Somewhere, now at this moment, Gerard Manley Hopkins comes to mind, naming heaven as a place longed for and haven of beauteous rest:

> *I have desired to go*
> *Where springs not fail,*
> *To fields where flies no sharp and sided hail*
> *And a few lilies blow.*
> *And I have asked to be*
> *Where no storms come,*
> *Where the green swell is in the havens dumb,*
> *And out of the swing of the sea.*

And so, this is life, a season of musical notes played, of Lady Greyhounds racing the floor, of laughter at church and tears in memorial. And so, this is death, of a husband and father and friend and teacher. And so when life and death meet, all we can say is what an 80-year-old lady once said to me when her husband died, "A big hole is left that cannot be filled."

Did I tell you that a lone wildflower pushed up through the earth in Strawn near Pedigo Street and Highway 108 near a gas station there? And did I speak to you the joy of bluebonnets ushering in the glory of spring? And did I share with you that just the other day, a bluebonnet blossomed in heaven in a haven where Jesus resides at home where springs fail not, where no storms come, where fields swell with green, where calm soothes the soul in Peace? And did I tell you that a bright Light still shines even in dark hours?

Glorious Spring

I'm sitting here under the old oak tree, watching puffy clouds roll overhead like cotton balls floating in the air. The grandeur of God hovers like a butterfly over a flower as the spring season winds down.

Oh, glorious spring! It paints the world with colors—green grass, orange fruit, and purple flowers. The poet Gerard Manley Hopkins applauded spring: "Nothing is so beautiful as spring—when weeds, in wheels, shoot long and lovely and lush."

Spring hails as the season of drenching rains with the patter of water hitting your windshield or roof. Water refreshes the landscape, sprinkling earth with God's glory.

Farmers know beautiful spring as the season of sowing seeds. I once pastored a church in Locker, Texas. The community blossomed with simplicity—a white-frame church, an outhouse, rows of fences, grazing cows, rolling hills, and a Texas farm-to-market road.

Church leaders farmed to make their living. Peanut farmers told tales of planting seeds, harvesting crops, wrestling with rattlesnakes in bins, and hauling the crop to market. The locals celebrated harvest time; the climax of hard work came to fruition. No harvest, though, arrived without seed sowing.

Farmer Merle Taylor once offered this city boy some advice: "If you're gonna be a farmer, you gotta have faith. You till the soil, plant the seeds, and hope it rains. You wait a lot. It takes faith in God to be a farmer."

Jesus spoke of sowing seeds. He sat by the sea, unfolding a story of wonder. A farmer sowed seeds. Some fell along the path, some on rocks, some among the thorns, and some on good soil (Matthew 13:1-9). The seeds that fell on good soil produced a crop. Celebrate spring, that season of asking God to break up the hard ground of the heart, to plant his seed in the soul, and to send the rain of his Spirit to bear fruit. It takes faith to sow the seed and faith to bloom like Jesus where you're planted. Nothing is so lovely as spring!

Words and Deeds

I'm sitting here under the old oak tree listening for the sounds of spring. A sparrow perches on the barbed-wire fence and chirps. A lawnmower grinds, and a weed trimmer whines in the distance. The wind whistles as the grass blows furiously on this day. I hear the echo of words in my ear.

I think of Jesus' words which evoked power.

To seekers on a Galilean hill, Jesus taught with words: "And he opened his mouth and taught them saying, 'Blessed ...'" (Matthew 5:2-3).

To the self-righteous, Jesus gave a warning: "Do you not therefore err, because you do not know the Scriptures, neither the power of God?" (Mark 12:24).

To the demonic, Jesus spoke strong words of retreat: "Come out of the man, you unclean spirit" (Mark 5:8). To the commoners, Jesus told stories to awaken the senses and warm the soul, "And he spoke another parable to them, saying, 'The kingdom of heaven is like ...'" (Matthew 13:33).

To the crippled and sick, Jesus spoke healing, "Rise, take up your bed, and walk" (John 5:8).

To the boastful proud, Jesus uttered an urgent rebuke, "Get behind me, Satan."

To the confused and hurting, Jesus encouraged, "Let not your heart be troubled; you believe in God, believe also in me" (John 14:1).

Not long ago, I taught my daughter to drive her five-speed *Ford Mustang*. I spoke words of instruction, "Let your foot off the clutch slowly when you shift gears." With a bump and a jump, she learned in the throes of anxiety and with many words.

Recently, doctors diagnosed my neighbor with lung cancer. A voice of concern and care flowed from the lips of the family.

A bunch of guys from the church teamed up and mowed their yard. That's what a Christian community is supposed to do. Words speak. Deeds live. God's face connects words and deeds. One guy prayed with the cancer patient, a man now struggling through chemotherapy, radiation, and sleeping with oxygen tubes connected to his nose. The prayer connected heaven and earth, the voice of a struggling man and the heart of God in hope for recovery. Words enliven.

Just last week, my friend and mentor, Joseph McClain, passed away. He taught me Greek in my college days. He taught me the value of words—their etymology, their underlying interpretive force from historical settings, and their meanings in contemporary culture. He asked me to deliver the eulogy at his funeral by mining the depth of meaning from the words of 1 Corinthians 13. He urged me to highlight the supremacy of love. He taught me that love is more than noise. Love is listening. Under his tutelage, I learned to listen to the rhythms of words in the Bible and the rhythms of God. More than what you know, love is *Who* you know: Jesus. And more than giving, love is a gift. Words spin a story in the gospel of Jesus' love.

Dr. McClain shared wise words: "The really smart person does not know everything but knows where to go to find something." He introduced me to wordsmiths and scholars with the names of A.T. Robertson and R.C.H. Lenski. Their written words inspire me to this day. Dr. McClain's faithfulness to God in teaching about words lives in me and with me. Words link heart and soul in a common bond.

In the midst of words, I seek to understand circumstances—teaching my daughter to drive; agonizing with a neighbor in a time of sickness, uncertainty, and anguish; grieving in life's shadows in the memory of words. I also look into a face when confronted in an exchange of words. Sometimes I see the face of God amid words.

As Emily Dickinson says of circumstances and of God: "All Circumstances are the Frame In which His Face is set."

So, here I am under the old oak tree, penning words. Do words make a difference? Do they challenge? Do they motivate change? Do words have a face?

Nineteenth-century poet Christina Rossetti speaks to me in the 21st century. Her words penetrate to the core of the gospel story and to the heart of the supremacy of love: "Words are spoken: deeds and lives speak." In life, words are spoken, and deeds and lives speak. What are you speaking?

John D. Duncan

There is no "I" in Team

I'm sitting here under the old oak tree musing with madness over March.

"March," the poet Emily Dickinson once said, "is the Month of Expectation." The college basketball playoffs soon begin. "March madness," the hoop-it-up prognosticators call this college basketball hoopla. My expectations fade, as my favorite North Carolina Tar Heels do not look to make it into the playoffs.

My mind eases back into the days of my youth. 1978 stands out as quite a year. I was a junior in high school that year. Jimmy Carter served as president, bell-bottom pants and Afro hairstyles were "in," "Inflation" became a household word. Mickey Mouse celebrated his 50th birthday at *Disney*. NASA prepared for test flights for the first space shuttle. In sports, the Pittsburgh Steelers beat the Dallas Cowboys in Super Bowl XIII in Miami, MVP Bucky Dent and the New York Yankees won the baseball World Series, while the Wes Unseld and the Washington Bullets won the NBA championship.

In Hurst, Texas, a championship basketball season unfolded for the 1978 L.D. Bell High School Raiders boys' team. Led by Coach Ray Debord, the talented team won 29 games with only four losses. The season produced Coach Ray's first championship season at Bell. The team meshed and molded through long, hard workouts and the classic motivational speeches of Debord. He preached strong defense, finding the open man with a pass, fierce rebounding, and balanced scoring. Ray's assistant, Mike, reinforced the defense with gruesome drills. A piece of paper on the locker room office window declared Debord's philosophy, "There is no 'I' in 'TEAM.'"

The team went undefeated in its district games, defeating opponents from Wichita Falls, Denton, Lewisville, and arch-rival

Trinity—twice. The team was ranked No. 10 in the state before losing a bi-district game in Stephenville. The team possessed the passion and skill to complete a championship season.

The 1978 Raiders produced an unforgettable season with this unforgettable team, producing a team of winners not just on the court but also off the court. That team made it to the Hall of Fame. The Hurst-Euless-Bedford Sports Hall of Fame recently inducted the 1978 L.D. Bell High School champion boys' basketball team.

My older brother George starred on that team. He served as the team's point guard, making passes to the likes of other high school stars with the names of Davis, Callaway, Alsup, and Hammonds. The echo of "We are the Champions" reverberates in my ear as I recall those high school days. I still remember walking through the locker room and seeing that white piece of paper on the locker room wall: "There is no 'I' in 'TEAM.'"

Some 24 years later, I sit here under the old oak tree thinking about the church. There is no "I" in "CHURCH." Jesus said, "The greatest among you shall be your servant." The Apostle Paul addressed the church as a body, "The church is the body of Christ."

Paul preached the value of every person of the body fulfilling a role and being important to the church. No church can do God's work without every member finding and fulfilling God's call. It takes people to build a church. It takes understanding Christ as the head of the church for a church to effectively minister.

It's a long story, and we do not have the time, but I guess I should tell you that I was a toenail on that 1978 team. I made the team but never played one second that season. I spent the whole season on the junior varsity team and was moved back to varsity for the playoffs at the end of the season. My only contribution was that Coach Ray asked me to referee during practice. He had referees for practice long before Mark Cuban, owner of the

Dallas Mavericks, hired them for his team's practices. Coach Ray was always ahead of his time.

So here I am, pastoring a church and savoring the days of my youth here just before the month of expectation, knowing that whether you are a knee or a finger or a foot or even a toenail in the Lord's church, as long as Christ is the head of the church, every single member is important, even the tiniest parts.

Amid the memories and echoes, Oswald Chambers comes to mind, "There is no joy in the soul that has forgotten what God prizes."

Today I am full of joy, an under-the-oak-tree sitter looking at my toenails and full of joy that God prizes each person, each of us, even me, in the love and wonder of his grace. By the way, there is no "I" in Jesus either, but there is much joy when he's in you.

Running Wild

I'm sitting here under the old oak tree, wondering about things running wild. According to the headline in the local newspaper in our town, a man claiming to be the notorious outlaw Jesse James showed up on the town square. The man wore shorts and appeared to reach for a gun. Six police officers subdued the man with pepper spray and their combined brute strength. Officers took him to the hospital for treatment. The mayhem, which occurred around 3:25 one morning, created quite a stir. For a brief period of time, emotions ran wild. The Brazos River runs through our town. The spring rains filled up the river, which feeds Lake Granbury. Fish run wild. Fishermen seem excited. Boaters have begun their lake cruises. Soon jet skiers will zig and zag across the lake. As I drove across the bridge near *Wal-Mart* the other day, I noticed the movement over the lake. The lake currents cruise along at brisk speeds. I guess you could say that the river upstream and the lake run wild.

The rain showered my yard with spring blessings. The grass sang hallelujah. I cranked up my lawnmower and cut the grass. I fired up the string trimmer and chopped weeds. The rain set nature in motion, and the grass and weeds have run wild. Spring has run wild, and the wheels of nature spin the glory of spring into a dotted landscape of color and pizzazz! G.K. Chesterton once spoke of Christianity. He said, "And the more I considered Christianity, the more I found that while it had established a rule and order, the chief aim of that order was to give room for good things to run wild."

Jesus spoke of good things running wild—the good news of God's kingdom; trees bearing good fruit; good gifts coming from the heavenly Father's hand; good men out of the abundance of their hearts producing good things; saints sowing good seeds that take root in good soil; a Good Shepherd laying down his life for the sheep; faithful and good servants who hear announcements of "well done!" Jesus longed for the good things to run wild.

The Apostle Paul, too, yearned for the running wild of God's good things. He called them the fruit of the Spirit; fruit woven in the heart like vines woven around a barbed-wire fence while holding luscious grapes anxious to be plucked. Paul's vine exploded with good that abundantly overflows in the believer's life. It is also fruit that becomes sweet and delightful once tasted by others.

What good fruit did Paul wish to see run wild among believers in the church? Paul craved beauty to blossom and run wild like bluebonnets on a Texas roadside—love, joy, peace, longsuffering, gentleness, goodness, faith, meekness, and self-control.

Ah, spring—the season of resurrection excitement and bluebonnets blooming, the season when joy runs wild. Emotions run wild in spring. Rivers and lakes run wild. Weeds run wild in my yard. But more than any other thing, Chesterton puts our faith in Christ in its best possible terms: When Jesus blooms in the heart, his good things run wild. That's the good news for you today and, by the way, for Jesse James, wherever he is.

The House

I'am sitting here under the old oak tree, meditating with mirth about a house. Recently I visited my two aunts and stayed in the house my grandfather built in the mountains of North Carolina. He built a white two-story house in 1938 with the help of a carpenter and friends. Times sure have changed. Who could find friends to help build a house today?

The pastor/poet George Herbert from 17th century England once spoke of a house in The Familie: "But, Lord, the house and the familie are Thine, Though some of them repine; Turn out these wranglers, which defile thy seat, For where Thou dwellest all is neat."

Walk through this house of my heritage, and you will find the basics—a living area with a fireplace, five bedrooms, kitchen, dining room, and bathroom. As a man with a wife and three daughters, I cannot imagine one bathroom for the morning rush hour. That might give new meaning to the word "chaos." These days spoil us, but not so in 1938. You took what you earned. You took what God gave and thanked him for it. O, for days of simplicity! But, Lord, the house and the familie are thine.

The porch serves as the best part of the house. On summer days, you can sit on the porch or, better yet, swing on the porch swing. I used to lie on the swing and rock while the breeze blew in my face. Once, I was rocking along, and the chain broke. The quick ride to the ground jolted me into a mental state of sudden alertness. Thankfully, I was not hurt. Professionals fixed the swing. Nothing lazily passes the time like that swing. You could dream the day away though some of them repine.

The dining room formed good memories. I smell the freshness of corn on the cob, mashed potatoes, and green beans straight from the garden near the house. I smell homemade biscuits still warm from the oven. I taste pan-fried steak with gravy that makes you want to lick your lips. Then, of course, homemade chocolate pies from my grandmother's hands added a sweet taste for connoisseurs of delightful desserts.

Stories found their way around the circle—basketball in a barn; walking home from school in the snow; milking the cows; flowers for the decoration; what a good feller so and so was; skipping English class to play basketball; working at the knitting mill; planning picnics; the creek; the spring water; the mine across the mountain; the furnace; family pictures, smile, at the count of three and say "Cheese!"; about Grandpa Duncan; about the delightful taste of the chocolate pie; about skipping English again (the good stories always get repeated); about shortcuts across the mountain; about my great grandmother Ibbie praying at an open window so loud you could hear her down the mountain.

Families need more prayer. "To clasp the hands in prayer," theologian Karl Barth once muttered, "is the beginning of an uprising against the disorder of the world." Prayer combats disorder.

I needed prayer the day I was ordered to eat green beans. My aunt had long helped me smuggle green beans under the table so that I would not have to eat them. I detested green beans! I was creating disorder in preparation for the smuggling of green beans when my father commanded me to eat at least one green bean!

I protested but slowly slipped that green bean into my mouth and into my throat when I gagged. Disorder reigned. My father met me in the bathroom. Prayer ensued discipline, if you know what I mean. Sin takes prisoners. What memories in that house. Things change, though. Not far from the house, I miss the grocery store. The corner store where Scottie (the guy who owned it) worked and sacked groceries is gone. In the old days, guys would sit on the bench outside, smoke cigarettes, spit, and talk. *Wal-Mart* moved in, but you can still get the news.

I went to *Wal-Mart* the other day and heard the news. The greeter has heart trouble, a blood clot in her leg, and should not have been working on that cold day. Some lady walked in and announced, "I finished school." Seems her business closed, and she lost her job. She also lost her husband to an affair. Sin knows no limits. She divorced him, got her GED, started college, finished, and now teaches school. "I didn't think I'd make it," she said as she smiled, "but God has blessed me." God's grace tumbles over us like snow from heaven.

Oh, the guy at the checkout stand broadcasted a weather forecast of snow. By the next morning, snow tumbled from the sky like glitter falling. Things change, but you can still get the news if you listen close. I guess the more things change, the more they stay the same.

Turn out these wranglers, which defile thy seat. The house has changed a lot. The pine trees beside the house have been cut down. The boards in the house creak. The basement floods. On cold days, drafts spew cold air. Nails ease their way out of the wall and need a good hammer to find rest.

My mind drifts back—1938; 1965; 1974; 2003.

Imagine 1938: A man, a carpenter, and friends: Pass some nails. Throw me some wood. Son, get down off that roof. Somehow, my dad climbed on the roof while the house was being built.

Imagine 1965: I am a boy sitting in a chair with my brother, holding a box of cereal ready to go home to Louisiana. "Son, don't slide on that rail." One favorite pastime was sliding on the rail down the stairs.

Imagine 1974: My brother and I throw a baseball and jump the huge boxwood bushes in the sloped front yard. "Son, don't tear up those boxwoods." Sometimes we would not make it over the bushes.

Imagine 2003: Every night before you go to bed in that house, four things must happen—lock the doors, close all the blinds, read the Bible and pray. "Father, we thank you for love, life, liberty, grace, and your goodness."

Did I tell you that when hands are clasped in prayer that an uprising against the disorder of the world occurs? Did I tell you that what makes a house a house is faith? Did I tell you that order comes where Jesus calls? Did I tell you that my aunt had a vision of Jesus in a big blue sky standing over that house to protect it? Did I tell you how neat that house is, really?

God's protection knows no limits. For where Thou dwellest all is neat.

God's Message Board

I'm sitting here under the old oak tree, pondering friends. I remember friends from high school and college. Granbury, Texas, where I am privileged to pastor, has provided many a friend. Cambridge, England, serves as a place where new friends bless my life. But the friend I am thinking of is an old friend no longer on earth—Frank.

The Romans in antiquity possessed a quality of friendship called *amicitia*. Unusually, it included more than our common idea of friendship—talking, attending basketball games together, helping each other with projects around the house, like painting a room or repairing the broken lawnmower; sharing words in confidence and as a confidant; taking trips together. The Romans believed friendship created an invisible rope, an unspoken tie or bond of obligation to loyalty, to duty, and to common fellowship.

Friendship, for the Romans, was not a relationship to advertise but a lifelong series of obligations that deepened mutual respect.

The Roman poet Horace hinted at this loyalty in these poetic words: "Accept as such this life below, and, should these bitter winds that blow mark the last sun that shines, be patient, friend."

Friendship forever surprises when Christ links friends by faith.

Frank and I became friends by blind luck, or since I do not believe in luck, divine providence. Frank was God's message board, an angelic messenger with poetic messages from heaven's postal service near God's throne. That Frank and I even became friends at all shocks me still.

Frank appeared one day at a church. He just showed up in the church parking lot, like a mysterious angel from the television show *Touched by an Angel*, spilling some story about a truck wreck that nearly killed him; a story about his sick mother whom he arrived to take care of; a story about a truck-driving vagabond life; and an assignment to water flowers in the church flower bed.

"God," as Frank once informed me, "sent me here for a reason." Frank thought maybe one reason was to water the flowers at church. Frank watered the flowers at church, smoked cigarettes outside, invited Christ into his life, was baptized, and left messages.

When he lived, he wrote poetic messages to friends, nurses, doctors, and church members: "Your smile is worth all that is written as God's love working in you." "If we want to deal with God the right way, we have to learn to love the right way." "Friends are what makes humanity eternal." "Love is God made visible."

That was Frank—God's message board, always dropping messages like seeds while wishing for them to bloom like flowers in the soil of sandy hearts.

I do not want to romanticize this too much because I must tell you that Frank annoyed me from the beginning. He was sandpaper on the chalkboard, a fingernail on the chalkboard of life.

Frank's moods from the day I first met him swung from happy to sad, from despair to hopefulness, from anger to laughter, from messages of sincerity to messages which produced venom. Frank called all the time, morning, noon, and night. For all its preciousness, Time had no limit in Frank's imagination. Did Frank ever sleep?

My daughter once informed me that caller ID identified Frank as an 86-time caller in one week. Has anyone ever called you eighty-six times in one week? Never mind if the whole world sleeps late on Saturday, Frank called at a little bit after 7 a.m. with words of greeting, "My friend, John, I've got to read something to you. ..." The message board had an urgent message.

I learned to dismiss Frank politely and to calm his venomous messages. He once declared, "John Duncan, this is the last time you'll hear from me. You'll never see me at church again. You people don't have time for me. You don't have time for me. You're too busy for me." I feared that Frank was right. I take such messages seriously and thought maybe the reason Frank showed up was so that God could deliver me a message: Be patient, friend. Silently, quietly, like thread slipping into the eye of a needle, Frank wove his colorful threads around my heart. Frank, he got under my skin. Frank, he got into my heart.

Time and messages revealed that bitter winds had blown in Frank's life—alcohol addiction; alienated from family; a windswept pain that poked like a needle in your belly (hurt people hurt people and cannot often help it); a tragic truck wreck; the loss of a job; debt piled higher than a stack of boxes; brain surgery; and the dreaded poison—cancer. Frank and my wife, Judy, shared the sadness of treacherous cancer cells traveling lifeline blood supplies. Maybe, just maybe, this was another silent thread bonding us together in the shadows of life while we grasped and groped for ropes of Light.

Frank drove an old blue beat-up Cadillac that he once announced to me might have been repossessed. Frank was blue and beat-up himself—by life, by pain, by bitter winds that blow like hailstorms in a pitch-black night. St. John of the Cross called it the dark night of the soul. The pastor/poet referenced it as an affliction of tears: "If all men's tears were let into one common sewer, sea, or brine, what were they all compared to Thine?"

Augustine asked a question in his struggle while speaking of a storm that broke within, followed by a deluge of tears: "I longed for a life of happiness, but I was frightened to approach it in its own domain; and yet, while I fled from it, I still searched for it."

Frank, old buddy, darkness penetrated his heart while tears ran together in a speeding, streaming flash flood of anxiety and pain. He ran from happiness yet searched for it, grasping desperately for a rope in the dark. And the rope was Christ. And so Frank searched for relief, for happiness, for peace. He crafted words into poetry. Before he died, he even told the funeral home director, "I am a truck driver and a writer of poetry." And so Frank penned messages: "Suffering is our crucible of faith so that we may comfort others in their time of need."

Had Frank borrowed from the Apostle Paul in 2 Corinthians 1:3-4: "Blessed be God, even the Father of our Lord Jesus Christ, the Father of mercies, and the God of all comfort; Who comforts us in all our tribulation, that we may comfort them which are in any trouble wherewith we ourselves are comforted of God. And gently God spoke to me, 'Be patient, friend,'" and in Frank's words, "Never miss a chance to read a story to a child." And another thread tied a knot around my heart. Frank's cancer raced through his body. Frank phoned me the day doctors told him the news of his impending death. "John, come NOW. I need to see you."

"Frank," I replied, "I cannot come now. I have a funeral. I'll come after the funeral sometime after lunch."
"I won't be here. I'm going to die. I guess I'll never see you again," he whispered as he breathed heavily into the phone. The message board reverberated in my ear; an old message resurrected, "John Duncan, this is the last time you'll ever hear from me. You'll never see me at church again. You people don't have time for me. You don't have time for me. You're too busy for me." A voice kept repeating an old message Frank once mumbled to me, holding back a wall of tears, "John, I am lonely. I hate being alone."

Loneliness broods a melancholy madness in the mind, a darkness that screams. I finished the funeral. I raced to the hospital. Frank told me the news. Doctors explained that he had two months to live. In the hospital room, peace washed over Frank. A tear trickled down his right cheek like a drip from a leaky faucet. The rope tightened in a bond of friendship, a deepening sense of mutual respect. Frank at times angered me, frustrated me, puzzled me, and made me laugh. Now tears and an invisible bond forever linked us. The bond was Christ.

Frank died almost two months to the day after he got the news. He became a child again—helpless, dependent, a child wanting a story read. One day, he told me to sit down. He began, "My friend, John, I've got something to read to you." Had I heard this before? "Never miss a chance to read a story to a child." Frank read me jokes, one with the punch line about a child and some preacher preaching at church, "Mommy, if we give him money, will he let us go?" and another with a punch line of some elderly lady saying in church to some guy who pledged to give to the building campaign, "Hit him again, God, hit him again." Frank laughed. I laughed.

He gave me a message in an envelope before he died, words from Saint Francis of Assisi: "Lord, make me an instrument of thy peace ... where there is hatred, let me sow love; where there is injury faith; where there is doubt faith ... for it is in giving that we receive; it is in pardoning that we are pardoned; and it is in dying that we are born to eternal life."

God hit me again with a message from Frank, that was the message from the message board: Make me an instrument of thy peace.

On the day Frank died, I did not pass up the chance to read this man-child a story. We read Isaiah 40, with the Lord we will fly like eagles; Psalm 37:4, "Delight in the Lord, and he shall give you the desires of your heart." At long last, the desire for delightful happiness ended; Frank's search found solace in a

Savior; a peace that purifies the past. Quietly, silently, like thread slipping into the eye of a needle, Frank died, an invisible rope of Light reached down and pulled him into heaven. Frank slipped from the surly bonds of earth to clutch the hand of God, no longer afraid, no longer alone.

Sometimes in life, God sends us a Frank, a mysterious unknown messenger, to remind us that he was lonely once, rejected many times, and still possessed the power to love; the bond to forgive; the joy of hope in the shadow of darkness while on the cross. The message plants and seeds that blossom into a flower by which we become instruments of thy peace.

Frank sent one last message: "Just wish we had longer time to know each other better! The Lord will save us a table, and plenty of time to do just that." Well, the Lord saves us a table. The Son at last shines. The invisible rope still links earth to heaven, heaven to earth. Mark the last sun that shines. Be patient, friend.

The Days After Easter

I'm sitting here under the old oak tree, wondering about the days after Easter. Spring sprouts with the haze of bluebonnets and green grass. Lawnmowers fire up after the chill of winter. And in our town, workers dumped loads of chlorine in the city pool in preparation for teenagers to hang out. I dub this the "hang out generation" because everybody just wants to "hang out." Do you hang out?

The gospel writer John tells about the days after Easter—of Mary leaving the empty tomb of Jesus and her encounter with two angels dressed in dazzling apparel prettier than a prom dress. She also encountered Jesus, whom she thought was a gardener. The Bible gives details about the realities of daily life—weeping women grieving at an empty borrowed tomb, parables of farming and seed sowing and laborers in the vineyard, and a case of mistaken identity, Jesus confused with the gardener (John 20:18). Did the garden need to be de-weeded? John then tells us about Mary as she ran to share the good news.

Do you not love good news?

Good news brings laughter and a lift to the human spirit. What about Jessica Lynch and seven prisoners of war rescued from captivity in Iraq? When Jessica's family and the other POWs' families received the news of the rescue, do you think they jumped over the couch in elation and happiness? Good news brings relief, like receiving news from the doctor that your test results from all that poking and prodding on your body came back OK. Good news delivers a smile to the soul, like discovering that your checkbook balanced when you just knew that it was overdrawn. Good news demands a hearing, like what you shared when your baby daughter entered mother earth through her birth canal. Some things have to be shared.

John tells us Mary shared the good news with the disciples. It happened in the days after Easter.

The gospel writer and medical doctor Luke tells us of the first few days after Easter. After Easter, the lightning and thunder of Friday, the gory cross, the silent tomb, and the explosion of joy on resurrection morning behind, Luke simply records, "And they remembered his words" (John 24:8).

Here I am on the days after Easter thinking of all the things I forget—the grocery list, my car keys ("Where did I put them?"), my phone ("Has anyone seen my phone?"), a meeting ("It was when?"), and once upon a time, my daughter. I called my wife on the cell phone: "Do you have our oldest daughter? Honey, you have her, don't you? Please tell you do have her!" "No, I told you to pick her up." "Are you sure? Well, I guess I forgot, but I remembered before I got home and am now turning around to go back and get her."

She waited patiently at church.

I can only imagine how much would be forgotten were it not for cell phones in today's world. How did the women at Jesus' tomb and the disciples remember if they did not have cell phones? How do you remember without a cell phone? How do you remember if you always forget? It took an awful lot of forgetting and two shining angels delivering dazzling words for them to remember that Jesus said he would rise on the third day. He arose.

Old Luke tells us that Peter marveled, which means that he too had forgotten and now remembered and decided to spend the rest of his life dispensing the good news. Today we call that a preacher, but every Christian after Easter ought to have some good news to tell.

Then Luke tells us that Jesus walked a road, vanished, and ate a breakfast of broiled fish and honeycomb. My late grandmother once declared: "You should always eat breakfast. It is the most important meal of the day." Holy cow, she learned it from Jesus. After Easter, Jesus ate breakfast. Remember breakfast. Remember the resurrection every time you eat breakfast. I would skip the broiled fish and go for donuts and cereal, though.

Matthew records how the Roman guards tried to distort the good news with bad news. He tells of meeting in back rooms filled with smoke and plots to lie about Jesus' body and bribes, the jingling of silver coins rolling around in soft money bags. Still, one can only hear the echo of Jesus' own words when Matthew describes the sinister plot: "Rejoice!" (Matthew 28:9). Can we do anything but rejoice in the days after Easter?

Mark grieves with his after-Easter words: "And they went and told it to the rest, but they did not believe them either."

Easter joy aims to open a window of belief, letting light into the soul. Easter reality closes a window of darkness to the stark reality that even after all those Easter musicals and swelling Easter crowds at churches and Easter sermons where preachers preach their hearts out and Easter lilies blooming like angels in dazzling apparel and "The Ten Commandments" on television every year, some people still do not believe. They simply forget. They forget Jesus.

Jesus even rebuked his own disciples, who by now were remembering everything Jesus had said and were getting an earful at the table for their "unbelief and hardness of heart" (Mark 16:14). After Jesus got through with them, I do not think they ever forgot. An earful at the table has a way of heightening the senses and alerting the memory. You never forget.

If all this talk about the days after Easter and forgetting and remembering does not make sense to you, I am not sure it makes sense to me, either. But one thing I know, Jesus' resurrection does not make sense either. Still, I believe in it and him by faith with all my heart, and it helps me remember the most important things in life and causes me not to worry about sinister plots. It makes me rejoice every morning when I eat breakfast.

John D. Duncan

Oh, by the way, I never miss breakfast.

Pastors and Mavericks

I am sitting here under the old oak tree, pondering the powerful playoff run of the Dallas Mavericks and the precipice upon which pastors stand.

Do basketball and pastors coincide? Like coaches in today's society, pastors live on the edge of a precipice, ready to step into the glorious, promised land, or they gingerly step toward the not-so-ready dangerous fall into oblivion. Pastors possess the joy of a higher calling, but for many, pressures mount.

Not long ago, after a draining playoff game, Dallas Mavericks coach Don Nelson talked about Los Angeles Lakers' coach Phil Jackson, who had a medical procedure after heart trouble. Pastors work with people who have heart troubles of numerous kinds.

Nelson remarked that on a scale of 1 to 10, a coach's job is a ten on the stress meter. Nelson followed his remark with a telling statement: "It's not just the pressure you put on yourself, although that's the most of it. It's the whole environment, the competition, the press, the radio talk shows-for nine months of the year; everybody's killing you. And if they're not, you're killing yourself."

I have pastored only three churches, which may not completely qualify me to stake my claim, but pastors today face pressures like coaches in a playoff run. I remember and appreciate with fondness the churches that I have been privileged to pastor--the country church of my college days, my first full-time church, and the growing church I now pastor, a church where God amazes me daily by his grace.

I also think of the precious people--Merle, who taught this city boy the difference between sheep and goats; Earl and Emma, who defended their 19-year-old peach fuzz preacher as not some "little preacher boy" but "our preacher" and served me pecan pie; Mack, with his winsome spirit of encouragement that carried me on low days; Cooter, who laughed and forgave me the day in which I plowed over a water pipe while mowing the churchyard; Elsie, who appreciated my trips to the nursing home; an unnamed East Texas lady, who once served up these words: "You young! The Laud done gone and sent you out early"; the Lees and the Smiths, who invited us over for games and fun; Sam, who allows me to be myself whether good or bad; and a host of other unnamed saints at Lakeside Baptist Church, who have helped me hold on to Jesus in the joyous roller coaster ride of 16 years here at Lakeside in Granbury.

The struggles, the mostly highs, and the joys of 16 years in the same place and two other churches still cause me to appreciate God's work, his call, and pastors on the edge of a precipice in the pressure.

I remember through the years numerous pressures and a few not-so-precious saints--a couple of anonymous letters; the guy who once declared, "You'll never make it as a preacher"; church financial pressures; people and personality pressures; growing pains and the pressures of growth; lectures from my parishioners; saints worried about bathroom toilet paper supplies and worship temperatures (Too hot! Too cold! All on the same Sunday!); crowded parking lots; watching the sails rip off of families falling apart; families in other crises like job layoffs; and the ever-present joys of music and worship in this complex 21st century, to name only a few. I learned the pastor's greatest challenge--knowing what to accept as truth and what to ignore or dump into File 13 of life. Satan often comes cloaked with shining wings.

I often ask, "What is the greatest pressure pastors face?" Is it sneaky spiritual warfare that aims to destroy? Is it crises like death and marital straits which aim to rip the sails off marital lifeboats? Is it people who stir trouble in the church? Is it a lack of experience or a lack of knowledge about a church's particular history? Is it a lack of Bible knowledge or spiritual discipline? Is it not enough of Emma's pecan pie?

Or do pastors get beat up by incipient competition between churches? After all, Eugene Peterson once quipped of the dangers of always wishing for "something bigger," or, in his own words, that eternal quest for the perfectly desirable church of the pastor's imagination, "a tall steeple church with a cheesecake congregation."

I think Don Nelson must have been preaching at a pastors' conference. Preachers, pastors, and staffers sometimes get beat down, but most spend a lot of time beating up on themselves, if the truth be known.

For all this talk about coaches and preachers and playoff run by the Dallas Mavericks, two things must happen in the boiling pressures of ministry. Eugene Peterson admits: "Hang around (the church) long enough, and sure enough there are gossips who won't shut up, furnaces that malfunction, sermons that misfire, disciples who quit, choirs who go flat-and worse. Every congregation is a congregation of sinners. And if that weren't bad enough, they all have sinners for pastors." Peterson calls for God's servants and his people, albeit all sinners, to develop two things--holiness in relationship with God and a passion for his calling. These two essentials appear to be missing among pastors and people today amid life pressures.

So here is to all pastors whose sermons have misfired and whose ministry passion has fizzled: Develop holiness in relationship to God again. Ask Christ to renew his joy in you. Beg for his Spirit to rekindle the flame of his passion and calling in spite of the pressures.

So here is to all the people of churches all over the globe: Trust God in your pressures. Recognize the pressures your pastor faces, even amid the beating up of the inner self. Encourage your pastor today. And, by all means, stop looking for cheesecake congregations. Invite your pastor over for pecan pie. It will do you wonders, and it sure will bless your pastor. I sure miss Emma and Earl and that piece of pecan pie of shared fellowship in Christ.

Finally, to Don Nelson, I say, "Go, Dallas Mavericks!"

Snowflakes Falling

I'm sitting here under the old oak tree, thinking of snow. Just a couple of weeks ago, snow covered this old oak tree in Granbury. Three inches of snow made Granbury postcard pretty, if there is such a thing.

In the North Carolina mountains, where my family history plunges deep roots in the soil, blizzard conditions dumped snow like loads of white sand on the earth. Roads closed. The rush to *Wal-Mart* to stock up on groceries before the snowstorm hit was unbelievable. The icy conditions meant that a few folks could not escape their mountain homes for a few days.

A couple of days ago, I woke up on a chilly Sunday morning in Cambridge, England, to snow falling like cotton balls from the sky. The glistening snowflakes tumbled from the sky at hurling speed like meteor showers against a dark sky. The snow in Cambridge rushed to the earth fast and furiously and beautifully blanketed the common areas and the towering buildings where schools like King's College stand. The ground, the buildings, and the snow painted the Cambridge morning white like a big wedding cake ready for the celebration.

I love it when God paints the world and brushes his finger stroke of beauty on the earth. I love it when God paints the earth with his grander. I love it when God paints the heart white in a world so often black with terror, violence, sadness, sorrow, sickness, and sin.

I have not yet seen the movie *The Passion of the Christ*, but I hear the buzz. While in Cambridge, I checked *CNN* news and its website, and the movie was all the rage in America. At teatime at the *Tyndale House Biblical Research Center*, the chaps in Cambridge talked about the movie's theme, its brutality ("the worst film for brutality ever made," as one theologian stated), and the chance to see it when it arrives for showing at a local theater. I looked on a movie website, and the movie arrives in Cambridge at the end of March.

My teenage daughter watched the movie minus popcorn and soft drink. *The Passion* is not a popcorn-and-soft drink kind of movie. Maybe that's what's wrong with the world. We have a popcorn-and-soft drink mentality when we ought to cherish Christ's passion. Enough of that sermon.

Anyway, my daughter talked to me on the phone about *The Passion*. She explained that the movie had lots of blood but that the flashback scenes were really good. "I won't give too much of the movie away. You'll have to see it for yourself," she observed. I guess she did not think that after all these years as a preacher, I probably knew the plot line to Christ's passion. I cannot wait to see the movie.

She talked about *The Passion*, I listened and talked about the beautiful, wintry snow that painted Cambridge like a picture-perfect postcard.

This talk about *The Passion of the Christ* and snow leads me to one thing: I hope the movie has one snowy scene in it, like a postcard from Granbury or Cambridge; blanketed by snow, or a mountain covered with rolling white flakes piled high and looking like a snowman, or snow glittering a building to look like a wedding cake in Cambridge.

Why? Because for all the passion, as Easter soon approaches, it is the snow of the Christ of the cross falling on hearts and glittering them with grace and washing them as white as snow. Like falling snow by this old oak tree, Christ brings child-like wonder of happiness and joy. Like sow flakes falling, Christ's snow changes the landscape of the mountain of the heart and soul, decorating it anew. Like snowflakes tumbling, Christ's snow gives cause for celebration, like eating a piece of wedding cake amid the laughter and cheerfulness of two hearts uniting in marriage.

I hear Isaiah's (1:18) plea for snow: "Come now, let us reason together," says the Lord: "Though your sins be as scarlet, they shall be as white as snow; though they be red like crimson, they shall be as wood." Isaiah's words tumble on my heart like snow falling like cotton balls, and I pen these words. May snowflakes fall on your heart:

*Snowflakes falling

Gently falling
Falling Gently
From heaven above.
*Snowflakes falling
Softly falling
Falling softly
On earth below.
*Snowflakes falling
Quietly falling
Falling quietly
On my heart today.
*Snowflakes tumbling
Humbly falling
Falling humbly
On my soul in a fresh way.
*Snowflakes falling
Gently falling
Falling gently
To wash my sins away.
*Snowflakes falling
Softly falling
Falling softly
To bring the joy of life.
*Snowflakes falling
Quietly falling

*Falling quietly
To usher peace without strife.
*Snowflakes falling
Humbly falling*

*Falling humbly
"Come let us reason," the voice of God does know.
*Snowflakes falling
Gently falling
Falling gently
"Though your sins be as scarlet, they shall be as white as snow."
*Snowflakes.
Falling
Falling
Falling
Falling
Falling
Falling
Above
Below
Today
In a fresh way
To wash my sins away
To bring life
To end strife
"Come let us reason,"
That's what God says,
"Though your sins be as scarlet,
They shall be as white as snow;
Though they be red like crimson,
They shall be as wool."
*Snowflakes falling
Falling*

*Falling
From heaven above
*Snowflakes packing
Packing
Packing
The earth below.
Like wood and cotton balls,
*Snow falls
Pure white
In sight
On me.
Snowflakes falling, falling, falling on you and me.

John D. Duncan

The Quality God Blesses

I'm sitting here under the old oak tree, asking what one trait does God always blesses? As I ponder deep thoughts, the world spins out of control.

I write with the news fresh on my mind. Bush and Kerry drive toward the upcoming elections by plotting their economic strategies for American consumers. Do they know that consumers pay $1.44 for bread at Wal-Mart and $1.59 for unleaded gas? A 9-11 panel is still trying to solve the terror attacks on New York in September 2001. While they meet, an influential Shiite cleric from Iraq declares the terror attacks of Sept. 11 a "miracle from God." He must worship the unknown God of Acts 17 because my God takes glory in abundant life, not explosive death.

The push for the Final Four rattles television sets across America. Who will win? Will it be Duke or the University of Connecticut, Georgia Tech, or Oklahoma State?

Michael Jackson and Kobe Bryant still await trial, and the news will not let up. In our small town, the newspaper's front page printed a story about a young lady awaiting trial for a "murder for hire" on her husband. The news causes hair to stand up on the back of my head.

A cat birthed a kitten with a genetic defect in Germany. The four-eared kitten finally found a home. Oh, the joys of a kitten finding a home where a little girl can sneak the kitten into her room at night, cuddle it, and let its soft fur sleep next to her gentle face.

Drizzle drips from the sky, and rain soon comes to paint mother earth the colors of spring, which means, of course, that Daylight Savings Time comes, and we will all lose an hour of sleep. I have not found the hour of sleep that I lost last year.

The news rattles the earth, and I am thinking of that one quality God always blesses.

Not too long ago, a relative in the mountains of Spruce Pine, N.C., died. His name was Adam Duncan. He was my father's uncle. He drove a dump truck all over the Blue Ridge Mountains, hauling dirt, quartz rock, flint, sand, and asphalt. He once upon a time cultivated bees that made honey. I once saw him put on a silver suit with a mask that looked like something a knight wore while fencing in the Middle Ages. He donned the suit, reached in the white wooden box with gloves, and pulled out a honeycomb. He combed the honey and put it in a Mason jar for putting on homemade biscuits.

He took popcorn on Friday nights to my two aunts, never missed church, and often led the singing. If the car broke down, he would be the one to call. If the roof leaked, he would be the one to phone. If a snowstorm blew in and you needed groceries from the local store, he would risk his neck to make sure you had groceries.

He loved to sing the old trusty hymn *Trust and Obey* adult men talked about Adam when he died, describing him: "I would choose Adam Duncan as the most faithful man in church." God blessed Adam. His most faithful task was being the first to arrive at church and the last to leave the church. Why? Adam locked and unlocked the church every Sunday, come rain or sunshine, snow or sleet, drizzle or fog.

And so here I am under the old oak tree, pondering faithfulness. The Bible says, "Moses my servant was faithful in all my house" (Numbers 12:27). Adam exhibited faithfulness. Faithfulness is taking the trash out on trash day. Faithfulness is turning your homework in on time. Faithfulness means remembering your daughter's birthday. Faithfulness is doing the laundry before it piles too high. Faithfulness is changing the oil in the car every 3,000 miles. Faithfulness is daily Bible reading and daily prayer. Faithfulness is the consistent doing of necessary things, even when you do not feel like it. Faithfulness is trusting and obeying Jesus, even when the world spins out of control.

The old oak tree does not have a lock and key for Sunday, but churches need to be opened and unlocked. Doors need unlocked and locked on Sundays, but more than that, God needs the faithful and their faithfulness. It is the one quality God always blesses.

Simple Things

I'm sitting here under the old oak tree, thinking about simple things. The British poet John Keats once quipped, "Stop and consider! Life is but a day; a fragile dewdrop on its perilous way."

I'm sitting here with morning dew under my feet, pondering the simple things in life. Jesus used simple things to discuss the kingdom of God—golden treasures stored in lockboxes; wedding banquets in their gala and festive joy with wedding garments like white dresses and a banquet table loaded with delicious food; fruit trees minus figs for a story; plush seats at banquet tables and rough roads with potholes on a narrow way; lamps full of oil for light; a widow sweeping the house while looking for a lost coin; a shepherd searching in the open fields for a lost sheep; farmers plowing fields and planting seeds in expectation of a bountiful crop; storms that blow in at midnight and houses built on a rock; a mother crying over her wayward son and a troubled son who leaves home and returns amid tears and a party on the porch; bread and lights on a hill and simple words like, "Follow me."

My favorite simplicity of Jesus is the time a small child crawled into his lap, and he stated the kingdom of God is such as this. Was Jesus saying the kingdom of God is about toys like an *X-box* or a dollhouse or a motorized car and bicycles and kites with tails dancing in the wind? Was Jesus saying the kingdom of God is about trips to the park where your mother pushes you in a swing and baseball games where dirt soils your socks? Was Jesus saying the kingdom of God is about soccer games and skinned knees and bandages and ice cream cones and ordering a *Happy Meal* from the drive-through window at *McDonald's*?

No, Jesus was saying that the kingdom of heaven is about simple things—child-like wonder and innocence and faith like when your daughter jumps off a ledge into your sure arms and trust that trusts even when the future is unclear. Children possess kingdom qualities because they believe in the simplicity of all that Christ can do. Who could ask for anything more?

The dew sticks to my shoes, and I am thinking of simple things—the chirp of a bird feeding her young on a spring morning; the rise of the sun in its beauty in the crispness of a new day; the glory of a sunset sparkling light over the lake and singing in all its splendor of the joy of a day passed ("Stop and consider! Life is but a day ..."); the push and pull of oceans tides as the whitecaps stand tall in the wind, and as the foam, seaweed and even seashells roll in with the tide; simple things like mountains pointing to God who made heaven and earth; the drip of rain on the gutter while rain pours amid thunder and lightning; the laughter of friends; the tears shared in sorrow among family; the high fives of fans watching their favorite sports team in the elation of victory; the laughter of children; words shared among friends and family that bring healing; parents kissing their kids on the cheek at bedtime; and living each day to its fullest.

Jesus invites us to live life to the fullest. The dew is on my feet, and complexity heightens my senses. From where does the dew come? Did rain fill the earth like water poured into a bowl, and did the bowl overflow to the ground this morning? Did God cry in his grief, and his tears sprinkled the earth with teardrops of dew? Did clouds collect water and quietly drop them one by one on the earth like dripping rain from the roof of a house? Did the oceans roll and tumble, toss and turn, churning sand beneath the ocean's surface and suddenly push dew drops toward the shore like a starfish or a bottle floating to the sea's shore?

Maybe, just maybe, God sent a child in smiles and laughter with a dropper like one for putting drops in your eyes to moisten them, and the child sprinkled the earth with God's dew. Or did the morning dew kiss the grass as if to say, "Stop and consider! Life is but a day; a fragile dew-drop on its perilous way."

The psalmist says: "This is the day the Lord has made. Let us rejoice and be glad in it!" (Psalm 118:24)

So, in simplicity, I decided not to try to figure out how dew reached the grass or my shoes on this day. Today, I simply thank God for simple things—God's love and forgiveness and strength and grace and wisdom and power and family and friends and church and wide-eyed wonder and faith and trust and the morning dew.

Hey! Praise the Lord. Give thanks. Watch the sunrise. Enjoy the ocean tides and mountain beauty. Let a child climb up in your lap. Speak simple words. Stop and consider; life is but a day.

John D. Duncan

Dad's Old Glove

I'm sitting here under the old oak tree, thinking of Father's Day. Actually, I'm thinking of a glove. Imagine a leather baseball glove. Hear the sound of the ball popping the leather. Smell the leather.

I think back to the '70s when I was a teenager. I am leaning against a steel chain-link fence on a softball diamond. My father wears a yellow jersey with blue letters on the front and numbers on the back. My father is wearing tennis shoes. A baseball glove fits nicely on his rather large left hand. I do not know if his team won or lost. I remember the game was played on a spring evening as the sun set.

Fast forward to a spring evening in 2004. Two of my teenage daughters sit in the stands behind a steel chain-link fence on a baseball diamond. I wear a red jersey. The jersey has black letters and no numbers. I am wearing cleats. A baseball glove fits nicely on my rather large left hand. My church softball team is winning. On this spring evening, the sun sets as the baseball diamond lights slowly come alive with the bulbs shining on the field.

I should tell you the baseball glove is my father's, the one he used when I was a teenager. The softball guys give me a hard time about my glove. It has been restrung, tied with shoestrings, and looks like it has been left out in the rain a dozen times. Just the other day, a hard-throwing teammate threw the softball so hard it broke the webbing. I cut a shoestring, fixed the broken webbing with a knot, and played the game with that glove.

In one of his poems, the poet Percy Shelley has a line, "God dawned on chaos." My glove has been fixed so much it looks like chaos. I need to purchase a new one, but I guess I am sentimental. I like that glove because my father passed it on to me.

Father's Day arrives in the glory of a Texas summer. I am thankful for all that my father passed on to me—love, care, grace, hope, life, laughter, eternal things, not just things you can stuff in the garage or attic, not just baseball caps, bats, and a leather glove.

When I think of my father, I think of the words of C.K. Chesterton, "The secret of life lives in laughter and humility." My father discovered that secret. I thank the Lord for him and remember him every time I put on my baseball glove. I remember him on this Father's Day.

Who knows, maybe I'll call him and see if he wants to come over and play catch.

John D. Duncan

Bonnie, a Flower in the Desert

I'm sitting here under the old oak tree, remembering Bonnie, a flower in the desert of my life.

The year was 1987. In those days, life was a seed planted and soon to sprout. I pastored a small church in a rural community. The world at large buzzed with news—nuclear testing in Nevada; a plane crash killing 156 people in Detroit; the first heart-lung transplant in Baltimore; Fred Astaire died; Hillary Duff was born; Prozac made its debut in pharmaceuticals; Lethal Weapon was a popular movie, and Wal-Mart planned to build a Super Wal-Mart here in Granbury.

One hot August day in 1987, I stood on a porch. The boards creaked when I walked up the steps. I knocked on the door. Bonnie opened the door and invited me inside.

I spent time with Bonnie and her husband, Burl, in the ensuing years. I think of the words of the poet Walt Whitman when I think of Bonnie: "I anchor my ship for a little while only, My messengers continually cruise away or bring their returns to me."

I anchored my ship in Bonnie's living room on many occasions. She was my messenger, often giving insight into God's ways, church talk, her strong opinion about the way things ought to be, and encouragement for the journey—during a time when my pastorship sailed rough seas.

The church declined in 1987. My pastoral skills required excelled growth. The likes of Riley, John and Ruth, Dorothy, and Bonnie directed my life like a compass. They advised me to spread wisdom and poured water on my weary, dehydrated soul.

I anchored my ship for a little while, myself the skipper, in the words of Whitman again, "How (I) the skipper saw the crowded and rudderless wreck of a steamship, and death chasing it up and down the storm." The church declined. Like a stern ship, the church appeared crowded and rudderless, a church ship on a wrecking course. In my mind, at least, the church seemed like death chasing it up and down the storm. The storm winds blew. The lightning and thunder raged. The storm rocked the ship, tossing it like a bottle on the rolling, ferocious waves.

Then suddenly, the storm calmed. The church ship found a harbor of peace. The church suddenly grew, the church ship alive, vibrant, active, and full of joy. And there, on the shore amid the desert of my life, a flower bloomed. Her name was Bonnie.

I stood at her gravesite just the other day. Bonnie lived 84 fruitful years. She once vowed after a storm on her farm never to shortchange God. She once told me I was the best pastor she ever had, "my brother John," she boasted. She once helped calm a storm in the days of my youth. She once wrote a note in her Bible given to her by her son, Tom, one Mother's Day in the 1960s. She wrote about God's "true book." She once instructed the preacher which verse to read at her funeral.

Now, almost 18 years later, I stood in the sunshine at the cemetery. In the words of Emily Bronte, life lengthens, "shadows on shadows advancing and flying!" The sun lengthened the shadows. The family walked through the valley of the shadow of death. And memory flooded my mind.

I remembered the porch, the door swinging open, the words, the night her husband, Burl, died, the storm, and the flower in the desert. And somehow, somewhere, her words came rushing afresh, like a flower in the desert, like dew on fresh-cut grass, like a cool breeze wisping over a calm sea, the ship afloat in the calm. What were her words? Her words were similar to those she instructed to be read at her funeral, "Let not your heart be troubled; you believe in God, believe also in me."

John D. Duncan

    I stood at the gravesite and gave thanks to the Lord for flowers in the desert, of whom Bonnie was one, a flower that blossomed in my life one August day.
    Tom told me that she went peacefully, he slipped his hand into hers as she gasped for her last breath. As she breathed her last, she slipped quietly into God's hand. And that's where she is now—no longer a flower in the desert, but a flower radiating and wafting a scent of sweetness in heaven. And sometimes, yes, sometimes, that's how life goes.
    Let not your heart be troubled.

King Jesus

I'm sitting here under the old oak tree, reflecting on the days after Easter. I find myself thinking of Jesus as "King."

Recently I traveled to Cambridge, England. The main tourist attraction in Cambridge remains King's College, founded on Easter in 1441. On Easter, the first stone was laid by a young, vivacious Henry VI. King's College Chapel took over a century to build. A king laid the stone.

While in England, I toured the Tower of London. I stood in line as I waited to see the crown jewels. While in line, the Tower of London tour guide shows a video.

The video unveils the pomp and circumstances of Queen Elizabeth's coronation, the placement of a golden crown on her head in the crowning of a queen in splendor. After the video ends with the people of Great Britain celebrating the queen's coronation, you are privileged to walk through what looks like a bank vault. Inside the vault, in glass casings, you will find scepters, golden swords, and crowns decorated with rubies, sapphires, and diamonds inlaid in gold—the crown jewels. The queens and kings of Great Britain of days past display their wares in the glory of Great Britain. The queens and kings bask in the glory of jewels worn in crowns.

All this talk somehow leads me to think of Fredrick Buechner, who, at the age of 27, stumbled into Madison Avenue Presbyterian Church in New York City. He attended a worship service at the time of Queen Elizabeth's coronation. He heard a sermon by the great Presbyterian preacher George Buttrick.

Buechner writes: "And then with his head bobbing up and down so that his glasses glittered, he said in his odd, sandy voice, the voice of an old nurse, that the coronation of Jesus took place among confession and tears and then, as God was and is my witness, great laughter, he said. Jesus is crowned among confession and tears and great laughter, and at the phrase great laughter, for reasons that I have never satisfactorily understood, the great wall of China crumbled, and Atlantis rose up out of the sea, and on Madison Avenue, at 73rd Street, tears leapt from my eyes as though I had been struck across the face."

God as king crowned him with grace—a crazy, holy grace.

Still, here I am in Texas, pondering Jesus as king. Spring will paint the earth a glowing green in a few days, and bluebonnets will dot the Texas landscape. Yard mowing season will begin. In our town, jet skis and boats will zip across the lake, and for $15-a-carload, movie watchers will catch two movies at the outdoor drive-in named the *Brazos Theater*. All told, Jesus will still be king.

Yet in these days after Easter, I find myself thinking of Jesus as king, a humble Savior riding into Jerusalem on a donkey; a brutalized king crowned with thorns while blood dripped off his nose; an entombed king quietly placed in a grave with the fanfare of a funeral with one attendee; a risen king who stepped out of the tomb while an angel white as snow sat on the stone rolled away.

And all I can do is live in wonder—of sunrise in the glory of spring; of bluebonnets popping up all over the hillsides; of birds sailing and singing in the early morn; of Jesus as king loving and living and forgiving and rejoicing in the hearts of those who live in the wonder of his friendship. He is king. I bow down and worship and serve in the joy of his crazy, holy grace. And all I can do is say, "Hail King Jesus."

And you?

God's Fingerprints

I'm sitting here under the old oak tree, pondering the finger of God. His fingerprint makes an imprint on all the earth.

When a child is born, a doctor counts toes and fingers. Weddings find celebration when the bride and groom speak vows and place a ring on each other's finger. Children love to paint with fingers an array of blues, greens, oranges, yellows, and browns in a kaleidoscope of finger-painting that ends up on refrigerator doors. In order to type this article or build a porch on the back of your house, wash dishes, or help your child with their math homework, each respective activity requires fingers. Each finger possesses a fingerprint. A fingerprint unveils the uniqueness of you.

In 1997, I visited the Sistine Chapel in Rome. It has been in the news—a meeting place for a college of cardinals, votes cast in a shroud of secrecy and white smoke. The Sistine Chapel was built in the 1400s in the same dimensions of Solomon's Temple as described in the Bible. Paintings decorate the walls and ceilings.

I remember our visit to the Sistine Chapel vividly—the press of the tourist crowd ("no cameras, please"), my weary daughters wondering if we could purchase something to eat, the famous paintings of The Last Judgment, The Twelve Apostles, and Michelangelo's work, the tour guide Giorgio, and the finger of God painted dead center in the top of the ceiling.

The finger depicts God's hand, his fingerprint on creation. Spring has come, and God's creative wonder comes alive: birds chirping, bees buzzing, flowers blooming, fish zipping through the oceans and rivers, and the moon and stars, the sun's rays showering the world with the delight of God's glory.

The 16th-century theologian John Calvin called creation the "theater" of God's glory. The Psalmist declared, "You (Lord) have set your glory above the heavens. ... I consider the work of your fingers, the moon and the stars" (Psalm 8:2-3). God's fingerprint paints the world like a child's finger-painting glowing in a dazzling array of colors.

Yet, when I consider creation, I ponder human beings, people God created—a world of happy people, sad people, angry people, joyful people, hard-working people, lazy people, and, well, just people. I think of the people in the Sistine Chapel on that July day in 1997. And I think of people I know personally. And I think of fingers, but more so the finger of God. "What is man that you are mindful of him? The son of man that you take care of him?" (Psalm 8:4).

All in all, I know God's fingerprint is on our world, his people, and even me. Who could ask for anything more? Who could ask for anything more?

Life as a Pastor

I'm sitting here under the old oak tree, thinking of my life as a pastor. In *The Church Porch*, George Herbert writes, "... dress and undress thy soul ...," and earlier in the poem remarks, "Join hands with God to make a man live." Such is the life of a pastor—soul work and helping people join hands with God.

I recently preached on the wisdom of God. I shared with our church that (a) we should live under the sun but seek wisdom above it; (b) all the rivers run into the sea, but only One River, Jesus, satisfies; and (c) we should plant spiritual seeds, develop roots and live a life of purpose under God's care. Life, like the sea, never fills up or fully satisfies apart from Christ. I mentioned life as repetitious sameness, ceaseless change, and a variety of people in places with Christ at the center.

I even quoted Sue Monk Kidd in *The Secret Life of Bees*: "There is nothing perfect. There is only life." I added: "There is nothing perfect. There is only Eternal life." I spoke to graduating high school seniors, of which my daughter, Jenifer, was one. After the service, what do you think stuck like peanut butter to the brains of my hearers? My comment that we live in the "flip-flop generation," one where girls will get married wearing $500 dresses and $2.99 flip-flops from Wal-Mart. I preached soul work and wound up with a flip-flop sermon. I invited the church to join hands with God.

The next day, God welcomed in his gentle hands Tom, a church member and a prominent member of our community. Tom loved his motorcycle, and God called him home in a terrible accident. The Psalmist says: "You number my wanderings; Put my tears into your bottle." Gerard Manley Hopkins dramatically pictures grief, "My cries heave, herds-long; huddle in a main, a chief-woe, world-sorrow; on an age-old anvil wince and sing—Then lull, then leave off." I grieved with the family and prayed while sitting at the table, holding hands in a circle while their fluffy black cat rubbed his fur in my face. The sea may never fill up, but the tears of the soul fill many a bottle. God's hand holds it. Soul work sprinkles raindrops.

The drama of this pastor's life flows like a river—a church member waiting for a liver transplant; another with appendicitis; back surgeries; gall bladder operations; cancer; chemotherapy; a baby near death from respiratory failure; and the calling of a new minister to students. All these things dip into the same river—the River of Life, Jesus, and soul work, and won't you join hands with God to make a life?

Tomorrow comes, and I will stand at a gravesite and eulogize the fishing guide, Jim. I will read from the 23rd Psalm and talk about, in his wife's sweet words, how he lifted his hands toward heaven and prayed and spoke words. Simple words, "I've had a great life, loved fishing, my family and kids." The sea tides roll.

The next day I will stand and fill up a bottle with tears as I grieve the loss of Tom at the memorial service. I will remember his strong will, bright smile, and riding in his race car at 90 miles an hour. I'll remember him stopping the car and walking me over a piece of property overlooking the lake and his tall frame looking into my eyes and saying, "Preacher, tell me why I need to be baptized." I did, and later we baptized Tom. I think of the race car and the motorcycle and life's great race and the finish line and a bottle of tears. All rivers run into the sea. The soul flows.

So here I am under the old oak tree, thinking about my life as a pastor not too far from the church porch—four weddings in nine days, funerals, sermons, high school graduation, life, the laundry, mowing the yard, the checkbook, changing the diapers, holding a baby ready to breathe its last breath, and bottles. Eugene Peterson says it best, "Pastoral work takes place between Sundays, between the first and the eighth day, between the boundaries of creation and resurrection, between Genesis 1 and Revelation 21." Soul work happens between Sundays.

I love my life as a pastor—the drama, the dressing of souls, souls joining hands with God to make their lives like 8-year-old Joseph did last Sunday, the joy, the laughter, and filling up bottles.

This week, I will fill up bottles, but in the midst of it all, nothing will compare to the tears of joy that will flow from the river of my heart when Jenifer walks across the stage and graduates from high school. Congratulations, Jenifer. Live. Celebrate. Dress your soul. Swim in the River. There is nothing perfect, only abundant Life. Join hands with God and make a life! Welcome to the flip-flop generation.

John D. Duncan

Grace Reigns

I'm sitting here under the old oak tree, remembering Don Knotts in his passing at 81 years of age and Mayberry RFD. I must tell you that I did not spend much of my childhood watching programs like the *Andy Griffith Show* and the nostalgic town Mayberry. Later in life, I learned to watch cable TV's *Nick at Night* and see Don Knotts in his quirky role as Deputy Sheriff Barney Fife. Laughter reigned.

I find myself reflecting that we live in the dream of a Mayberry world that is an *iPod* world in actuality. I live in Granbury, Texas, a place where people once referred to our town very much like Mayberry. After all, we had a *Dairy Queen*, a drive-in-theater, a local radio station that aired high school sporting events, old roads where once in a while a tractor slowed traffic, and a lake where fishermen could fish on the grassy banks on a warm day. Mayberry reigned.

iPod has arrived now in the 21st century. *Dairy Queen* has been replaced by *Chili's*. The drive-in theater is still open, but a newer theater with stadium seating airs the latest flicks. The local radio station has surrendered to the satellite radio in cars and computers. Sprawling roads and busy intersections now slow traffic, and drive time takes longer than it used to, no matter the destination in our town. Fishing has even changed—high-powered boats and sophisticated technology that measures the lake's depths and tells you if a fish school is nearby. Just the other day, I saw a young man jogging on the street with headphones in his ears and his *iPod* blasting the musical tunes of who knows, Lifehouse? Carrie Underwood singing *Jesus Take the Wheel*? Or maybe Coldplay? Or just maybe, Casting Crowns belting out Lifesong. *iPod* reigns.

I remind myself of the old quote: Three things in life remain constant—death, taxes, and change.

I sit here and ponder the church of the 21st century: Do we long for a Mayberry church in an *iPod* world? Anyone who lived in the fabulous '50s would probably answer a resounding yes. But what about a person born in 1990? They much prefer *iPod*, I am sure.

The landscape in Granbury changes daily: *Home Depot, Loews*, new roads, new construction, new schools, and traffic with drivers zipping about while talking on cell phones. The landscape of denominational life, church life, and Christian life changes daily, too. Pity the poor pastor who faces the challenges of navigating the worship styles, the expectations, the challenges, the struggles, the shifting dynamic of stewardship (from giving tithes to giving to a cause), and the complex problems churches and people face. Or celebrate the fact that Christian leaders stand on the brink of the greatest opportunity to produce life change by the power of the Gospel.

God's truth remains. Jesus is our One constant. And the gospel speaks to an *iPod* world just like it did in a Mayberry world.

So here I am, sitting under the old oak tree, sipping lemonade. In a Mayberry world, lemonade was lemonade. In an *iPod* world, lemonade might be raspberry or strawberry or the pick of your choice. We live in the age of multiple choice. Yet one simple constant remains: Jesus Christ. I long for a Mayberry world, but I live in an *iPod* world, so all I can do is adapt to the times' complexity, but cling to the glory of the gospel in its simplicity.

Augustine in his *Confessions* in the fourth century spoke of God's light, change in his own life, Jesus his anchor, and concluded that thirst and hunger for God answered his deepest questions in the complexity of life: "In this way, O Lord, you create happiness and give it to us to ease our lives." In a Mayberry world

John D. Duncan

where people often long to go back to remember happiness, Augustine invites us to live in the present moment and to look toward the future to discover our true happiness and ease in the light, strength, and humble mercy of God. May God's grace reach us to find happiness in him. Grace reigns!

Ascension Gifts

I'm sitting here under the old oak tree, thinking about the ascension of Christ. "Ascending" sounds like something you do when you climb a ladder. "Ascending" sounds like an eagle riding the wind to new heights. "Ascending" is what my middle daughter did when she was young, and she climbed on top of the refrigerator.

The thrill of Christmas and Easter buzz like sirens around the church and even in the world. Rightly so because, as Christians, we circle those dates on the calendar and celebrate them in the glory of Christ. Ah, what glory it is! The poet Gerard Manley Hopkins once said, "Glory be to God for dappled things." I looked up "dappled" in the dictionary. It means to mark with different colors. Christmas and Easter add color to the Christian calendar, the church, and the Christian life. Where would we be without those dappled things? And, how drab and dull and colorless our lives would be without Christ in Christmas and Easter?

We find in the Bible after Jesus' resurrection appearances in Galilee, where Jesus ate fish with his disciples, that Jesus went to a region near Bethany and ascended. Paul writes to the church at Ephesus and indicates, "Jesus ascended and gave gifts to men" (Ephesians 4:8). What gifts were given? After all, of the ascension, we only know that Jesus lifted up his hands and blessed the disciples and parted from them, and was carried up into heaven (Luke 24:50-52).

Like Elijah, did he ride the whirlwind, summoned by a chariot of fire and horses of fire? Did he suddenly disappear like Enoch, as the Bible says, "And Enoch was no more"? Did a giant hand reach down and carry him to heaven? Did he fly in the air with grace like Michael "Air" Jordan in his heyday, rising for a basketball dunk only to ascend and never return from flight to earth? We do not know. The Bible says simply: "... he went up ..." (Acts 1:10).

When my daughters were small, Easter approached. The church discussion surrounded the story of Christ and his resurrection and, apparently, the Trinity, God as Father, Son, and Holy Spirit, three-in-one.

At this point in the story, I should tell you that I have three daughters—Amy, Jenifer, and Melanie. Amy is the oldest, the one who always asked theological questions. Once when we had the Lord's Supper, she asked, "Mom, is this the last supper?" and she is also the child who, when seeing Jesus hanging on the cross in a children's book, blood running down his forehead, exclaimed, "That's gross!" Theology speaks.

Jenifer is the child who climbed the refrigerator, the happy child forever laughing and smiling and, like her mother, bringing the fun to life. She once told me, "God is in our heart—and so is Santa Claus!" Faith and fun capture the beauty of her essence.

Amy and Jenifer are in college. Melanie, the youngest, is in high school now. She, to this day, is the child full of answers, the right word for the right moment that will cause you to think seriously or fall out of your chair with side-splitting laughter. Her quick wit illuminates the world. Melanie once asked me, "Daddy, what is joy?"

"It's kind of like happiness on the inside but more than that," I replied in simplicity.

"Well, I've got lots of that, don't I?" she responded without a thought. And she does have lots of joy!

When my daughters were younger, the eldest two in elementary and Melanie in kindergarten, Amy, the theologian, asked the question in the days before Easter: "Daddy, I don't get the Trinity, how can they be three in one?"

"Wait here," I said, eager to explain as Jenifer and Melanie listened and observed.

I walked over to the refrigerator, found an ice cube and an egg, and returned to the table where all three daughters sat. I began to explain: "It's like this: Father, Son, Holy Ghost, three-in-one." I held up the ice cube: "Three-in-one, frozen it is ice; it can also be vapor; melted, it is water; three-in-one!" I threw the ice cube in the kitchen sink.

I held up the egg: "Three-in-one: the egg is a shell, a white and a yoke; three-in-one."

Satisfied, they all watched, listened, and responded nonverbally as if to say, "We got it!" I often encourage parents to give simple answers to deep theological questions with children. I had done that myself. Simplicity rules! No more questions emerged, and they went about their business until the Saturday before Easter.

On Saturday before Easter, all three girls stood at the kitchen table while their mother, Judy, helped them dye, decorate and color the eggs, making them "dappled things" in Easter glory. They colored the eggs when, suddenly, one of the eggs cracked. Melanie, ever ready to answer the moment with words, stood back and shouted as the cracked egg leaked its yellow yoke on the table, "The Holy Spirit is leaking out!" three in one had stuck in her brain from the Trinity discussion. Now one of three leaked out of the cracked egg—in her mind, the Holy Spirit.

Ah, childhood moments of memory. Ah, the glory of dappled things and words fit for the right time. Ah, oak trees and Easter and cracked eggs and the Holy Spirit leaking out! Ah, the death (gross!) and burial and resurrection and ascension of Jesus.

Jesus ascended, and he gave gifts to men. Christmas dapples the world with the story of Christ's birth. Easter dapples the world with glory. The ascension is when the Holy Spirit leaked out.

The Holy Spirit hails as one of the great gifts. The Spirit convicts, commends, guides and comforts. I am not sure how nor what specific steps to take to get the word out, but the 40 days after Easter remind us of the message of the gift of the Holy Spirit who has "leaked out" in believers and who moves like mist over the waters and shows up to bring grace and help just in the nick of time.

    Jesus went up, and the Holy Spirit leaked out. And we daily sense the blessing of this great gift. Daily he gives gifts. Will we receive them with thanks?

Sweet, Sweet Pie

I'm sitting here under the old oak tree, thinking of pie and crust, of sweetness and hardship, of happiness and sadness. On numerous occasions over the years, I have written about Ruth when writing this column. She played the organ for our church many years ago. She passed away not long ago. I dedicate this column to her daughter, Kathleen.

Ruth died two days after her 96th birthday, born on April 26, 1910. She was born to J.L and Cora. J.L. was a Baptist preacher and carpenter.

On a March day in 1930, Ruth climbed out of the bathroom window to elope with her beau, John. John was the crust of the pie, a man of the Depression, a frugal man who worked hard for everything he possessed. And he also mixed the sound for recordings of church musicals while producing numerous albums.

John passed away one March day in 2004, four days shy of his 74th wedding anniversary. He liked to invite me into his home, turn on Pat Robertson videos he recorded, and discuss the end times. I would be a rich man if I had a dime for every time John asked me the question, "Don't 'cha think we're living in the last days?" He smoked a pipe, loved to discuss the end times, and was a crusty old character who served up opinions on life, politics, church, "the fundamentalists," "the liberal politicians," the Southern Baptist denomination, music, and the end times. He swung at those topics like a first-time tennis player swinging at tennis balls, hit and miss, hit, hit, hit, miss, and ka bang! The big hit over the fence!

John was the crust of the pie, hard on the outside but soft when you understood his background and his fears. He once said, "Preacher, I'm afraid." John's hardness probably resulted in deep fear, yet he had peace in Christ. It happens so in some people. He spoke of the fear of sickness and death. He died and donated his body to science and requested no funeral. You could say, in the words of the poet Percy Shelley, "Music when soft voices die, vibrates in the memory." John's melodious voice still resonates in my memory, "Don't 'cha think we're living in the last days?"

"Get some dessert!" John said on our first lunch meeting. We, meaning John, Ruth, and I, piled in their 1965 Mustang one June day in 1987. It was my first year at Lakeside Baptist Church, a church I have pastored for 19 years. Things were not going well, and it showed on my face. John became my ally in the war, my flashlight in the darkness, my song in the shadows, the one who turned the joyous knob of encouragement in the dissonance of my sad-song struggle. The crust tasted good and good for many years as we shared friendship. He let me be myself. What a great blessing in life when people let you be you and the you that God created!

Oh, but where would the pie be without the crust?

If John was the crust, Ruth was the pie. Ruth trained as a concert pianist before her exit from the bathroom window. She used those skills to play the piano and organ for churches most of her life. She played the organ at Lakeside into her eighties.

She once played for our late former minister of music, Randal. He was known for singing on the spur of the moment, tunes like His *Eye Is on the Sparrow*, his favorite. He would tell the organist what he planned to sing, never practice, and "old leather lungs," as his friends called him, would belt out the song without the blink of an eye. Except, one Sunday, all eyes blinked.

Randal told Ruth which song he was going to sing before the worship service. She heard one song, and Randal sang another when the time came for the special music. Ruth played. Randal sang. Neither of them stopped. They played on, sang on, and plowed on. It sounded like an old tin can rattling in offbeat.

If I can be so kind, it was the worst sounding mess of a song I have ever heard in any worship service. Neither of them blinked, but the church blinked, fidgeted, squirmed, and made faces like you see when a baby sucks on a lemon. We all laughed about it later. Life brings moments etched in the memory forever. That was one of them.

Then another Sunday, I told this great story about baseball player Babe Ruth. I told the story, rising high and low with voice intonation, when, suddenly, to make my point, I gestured with my hand toward the congregation and clearly stated, "The problem with Ruth was that he made a mistake!" Ruth, the organist, looked at her husband, face ashen, and whispered, "I made a mistake. I made a mistake?" John, never one to be quiet, within hearing told her, "No, Ruth. He's talkin' about Babe Ruth. Babe Ruth made a mistake, not you!" Ruth loved to tell that story every time I saw her. She rarely forgot, saved every card I ever sent to her from church or Cambridge, England, and loved to repeat stories a thousand times. And she shared the gospel story to every living soul who ever walked in her home, called on the phone, including phone sales solicitors and even people she did not know at restaurants. The gospel resonated within her heart and created wonderful notes on the musical score of her life, notes of grace and kindness and love and sweetness and humor.

Ruth had a great sense of humor. One summer Sunday night at Lakeside Baptist Church, the worship fizzled, and the sermon ended with a dud like the fizz of a firecracker that never ignites. I prayed, and the song commenced, *Set My Soul Afire, Lord!* The minister of music waved his arms for congregational singing, Ruth played the harmonious tunes of the hymn, and I watched and smelled a burning smell when suddenly, the organ caught on fire! The music minister jumped over a rail, unplugged the organ, and God showed up in holy fire as the song ended! Ruth and I laughed about that for years. I now say, "Watch what you sing for because you never know when God might just give you what you sing for!"

Ruth wrote in her Bible the plan of salvation, sermon notes, outlines, and her favorite verse, Lamentations 3:22-23, "It is of the Lord's mercies that we are not consumed, because his compassions fail not. They are new every morning: great is thy faithfulness." She used an old King James Version because, in her day, that was the only thing going. And John loved the King James as much as he loved Ruth, and Ruth wanted to please John, so she used KJV.

I spoke at Ruth's funeral and shared all the changes she had experienced in her life: From Model T cars to sophisticated automobiles with navigation systems; from black-and-white televisions that fit on the coffee table with rabbit ears wrapped with aluminum foil to wide-screen plasma televisions connected to the world by satellite dish; phones with rotating dials to cell phones with digital pictures; Elvis Presley to Shania Twain; big-church pipe organs with a genuine sound to synthesizers and keyboards with fake sound. Ruth witnessed change. One constant remained, though—Christ.

Ah, this is life. The spring sun shines, music still echoes in churches, and the Dallas Mavericks are in the NBA basketball playoffs, and encouragement is like a piece of pie, tasty and sweet, and life rolls on. And once in a while, someone comes along in life that helps put some music in your own heart, and the music lights a fire that sets the soul aflame with joy and peace and grace and life. And once in a blue moon, if the moon really turns blue, you, as a pastor, are privileged to do funerals where you say nice things, true things, and glorious things about God and his saints. And you do it with gratitude and are humbled by it.

So, when I think of Ruth, I see her smiling and grinning, and I think of John and the end times and set my soul afire, Lord.

And that's the way life goes: Make music in Jesus's name that causes the hearts of those who hear it to sing! I miss Ruth already. And next time I see her, I am going to say, "Ruth, where's John? Guess the end times have come. And Ruth, remember the time the organ caught on fire while we sang *Set My Soul Afire?*" And we're gonna hug each other and cry and laugh and slap our knees and sing our souls to life for all of eternity. Maybe she'll say as she did when last I visited her, "Sing *Amazing Grace.*" And I did. And I will. And we will. And we shall sing at the feet of Jesus. And we'll eat at the banquet table and eat with Jesus at the great feast, and old John will show up and say, "Get some dessert!" And we will talk about old times and Jesus, worship Jesus, sing and eat the pie and the crust, and laugh our souls to high heaven because we'll be there for all eternity!

The wind blows this spring morning. The green grass waves in the wind. A bird sings and chirps the joy of morning. And God loves to hear his people make music to him. And on this morning, I am. On this day, I will. Don't 'cha think we're living in the end times?

John D. Duncan

Awaiting Spring

I'm sitting here under the old oak tree, awaiting spring. The sun shines today. Birds sing the glory. And life like a river flows in the joy of ministry.

I mention the river in the flow of ministry because the life of a pastor is life on the move, full of twists and turns, ups and downs, power-packed with the pleasant and the unpleasant. Eugene Peterson was once asked what he liked about the church, and he replied, "The mess." C.S. Lewis says that in a Christian society, there are to be "no passengers or parasites," meaning, of course, that in the church, people are Christ-followers, pilgrims on the journey. Still, they are not to sit idly by and watch like mere passengers but to serve and act. They are not parasites that destroy the body but "little Christs" (C.S. Lewis) who build up Christ's body. In my years as a pastor, I have seen many passengers and parasites in the church.

We all know that Saddleback Community Church's pastor, Rick Warren, says the church is purpose-driven, and he is right. The Bible scholar Peter Stuhlmacher says, "The life of the church can and should appear as a sign of the righteousness of God." He is right, also. "Daddy," my youngest daughter once asked, "you're the boss of the church. Aren't you?"

"No," I replied, "I have a lot of bosses." Quickly I corrected my verbal joke by telling her, "God is the boss of the church." That is right, too.

The writer of Hebrews speaks of the church as an assembly, not to be neglected, but tells us of Jesus, the great, sympathetic High Priest to whom we can go to find grace and mercy just in the nick of time (Hebrews 4:14-16). I find the church is people in relationship with God in Christ through the Holy Spirit, and because of Christ, people who relate to one another. So, the church is people who have a relationship with Christ and have a relationship with each other because of Christ. Without Christ, the church goes nowhere and dies like a person infested with a fatal parasite.

As a pastor, I have the privilege of helping individuals in their relationship with Christ and their people-to-people relationships. One thing I find is that people need an ear on the journey and a guide to lead them into Christ's light near the cross in an hour of darkness.

Not long ago, I received two calls on different days—one requesting a priest: the other requesting communion.

The first was a call from a lady who needed a priest. She tried for days to get the Catholic priest to come and see her, but he was too busy. I am not criticizing the priest, but merely stating the fact of her comment because I know that priests, like pastors, are busy people, and who knows but what he was ill or out of town or at the hospital visiting the sick? I listened as she talked, and she asked me to come immediately, and I did. A crisis keeps no calendar and shocks and often surprises, and Henri Nouwen, a priest himself, once said, "Interruptions are our ministry." This told, I drove my car to her house by the lake.

I drove, got lost, called her on the phone to get the directions explained again, stopped at a convenience store to look at a map, and finally arrived at her house. Her mobile home overlooking the lake provided a picturesque scene as I knocked on the door. She opened it, told me she was deaf and could not hear well, stated that she was 83 years of age, then finally invited me into her home and began to tell me the long story of her pain. Her house was like a mural, a mosaic, colorful with old carpet and stained walls, reeked of smoke with stuff piled everywhere. I intently listened as her wrinkled face winced, and tears streamed like a dripping rain down her cheeks while her dog sat at my feet. A picture hung on the wall—a picture of

Jesus with piercing eyes watching both of us. Jesus watches with eyes wide open.

I will not tell you her long story. It is much too personal, much too sad, and much too painful. She stated her case, though, as she completed her long story of sorrow in the shadows. "No one wants to listen to an old woman," she said, "but I just need someone to hear me because I need forgiveness."

I could tell the pain had swelled beneath her soul, and she, like a train chugging down the tracks of life carrying passengers and, who knows, maybe even parasites. Like a train, this elderly woman needed to blow off puffs of steam to relieve the pressure inside. We prayed to Jesus, who watched over us and begged forgiveness, and she cried simple, sweet, sad tears.

For some, life is a trinity, a triad of loneliness, grief, and sorrow. I once sat on a bus in Cambridge, England, one cold February day. A lady, aged and sad with lines on her face, looked at me and spoke, "My life is very lonely since my husband died." Life bursts with grief, too. Christina Rossetti, the poet, wrote, "My heart dies inch by inch; the time grows old, grows old in which I grieve." Langston Hughes once asked, "And ain't there any joy in this town?"

I left the lady's house. I sensed her loneliness, grief, and sorrow. She needed an ear, a listening ear to find in its depth forgiveness. All I knew to do was take her to the High Priest of forgiveness.

Then one week later, a lady called explaining that her daughter was dying and needed communion, the Lord's Supper. "I have been trying to find a preacher in this town for days who will administer the Lord's Supper. My daughter is dying." I listened and felt her urgency. She pleaded with me to come, "Please come quickly!"

I loaded my Lord's Supper supplies, which is not a common thing, because, while I have shared the Lord's Supper at nursing homes, I never had done so at the hospital. I arrived at the hospital, found room 112, introduced myself, and saw relief wash over a mother's face. She walked me over to her daughter, woke her, introduced me, and explained that her daughter's kidneys and liver were failing. The daughter looked gray and yellow simultaneously, a mosaic of pain as she winced and moved and shifted her small frame in the bed. We prayed, took the bread and cup in Jesus' name, and the mother wept while the daughter acted as if she were going to throw up. She did not and quietly slipped off to sleep. The mother thanked me and thanked me and thanked me as if gold had been given her or even as if I had delivered a new liver for her daughter. In their pain, the two ladies only wanted to be reminded of the great High Priest who once suffered pain, to feel the warmth of the one who gives comfort and sympathy by a shimmer of light from the cross, to know Jesus, the bread of life and Jesus the compassionate, suffering grace-giver in death.

Ain't there any joy in this town?

So, here I am under the old oak tree, scrambling beneath tears in the shadow of the cross. Churches find joy in forgiveness and the cross, and so do people. I called the lady I visited in the trailer home the other day. She seems fine, relieved from the pressures of her life. Her dog had been to the vet, and she thinks there was a card I sent somewhere in her piles. I heard, too, from the mother whose daughter was dying. She had been moved to the big-city hospital in hopes of finding a liver donor. And I talked to Jesus, my High Priest. After all, where would the church be without him? And where would I be without his forgiveness and his cross? Or you, for that matter? Where would you be? There is joy in the town! The joy is in Jesus. To coin a phrase from an old *Gatorade* commercial, "Is it in you?" Is it?

John D. Duncan

Where Would We Be Without Easter?

I'm sitting here under the old oak tree, watching the clouds pour the rain on mother earth. Drip, drip, drip. The poet Percy Shelley wrote about them in his poem, *The Cloud*: "I bring fresh showers for thirsting flowers, From the seas and the streams...." Today as I think of dreary clouds, I think of the sun behind the clouds. Forecasters say the sun will shine tomorrow.

I dedicate this column to pastors awaiting the sunlight of Easter in the clouds of ministry.

Every pastor lives between the cloud and the sunshine, between the dark blackness of Good Friday, as we call it, and the glorious light of resurrection on Easter Sunday. To be sure, every pastor lives between the sheer pain of Good Friday and the joyous excitement of Easter Sunday, between the depression of bad days and the good report of Easter Sunday.

I think of these, my years as a pastor. I think of the darkness—families breaking up, horrible deaths like teenagers in car wrecks, the tragedy of the loss of a baby, the gossip, the sickness in people's lives, the loss of jobs, the harsh words people spit out of their mouths, and the sin that stains all of us because all have sinned. I think of black Friday when Jesus died—the clouds, the thunder and lightning, the "darkness all over the land" as Matthew's gospel so clearly states it (Matthew 27: 45).

In the ministry, I have had darkness. One day almost 20 years ago, I sat in the church parking lot and cried. I had arrived at the church fresh and young, and enthusiastic. Now ready to win the world for Christ. I did not plan on taking the church from 140 people to 100 in six weeks, but it happened. I neither planned to incur a half-million-dollar debt with 60 giving families and praying like mad for God to help us deliver the mortgage payment on time. Neither did I plan on the advice of "Boy, we're going to teach you a few things." Boy, did I learn a few things in those tearful moments.

The darkest moments of a pastor's life pierce the soul with words that stick. One guy told me I would never make it in the ministry, and another lady remarked one day, "Preacher, we think you need to find another church." She did not put it to me that nicely, but that was the gist of her words.

Then there were the dark moments every preacher and minister experiences, the grind of ministry, the low-attendance Sundays, the dry baptistery, the drain, the weary Mondays, the hardscrabble world where pain shouts and tragedy in its darkness strikes with the speed of a lightning bolt at an inconvenient hour. So, the pain in people's lives often enters into a kind of darkness, and you join it. Eugene Peterson says, "When a pastor encounters a person in trouble, the first order of ministry is to enter into the pain and share the suffering." In the words of the African American spiritual, "Nobody knows the trouble I've seen!" Or, in the poetic words of Langston Hughes, "Well, son, I'll tell you: Life for me ain't been no crystal stair. It's had tacks in it. And splinters, And boards torn up...." Or add Shakespeare's words of "take arms against a sea of troubles." He may well have been writing about the darkness of pastors.

Oh, but the light pulsates with a rhythm in waves and moments of sheer ecstasy that flood like seas and streams, riding waves in rivers of joy. I think of that same church where I cried in the parking lot and shed tears after I had been there ten years (and now 20) and the time the church sent my family of five to Europe for 16 days. *American Airlines* called the trip the European Experience, but I called it sprinting through Europe on a breakfast of early wakeup calls and throw your clothes in the suitcase and breakfasts of hard rolls and "what great city are we in today?" It was sheer pandemonium and sheer delight!

I remember saying, "Ten years, and we've gone from almost being run out of town to a trip to Europe." My wife noted, "There's no proof that the airfare is a round trip. It might be a one-way ticket!" We laughed, and I cried and gave thanks for darkness and the light because Dietrich Bonhoeffer, who knew it all too well, said something like, "we in the ministry should learn to be thankful for the grace of all things, both good and bad." I am thankful to the Lord for his light.

I think of the fellowships, the laughter like the time the church presented me with a *Wal-Mart* greeter vest for my 40th birthday and the baptisms when people shake their wet-haired heads like a dog coming out of the bathtub and smiles and the good report of Sundays when folks joined the church and the response to sermons (one lady said one Sunday, "You preached like Billy Graham!") and the building campaigns and the joys of stewardship lessons and the numerous appreciation cards and staff and people with a wide range of emotion, enjoyment, and wonder, a river of seas and streams crashing in the euphoria of a ride in a raft on roaring rapids. Jesus caused his face to shine on more than one occasion. William Wordsworth once remarked, "My heart leaps when I behold a rainbow in the sky." My heart leaps when I think of the light, the joy, and the relationship with God and people in the ministry.

In the ministry, Easter keeps me grounded. Easter anchors hope in the darkness of a storm. Easter overpowers darkness with the light of joy and bursts through the hard stone of impossibility. Where would we be without Easter? Where would we be without Easter resurrection? Behind every cloud, the Son shines and radiates his glorious light!

I remember an old wise owl who once quipped, "When you feel like skinnin' 'em, love 'em; and when you feel like lovin' 'em, skin 'em," which was his way of saying in the darkness of ministry, show people the light of Christ's love, and in the light of good times do not forget to remind them of the darkness (of sin) and how Jesus can take care of it all in the light of his glory.

Of this light, Eugene Peterson again says, "The gospel message says, 'You don't live in a mechanistic world ruled by necessity; you don't live in a random world ruled by chance; you live in a world ruled by the God of the exodus and Easter. He will do things that neither you nor your friends would have supposed possible.'" My experience in the shadows of darkness and in the bright light of God's blessing is exactly that: The wonder, joy, and excitement of seeing God work.

Easter, I live and die and live again by it! But still, I cannot help but think of Easter without thinking of my grandmother Ruth Duncan from Spruce Pine, N.C. Her middle name was Easter, and she prayed with a hush and a whisper as the cool mountain wind strolled through the window. She prayed sweet prayers in hushed tones of God's glory in light, zapping the darkness and the care of the soul in the hands of God. Lightning bugs blinked near the window, but I always felt the rush of God's light when she prayed.

Today, I think of pastors who live on the axis of Good Friday darkness and Easter Sunday resurrection-light. I stand with pastors and applaud them for their faithful service in churches large and small for the glory of Christ. I praise God's work through them in darkness and light.

I sit here under this old oak tree and watch the rain in clouds of dark, but I always have the hope of knowing that the sun shines and the Son will shine in the light of hope. It's called Easter, and it encourages the called of Christ, and it calls the ones Christ calls. I must go. A dark cloud moves closer. I think I hear my grandmother praying. Ah, but in the distance, I see light. It's called Easter!

Summer

I KNOW NOT HOW IT FALLS ON ME

I know not how it falls on me
This summer evening, hushed and lone
Yet the faint wind comes soothingly
With something of an olden tone

Forgive me if I've shunned so long
Your gentle greeting earth and air
But sorrow withers even the strong
And who can fight against despair

Emily Bronte

Rome and God's Love

I'm sitting here under the old oak tree, peering into the beauty of the blue sky and thinking of the soon-to-be summer--south winds, heat waves, cotton-white clouds, and vacations. And I remember that once I traveled to Rome.

Our family awoke on Friday, July 18, 1997, ready for Rome. Well, actually, we were getting ready for Rome: I showered and shaved and put on pants, long pants because the churches we were to enter required it. My three girls dressed, making sure their shoulders were covered and wearing skirts. Judy, my wife, began the day by plugging her curling iron into the wall plug, 220 amp plugs common to Europe and unlike what we're used to here in Texas. She fried her curling iron and subsequently fried her hair, hair coming out in clumps. She's kidded me about a bald spot in the back of my head for years, and she got one before I did. So much for the risks of foreign travel.

We survived the morning--hair clumps, cold rolls, gross orange juice, and the usual jockeying for position by our girls to sit on the bus. You know the routine: "I was there first! I wanted to sit there!"

For me, this was the one place I could not wait to see. I purchased a Rome tour book explaining the glory of Rome--the Vatican City, the Roman Forum, the Palatine Hill and the Circus Maximus, the Triumphal Arch of Constantine, the Colosseum, the Appian way (mentioned in the Bible), and the catacombs.

When you tour Rome with a local guide, which the law requires, you get information overload. You learn interesting tidbits like "barbarians" comes from "barbara," which means "bearded ones," which were the invaders in the Roman region in the fourth century.

You learn history. The Roman emperor Constantine changed Rome forever. He conquered Maxentius at Milvian Bridge in Rome, saying he saw in the cloud a cross with the words, "Under this sign conquer." He divided his kingdom with Licinius in October of 312. He declared the Edict of Milan in 313. He embraced Christianity, stopped religious persecution, forbade crucifixion and gladiatorial combats, and defended Rome against enemy attacks. You learn more history than you want.

You learn unnecessary stuff. The River Tiber cuts through Rome and is the most written-about river in the world. Strangely enough, I've never read about the River Tiber except in weighty encyclopedias.

You learn that nothing ever changes. The Romans gathered at the Circus Maximus to watch chariot races, and wagering was common for those who watched. Gambling still wreaks havoc on society today. The Roman Forum was a government place with tall, white marble columns like those on government buildings in Washington. Does anything ever really change?

You learn that things generally stay the same. The Romans loved sports, races, fights, and athletic events. They gathered some 50,000 in the Colosseum for gladiatorial events, gladiators fighting like boxers for the prize. It was Las Vegas and the boxing commission all over again. And if it rained? The Colosseum had a hole in the roof, Texas Stadium-style, but if it rained, the maintenance workers erected in one hour a silk canopy to cover the hole. In Rome, let's call it the SkyDome (like the one in Toronto, Canada, with the retractable electric roof).

Legend records that Christians were thrown to the lions in the Colosseum. Georgio, our local guide, claimed it's all a myth. "It didn't happen," he said. I wonder if he thought Christ a myth too.

I stood in the Colosseum, realizing how small I am in the scheme of things, a mere drop in the bucket, a drip in the ocean of life. And I looked through the hole in the Colosseum, awed by the glory of Rome. And I peered into the blue sky, awestruck by the glory of God, that he loves a small drip like me. For God so loved the world.

And now, as I sit and as the wind blows against my face, I know that he loves you too.

John D. Duncan

Life is a Race

I'm sitting here under the old oak tree, pondering the race of life. What about a bike race like the Tour de France? I recently watched a bicyclist from Austin, Lance Armstrong, zip down paved streets of Paris, France, the victor in one of life's most grueling bike races.

What about the rat race? I once heard a guy talk about being caught up in the rat race.

I've never seen rats race, but I guess it's something to behold.

What about races with runners sporting spiked shoes? Recently a sprinter named Michael Johnson sought to qualify for the 200-meter sprint in the Olympics. He tumbled to the track in anguish as he pulled up lame while running the race.

Life is a race. The Apostle Paul asks, "Do you not know that in a race all the runners run, but only one gets the prize? Run in such a way as to get the prize" (1 Corinthians 9:24).

Today, I'm pondering life's race, and the cherished prize racers aim to clutch with their hands. I'm also thinking of *NASCAR* races with Jeff Gordon and Sheri Evans.

Sheri Evans?

Sheri Evans joined life's race on the starting line on the 31st day of July 1964. At the age of 3, this wide-eyed adventurer quietly slipped into her neighbor's home and put on make-up. The race was on. Before her 10th year, she went to the shopping mall with her parents and announced, "Don't hold my hand!"

Free spirit that she was, she once tried the Lance Armstrong thing, biking from Fresno, Calif., to San Francisco and across the Golden Gate Bridge.

Soon, though, like most of us, she was deep into the rat race thing--a cheerleader in high school; off to college to earn her associate's degree in nursing; marrying; working; cooking; doing the laundry; raising her precious son DJ, and loving just about anything connected to a race and a prize, like rooting for her beloved Oklahoma Sooners. She cheered "Boomer Sooner!" and all that stuff that Oklahoma fans do as they wish for their team to race to the top of the standings in football, baseball, or whatever. Her favorite thing, though, was stock car racing and watching No. 24 Jeff Gordon circle the *NASCAR* track at high speed with a loud roar.

In 1985, she did the Michael Johnson thing and groaned in anguish in life's race. She did not tumble in her quest for a gold medal but rather received the disappointing news that she had Hodgkin's disease. She struggled in the race--surgery, radiation, and recovery. Miraculously, God picked her up and put her back on her feet. Her diseased body made peace with her cancer for a season, ten years of remission joyously thrusting her back into the rat race.

I met Sheri in 1997 when she and her family visited our church. They later joined our church fellowship. I learned of her love for stock car racing and her body's renewed battle with disease during this time. Life's race shocks with flat tires, blown engines, and unexpected detours. Sheri raced for the checkered flag of victory as her body shouted in pain.

"God," C. S. Lewis once observed, "shouts in our pain and whispers in our pleasures."

In pain, was Sheri deflated in the race, Job's twin complaining, "My soul is weary of my life; I will leave my complaint upon myself; I will speak in the bitterness of my soul"? (Job 10:1). No, while slowing in the race, she endured without complaint.

She kept her eye on the finish line, determined to complete the race, whispering back to God, "I know that my Redeemer lives and that in the end he will stand upon the earth" (Job 19:25). Sheri gripped the steering wheel of faith. Her radiant smile hinted at imminent victory. And in this drama, Jeff Gordon cheered for her, sending an autographed T-shirt with an encouraging message: "Refuse to lose."

Then, on the 24th of April, 2000, amid tears of grief and joy with family gathered around, the checkered flag waved, and Sheri crossed the line of victory, entering the winner's circle of heaven.

Life is a race. The journey waves flags--green flags signaling "go"; yellow flags cautioning "slow"; red flags announcing "no"; and checkered flags calling us home.

Life is a race where little girls with wide-eyed wonder put on make-up, a grueling endurance test of uphill climbs and of rat races, and of anguished tumbling, which sends you sprawling flat on your face. Life shocks us with death.

When death comes, life troubles us. When life troubles us, God sustains us. When God sustains us, he comforts us.

And so as the shadows lengthen here under the old oak tree, I'm pondering the race. Run the race long and hard. Determine to live. Enjoy the company of family and friends in the race. Determine to love. Know how to win the race. Determine to live forever. Run in such a way to receive the prize, the upward calling of God in Christ Jesus.

Life, I've decided, is a race. Is your eye on the prize?

Motorcycle Man Carl Knows Peace — Don't Blink...

I'm sitting here under the old oak tree by the lake. The August heat prepares to bake the earth into hard clay on this early morning. A light breeze blows, reminding me that the Spirit blows where it wishes (John 3:8). The yellow grass longs to drink down water that stays stuck in the sky. White foam drifts on the shores of the lake. A teenage jet-skier whizzes by, his turboprop wide open. And a bird broods and sits on the barbed wire nearby.

I am reminiscing today about motorcycle man Carl. He stopped by my office one day. His wind-blown hair and filthy clothes gave the appearance of a weather-beaten man who had been on a troublesome journey. His leather coat and scuffed boots added to his roughneck aura. His wrinkled face could not compare to his battered heart as he shared his story.

"Preacher, can I see you for a minute?" he asked as he stood at my office door.

"Sure," I replied, knowing that when stragglers show up at church and ask for a minute, they usually take more than a minute and that my guard better be up because stragglers often spring well-spun stories for eager preachers anxious to hear.

"Preacher," he began as he sat in a chair across from me, "I've been to New Mexico and back in the last three days. Been riding my motorcycle. My wife left me. I've been riding and thinking, riding and thinking, and I don't know what to do. I can't get no peace."

"Um, um," I answered in a deep theological tone. "You don't know what to do?"

"That's right, preacher. I don't know what to do."

For years, I've tried to figure out why some people come to see me in my office. Motorcycle man Carl put it plain and simple that day: "You're the one to come to when I don't know what to do."

I guess that makes me the "preacher of I don't know what to do." I didn't know what to do with Carl, come to think of it.

"Tell me about your wife leaving you," I intoned as I put on my imaginary counseling cap.

"Said she don't love me anymore," Carl responded in his stylistic, get-to-the-point conversation.

"What do you need? Do you need food or money?" I quizzed as I placed the imaginary minister of benevolence hat upon my head. "We can always get you food, you know. You shouldn't go away hungry."

"Preacher, thanks, but I don't need food or money. I really just want my wife back, but she says she's not coming back," Carl moaned as a tear streaked down his cheek.

"Have you thought about giving your life to Jesus," I softly spoke. After all, he was calling me "Preacher."

"You know, I don't know why I came here, but I would like to give my life to Jesus," Carl said as he wiped a tear from his eye.

Right there in the church on the road that goes right by the lake, I shared the Roman Road to salvation, and Carl gave his life to Jesus. He prayed to receive Christ, walked out of the church, and rode his motorcycle home. For one month, every Sunday and Wednesday, Carl did not miss church. Our church baptized him, and we rejoiced in his newfound life. Then Carl disappeared.

This happens in life if you stick around the church long enough--the heat scorches the earth; the wind blows in the early morn; the grass sheds its green shade for yellow; foam drifts on shores; jet skiers take flight at break-neck speed; birds sit, and brood and church members disappear. Sometimes they don't know what to do, so they just disappear.

Six months later, as I was studying in my office, the phone rang. I answered. Carl spoke excitedly: "Preacher, I just wanted to call and tell you that I'm in North Carolina. I moved here to be close to my family. I found a good Christian woman who loves the Lord. And we got married. We go to church. I've never been happier since that day in your office. I'm at peace now. I've got peace."

We chatted, and as I hung up the phone, it was as if I heard the faint whisper of Jesus, "Peace I leave with you; my peace I give you. I do not give as the world gives. Do not let your hearts be troubled and do not be afraid" (John 14:27).

And so, when I don't know what to do, I quietly ask God to give peace. As the poet Gerard Manley Hopkins says, "And when Peace here does house, he comes with work to do, he does not come to coo, He comes to brood and sit."

John D. Duncan

Pride Goes Before a Fall

I'm sitting here under the old oak tree, thinking of my fourteen years as pastor of Lakeside Baptist Church in Granbury, Texas, and of all things, Paris, France comes to mind. I'm remembering with gratitude that our church once sent our family on a ten-year anniversary trip to Europe.

London, England, stands as the city of towers, robust towers which point toward the sky. Paris, France, glows as the city of light. Our journey from England to France carried us to the white cliffs of Dover. The white chalk cliffs hold back the water from the English Channel. Dover, which means water or stream, serves as the English Channel's most important port. A castle, the Dover Castle, looks over the English Channel. In ancient days, what historians call Norman times, the port and castle served as a port for the King and a fortress to protect southeast England. The site was bombed in World War II but later rebuilt and improved.

We crossed the English Channel on a ferry which carried huge buses as well as a host of guests. The 22-mile ride across the English Channel carried us to the port of Calais, France. Our drive to Paris carried us through the battlefields of World Wars. I realized firsthand the impact that war had on Europe, its soil, and its people.

Our trip to Paris led us to the Ibis Hotel. It's a chain of hotels like Comfort Inn or Holiday Inn. Two twin beds, one small shower with a restroom, and French cable tv filled out the French accommodations. Have you ever tried to get the Texas Rangers baseball game score in French?

One evening in Paris, we cruised the Seine River. The spectacular night view of Paris shone like beaming stars: Notre Dame Cathedral; the Eiffel Tower, built by engineer Alexander-

Gustave Eiffel in 1889 (Our tour guide kept repeating this, so I remembered this fact. I wondered if she received a commission for the number of times she said it.); the *Louvre Museum*; and the *Hotel des Invalides* which houses the tomb of Napoleon.

The next day, we toured Paris, riding an elevator up the Eiffel Tower, walking the art district in the famed Sacred Heart Church, and waltzing down the world's most famous street, the Avenue des Champs-Elysees. Paris is a city of perfect symmetry and architecture. Arches, bridges, monuments, sculptures, roads-all flow into a plan of beauty and precise grandeur. The Arch of Triumph symbolizes this grandeur, a huge stone arch that stood as an ancient entrance to the city but now serves as a monument to an unknown soldier.

France's motto is "Liberty, Equality, Fraternity." it sounds like a good motto for a church: Liberty in Christ; Equality through Christ, whosoever will may come; Fraternity and fellowship in the body of Christ. Why not?

Space does not allow me to tell all about France, but I will say getting lost in the Paris underground, a web of subway links and cable cars, improved my prayer life. Have you ever tried asking for directions when you weren't sure you were lost, but the person you talked to couldn't understand?

And so we toured Paris, the City of Light. Eleven thousand lamp posts light the city at night. One hundred fifty-five buildings shine with the aura of light. And Jesus said, "I am the Light of the world." Will you let your light shine among men that they may see your good works and glorify your Father in heaven?

Of all the things I remember, the echo of the words of our tour guide remain. We drove past the place where Napoleon's tomb lay. And our tour guide kept saying, "And Napoleon crowned himself." He thought no one worthy of placing a crown upon his head at his coronation, so "he crowned himself." And I am reminded that one of our greatest spiritual battles is pride, the snubbing of the nose at God and others, an "I'm-better-than-you-are" attitude that can creep into our craniums. As Napoleon discovered, "Pride goes before the fall." And Jesus came to strip away our pride so His Light can shine through us. Are you shining?

Glory and Reality

I'm sitting here under the old oak tree, imagining that I am in the cycling profession. I see myself flying through village roads in the French Alps, racing at 70 miles per hour down mountain roads while the rain and wind kiss my face, peddling furiously like Lance Armstrong toward the finish line in the Tour de France in Paris, France. I grab the Maillot Jaune, the infamous yellow jersey, as I bask in the glory of victory under the Arch of Triumph on the roadway known as the Champs-Elysees.

Suddenly, my senses come to me as I recall a July Sunday afternoon two summers ago when I experienced cycling inspiration only to realize that I was only a bicycle novice.

Inspiration seized me. I decided to shed a few pounds in 100-degree heat by borrowing my daughter's bicycle. The purple speedster with silver breaks set me on my course. The spiked pedals greeted my feet with delight as my legs pumped up and down like cylinders on a car engine. I turned left and then quickly right as I gained top speed on a straightaway. The sunshine flashed in my face, and the wind created a gentle breeze for a body pumping and perspiring.

As I enjoyed my biking cruise, I lost a sense of both time and distance. Oops! A sharp hairpin turn lay ahead. Quickly I steadied the bike, attempting as best I could to slow down with the brakes on the handlebar. However, common sense told me that if I tried to slow down too fast, I might sail into the blue sky. So, I slowed down a little, turned, and whiz--it was time for a split-second decision. Should I take the sharp turn and stay on the road, risking a wipeout on the asphalt? Or should I move into the gravel beside the road, through some tall weeds at a low spot, and then back up on the road? I chose the latter.

My decision proved, well, not so good. I turned, moved off the road onto the gravel, down an incline, into the weeds, and smack dab into a culvert hidden beneath the weeds.

What happened next seemed like what Walt Whitman in "Crossing Brooklyn Ferry" once called "dark patches": "Is it not upon you alone the dark patches fall, / The dark threw its patches down upon me also, / The best I had done seemed to me blank and suspicious, / My great thoughts as I supposed them, were they not in reality meager?"

The front wheel stuck in the ditch, stopped dead, fixed firmly in the mud, not moving, not spinning, not fulfilling its ordained function. The bike, though, is another story. It continued as best it could to thrust forward.

If I were an astronaut on the space shuttle, or maybe a pilot of an airplane, ejection in a moment of crisis is one way to describe this momentary dark patch. The bike flipped, I entered orbit for a brief second, no longer labored with thoughts of Lance Armstrong and the "Maillot Jaune," but hoping for survival, for life, and wondering if life after death and meeting Jesus soon to kiss him on the cheek at heaven's gate would be my final call.

Instantly, I landed on my head--with no helmet, of course. Thankfully, I landed on my head, the hardest part of my body. The blow gave me a sore neck but no more. I stood on my feet and looked around to make sure no one was watching. I shook the cobwebs out of my dazed cranium. I recovered, picked up the bike with a bent front wheel, and slowly climbed out of the tall weeds. A car drove by, and I waved, acting like life was normal.

I think, somehow, Jesus spoke: Think not great thoughts for yourself. Keep your goal focused on the narrow road. Watch out for curves, for dark patches that fall, and confess that your greatest thoughts are meager. And open your eyes to see what's ahead. The eye is the lamp of the body. So, if your eye is healthy, your whole body will be full of light (Matthew 6:22).

Grass and Weeds, Wheat and Tares

I'm sitting here under the old oak tree, watching the Texas heat bake my yard to a yellow crisp. I sit here drinking *Mountain Dew* and relaxing, having just finished mowing the yard. I breathe the heat. I feel the dust and yearn for dry roots to drink down rain.

I ponder the yard, but the weeds baffle my brain. Why does my yard die under the sun that dehydrates it? And why do weeds grow strong in places where grass should grow? Why, when I wish for grass to blossom in fields of green, does yellow crisp appear? And why do the weeds I detest crawl slowly across the yard, choking down the dust and shading my yard with patches of an ugly green?

Weeds, weeds, I hate weeds I hate weeds is one of my creeds.

Jesus told me this day would come (Matthew 13:24-30). Jesus compared the kingdom of heaven to a man who sowed seed in his field. Jesus' parable stated that while men were asleep, the sower's enemy clandestinely slipped into the field and sowed tares among the wheat. Soon the wheat and the tares grew together. Weeds greeted the wheat.

A slave of the landowner noticed the wheat and tares in the field. He reported to his master: "Sir, did you not sow good seed in your field? How then does it have tares?"

The landowner announced, "An enemy has done this!"

The slaves then asked the landowner, "Do you want us to go and gather them up?"

The landowner replied: "No, do not gather the tares lest you root up the wheat also. Let both grow together until the harvest when wheat will be gathered into my barn and then the tares can be burned up."

Jesus told me this day would come. He knew a man would sit under an oak tree and ponder weeds in the grass, tares in the wheat.

Jesus knew, too, that in the church, weeds would grow among the wheat; unbelievers would grow among believers. And so, I sit here waiting for the harvest. I keep sowing the good-news seed believing it will take root. I watch for the enemy slipping into the field at midnight. And I wonder, if you think the Texas heat is hot.

If all this weed and grass, tares and wheat discussion confuse you, then hear Saint Augustine. He spoke of God in his "Confessions" when he said, "You are most hidden from us and yet the most present among us, the most beautiful and yet the strongest, ever enduring and yet we cannot comprehend you."

Yellow crisp and weeds among the grass I cannot understand. The ways of God I do not always understand. Still, I look to the beauty of God and to his strength on this hot day.

Suddenly, I decide to water my yard. I realize that some things in life I cannot control, like weeds growing where grass longs to grow, like tares among wheat in the church. And as a pastor, I am determined to pour water into the souls of saints with His Word. I hear the echo of Gerard Manley Hopkins in my ear, "Mine, O thou lord of life, send my roots rain."

Boy, this *Mountain Dew* sure is good! I love Texas in the summer!

A Trip Down the River

I'm sitting here under the old oak tree, musing about the winding river.

I rode a canoe down the Brazos River one Saturday morning. We dropped the canoe near Lake Whitney and floated downstream. "You got a north wind, which is pretty unusual for this time of year," the canoe rental executive informed us. "Enjoy your ride, and remember the bridge is your stopping point," he added.

My cruise down the Brazos delighted my soul. The wind pushed us forward. The water was at a good height so that my canoe partner, Harold, and I did not have to exit the canoe and wade the water but one time. The sun shone high on that day. The blue sky formed a backdrop. The hues of green from the trees and grass painted the whole panoramic scene a wonder of color and joy. I am reminded that writer John Graves once described the rapids of the Brazos in *Goodbye to a River* as having voices, "Baptistly, poundingly, this one (rapid) was singing 'Beulah Land.'" On this day, the Brazos was the "Land of the Beautiful." Can rivers sing? Do they sing like Baptists?

The rapids sang, and a cardinal with its red bib chirped along. A deer flashed in front of our canoe, darting gracefully across a shallow part of the river while gently splashing water. A raccoon swam the river and dashed up an embankment, disappearing as fast as he appeared. Buzzards hovered and marked their prey as they caught the currents of the wind before diving for dinner. A cow mooed in the distance. Was a cow dinner?

Some of the other guys in our canoe caravan fished, but mostly, our canoe just cruised along. In one place, I wished I had brought a fishing pole because a 12-inch fish swam beneath our canoe. Soon another big one leaped out of the water. I'll call that fish "the big one that got away!" Every fisherman needs a fishing story. Or, in the words of John Graves, "In angling, as in reading, suspense is a quality worth having." For a brief moment, I wished for suspense.

Along the river, you could see car tires and junk just below the water's surface. Trash drifted here and there. It's amazing what you can find in the river: coke cans, candy wrappers, plastic bags, T-shirts, and an endless array of discarded mess floated along, pushed by the wind. Trees whipped by the wind, snapped like pretzels at a picnic, lay on their sides. Navigation around the fallen trees provided adventurous moments. Life is a journey, and sometimes all you can do is hang on and glide through the currents.

The sounds echoed down the stream with sunbirds singing, the rapids in chorus, tree limbs cracking, leaves whistling in the wind, the oar from the canoe splashing the water; and a little chatter from two men passing the time with talk, but, mostly, solitude. Ah, solitude, in the words of Henri Nouwen, "The careful balance between silence and words, withdrawal and involvement, distance and closeness, solitude and community form the basis of the Christian life and should therefore be subject of our most personal attention. Let us therefore look somewhat closer, first at our life in action, and then at our life in solitude." Have you ever looked at your life in solitude? Listened for it?

Ah, the sounds of solitude on the river. That old canoe cruiser John Graves says of the river's sounds and the crackling of logs on a fire by the riverside, "That gets to be one of the river's symphonic sounds, like owls and the gurgle of snag-thwarted water and the eternal cries of herons and the chug of tractors in unseen bottom fields." The river played in symphony on this day!

Near the end of our journey, we drifted and ate lunch. Harold had a sandwich, and I ate my ham and cheese, one with some chips, fresh bottled water, and two Oreo cookies. Lunch on the Brazos sounds upscale, but it was really quite simple.

All this river-riding got me to musing about Jesus. Have you ever stopped to consider how many times Jesus talks about fishing and water? Oh, the smell of those fishermen!

Oh, the tumultuous turn of rivers and waters in their streams and currents! Oh, all that talk of water that never runs dry and springs of gushers that bubble until eternity!

The Psalmist put it this way,

There is a river whose streams make glad the city of God,
The holy place of the tabernacle of the Most High.
God is in the midst of her, she shall not be moved,
God shall help her, just at the break of dawn (Psalm 46:4-5).

John, the beloved apostle of Jesus, saw a river in a vision, "And he showed me a pure river of water of life, clear as crystal, proceeding from the throne of God and the Lamb" (Revelation 22:1).

So, here I am under the old oak tree, reminded of a river whose streams make glad God's city; a crystal-clear river that sparkles with life. I am glad. I long for a river clear like crystal where Jesus dwells. Yet all I can think of is solitude, "Be still and know that I am God" (Psalm 46:10).

John D. Duncan

Where was God When the 'Twisting Wind' Came?

I'm sitting here under the old oak tree, thinking of God. I wonder what he's doing today. Is he making it rain? Is he making hay while the sun shines? Is he watching children swim and build sandcastles near the white-capped waves of ocean shores? Has God ever done the dishes or the laundry in mounds a mile high? Does he like to watch such chores as they are done? Is God on vacation? Hey, didn't Jonah once think God had forgotten him? That God had not been thinking of him? "I am cast out of thy sight, yet I will look again unto Your holy temple" (Jonah 2:3). Have you ever wondered if God sees you?

Here in Granbury, we have joined God in his work at Lakeside Baptist Church. We have been praying and giving, preaching and singing praise to God, and working and watching. Our new building in our new location has been under construction. Construction workers poured the concrete foundation. Walls joined hands and were raised. Roofers hoisted copper-colored sheet metal and made a glittering roof. A crane lifted the steeple to grand heights. Then, workers like bees began to buzz with things like light fixtures and painting and doors and carpet and tile in the preschool building because the floor needed to be easy to clean. We all know that babies make a mess when they spit up. We set "Opening Day," the first day in our new building, with grand festivities like those of baseball's opening day, but the game's stakes are much higher here. They have eternal repercussions.

Under the Old Oak Tree

Amid all this preparation, a storm blew into town. Much debate about the storm ensued. Was it wind? An earthquake? A fire? Weather prognosticators called it a "twisting wind." Neighborhood watchers said, "It had to be a tornado." One old local boy said, "Whatever it was, it was something else!!!!" The preacher speculated that Harry Potter and his demonic urchins showed up. I wonder if God watched some kind of unseen spiritual warfare battle above the church on that day. After all, we wrestle not with flesh and blood but unseen spiritual forces, against principalities, against powers, against the rulers of darkness of this world, against spiritual wickedness in high places (Ephesians 6:10). Assuredly, I can tell you that steeple was in a high place!

The wind ripped the steeple off the roof, snapped it in two, and drove the steeple into the roof of the new church building. An upside-down steeple in the roof and a hole resulted. Rain dripped into the new building, although huge trash cans caught the dripping rain to minimize the damage. We thank the Lord that no one was hurt. We press on toward our first services in the new building. We press on toward God's higher calling. We press on the upward way.

So here I am under the old oak tree thinking about God. Where was God while all this happened? I think he quietly passed by.

"And, behold, the Lord passed by, and a great and strong wind rent the mountains, and broke it in pieces against the rocks before the Lord; but the Lord was not in the wind. And after the wind an earthquake; but the Lord was not in the earthquake. And after the earthquake a fire; but the Lord was not in the fire. And after the fire, a still small voice" (I Kings 19:11-12).

God passed by to remind us that Harry Potter and Osama bin Laden and all the legions of destruction are not in control, but he is. God is at work. Are you listening to him? God is at work building his saints. In the words of George Herbert, "God

John D. Duncan

bless the Architect Whose art, Could build so strong in a weak heart!"

Roses, Thorns, and Silken Twine

I'm sitting here under the old oak tree, reflecting on life's roller-coaster emotions. The renowned English poet William Blake once captured the essence of these emotions in words: "Joy & Woe are woven fine, A Clothing for the Soul divine; Under every grief & pine Runs a joy with silken twine."

Life races with movements, twists and turns where you hang on for dear life, days where life's common thread produces grief and joy.

My wife, Judy, and I have been married for 20 years. We recently celebrated our 20th wedding anniversary. I took her to a fancy restaurant, one with silver forks and many choices of forks. "Work from the outside in," I heard my mom saying in my mind as I reached for the first fork. We both ordered Caesar salad and chicken-fried steak. My mind works in strange ways, but it occurred to me that Caesar, a Roman conqueror of history, and salad did not seem to go together. And it floated through my mind that there was no "chicken" in our chicken-fried steak but rather a breaded veal cutlet. We ate at a place called the *Nutt House* and enjoyed ourselves immensely. I paid the bill, which was no small task.

I then decided I would do something romantic. I drove my wife to *The Home Depot*, where we promptly purchased anniversary gifts. I bought her a three-foot stepladder. She needed the stepladder to reach grand heights of stuff placed in the cupboard and wipe the ceiling fans when they collected dust. She bought me a six-foot utility ladder. I needed a ladder to hang Christmas lights in December, wash windows in April, and change light bulbs all year round. She despises living in the dark. We do not usually buy practical gifts such as these, but on your 20th wedding anniversary, it pays to go against the grain. Our 20th wedding anniversary radiated with pure joy. Our anniversary produced a simple, nostalgic emotion-pure joy!

In the midst of Blake's accuracies about life, he also described our anniversary's dark side. In more recent weeks, we discovered Judy has breast cancer. Strangely enough, we learned of this news on the crest of a roller-coaster ride of thrill and excitement. Our church relocated and moved into a new building. How exciting! Everything was coming up roses—baptisms, church attendance, a growing church in a changing community. Then when the ride reached its apex, doctors who poked and prodded and tested and re-tested informed us that my wife possessed nasty little cells called cancer in her body. The roses sprouted thorns! A simple, dreaded emotion erupted like thunder and lightning against a dark Texas sky—pure grief.

Life weaves many threads. On the day of birth, someone ties a pink or blue ribbon on a package in honor of your arrival and your gender. On the day of your graduation from school, educators tie a black ribbon around your diploma. On the day of your first job, your new boss explains all the essential elements of employment as if to say, "Don't forget these things." You might want to tie a string around your finger so that you do not forget. On days of joy—birthdays, weddings, and anniversaries—ribbons wrap around gifts of gladness. On days of grief, ribbons wave in the wind as they hang from flower arrangements and decorated sprays. Twine holds the world together. That William Blake, he was on to something!

Saint Augustine once spoke of his grief: "What agony I suffered, my God! How I cried out in grief while my heart was in labor! But, unknown to me, you were there, listening." I have decided lo these twenty years of marriage that a common thread weaves through our lives, in the past, present, and future; the thread of God's listening love. The poet of the eighteenth century, John Milton, gently spoke of God's listening love in grief, "Oft he seems to hide his face, but unexpectantly returns..."

So here I am under the old oak tree pondering anniversaries and surgeries, absorbing God's listening love and waiting in silence with a pounding heart of love for my wife. Lo, these twenty years deliver both joy and grief, but as always, we're hanging on to Jesus, our common thread, knowing that his grace reinforces the sufficiency of his strength. And, somehow, we're discovering the grief of joy and the joy of grief. Thank you for your love, Jesus. And, Judy, if you read this, I love you! May God's Soul Divine with silken twine give strength in these roller-coaster days! I cannot wait until you can use that step ladder again!

John D. Duncan

Mowing and Praying

I'm sitting here under the old oak tree, pondering the lazy days of summer and working up the energy to mow my yard. The desert monks coined a word for laziness, "acedia," which means listlessness. "Acadia" has Greek roots, meaning "an absence of care." Today I am listless, but the yard must be mowed.

The poet Langston Hughes once lamented, "Life for me ain't been no crystal stair." When it comes to my yard, the grass grows, the flowers fade, and the yard must be mowed. My yard ain't no crystal stair." I guess I will jolt myself out of this listless state and start mowing.

When I mow, I pray. "Everything that one turns in the direction of God is prayer." Ignatius of Loyola commented. I mow the tall weeds, trim my grass, and turn stuff in God's direction.

I am mowing and praying—for the world; for the church, God's church; for kids on drugs; for soldiers in war; for families in grief; for a friend's son whose choices have catapulted his life into a whirlpool of descending trouble. I am mowing and praying and recalling that Langston Hughes also said, "Descent is quick; to rise again is slow." I am praying for my friend's son to rise again in the power of the Almighty. I mow and pray. The lawnmower throws grass in the direction of the ground, and I toss words in God's direction. The sunshine falls. Prayer rises.

I am mowing and pushing—grimace, grunt, groan. I agreed to mow my neighbor's yard. His yard takes longer to mow and challenges my body. I push the mower uphill, around trees while ducking under limbs, back and forth in ankle-thick grass, freshly watered by dripping drops of rain splashed into mother earth. Life ain't no crystal stair.

I am sweating and praying for my neighbor Bill that his company will renew his job. Companies lay people off, the economy sags, and I am praying that God in his economy will allow Bill to keep his job. The grass shortens. Prayer lengthens my soul. Jesus hears.

I am praying and dreaming because every time I turn a corner in Bill's backyard, I see the lake and his jet ski. Think of me as no saint. Mowing Bill's yard also means I receive the privilege of using his jet ski.

The heat withers my body, blades of grass stick to my legs, dust flies in my face, and I dream of zipping across the lake at break-neck speeds with the wind blowing through my thinning hair. Life ain't no crystal stair, but you cannot spend your whole life mowing the yard. A man needs jet-ski flair every once in a while. I have a dream.

I am jet skiing and praying. Now I zip across the lake and pray. Kari Barth once noted, "To clasp the hands in prayer is the beginning of an uprising against the disorder of the world."

I zigzag across a crystal lake as the evening sun glistens off the water as if a mirror lay beneath my path. I watch for approaching watercraft and enjoy the aura of God's creation. The heavens declare God's glory, not to mention the beauty of the lake. My handles tightly grip the handlebars on the jet ski, and my heart grips prayer.

I pray for an uprising against the disorder of the world—for grief amid pain in Israel where bus bombers create disorder; for soldiers in Iraq wincing in the chaos of ambushes and confusion; for peace in homes where Satan hurls missiles of disorder. I pray for joy to return to those who lost jobs as God in his economy provides new jobs and stable incomes again for struggling souls; for those climbing life's stairs and finding the uphill climb difficult like hiking Mount Everest.

John D. Duncan

Life ain't no crystal stair, but the yard must be mowed, jet skis need to come off the rack, and prayer needs to rise up against the disorder of the world.

Are you praying?

So now here I am, back under the old oak tree, drinking bottled water purified by mountain springs and praising my Lord the yard got mowed. Life ain't no crystal stair, but prayer makes life crystal clear! And Jesus hears.

From a Rock House

I'm sitting here under the old oak tree, pondering an old rock house. An old rock house sits in Pilot Point. The old rock house might be down some dirt road or out in the country or on an asphalt road near the center of town. I know not where that house sits. I do know that on September 14, 1940, Aunt Essie delivered her nephew, Cordell. Cordell had a last name---Parker. That rock house served as a conduit of education, values, and spiritual roots.

Not long ago, a speech teacher named Cordell died. Cordell taught at *Tarrant County College* and served as an educator for over 40 years. Today people change jobs faster than a lightning strike. Forty years at the same task and purpose is a remarkable feat. In the Summer of 1980, Cordell served as my speech teacher. He loved talking about life's most basic commodity—communication. Communication makes the world go around. Today S-P-E-E-C-H is on my mind.

S-Story. Life swells with laughter and drips with tears. Cordell could laugh. He loved stories, a part of the ever-flowing river of communication that puts characters and life into the drama and context of the flow of life. The ancient Greek thinker Heraclitus once said, "You could not step twice into the same rivers; for other waters are ever flowing on to you." Stepping into the same rivers twice is one thing, but telling a story twice is always permitted. Eugene Peterson once announced stories as pastoral care, understanding the people, places, and powers that influence people's lives. He called his visits with people "occasions for original research on the stories being shaped in their lives by the living Christ." Stories shape life. Telling stories influences lives.

Stories flow like a river—of treehouses; of wedding plans; of the church parking lot where Cordell met Irene, his wife; of swimming pools where a father tosses his daughter, Kippy, in the water, clothes and all; of wrestling matches where Cordell once dressed as a sumo wrestler, baring his body and soul to raise money for the *United Way*; of cards and Cadillacs and trucks spray-painted on a dark night; of life's No. 1 fear, public speaking; of Artem and monster trucks and hip-hop music with words like, "It's time to go"; of interest in the funeral home business and mortuary science; and of a rock house. Stories refresh and connect life like people gathering on a porch to talk while drinking cool cups of water from a mountain river.

P-People. In more recent days, I have concluded that life is really about people—the wired and weird; the stable and unstable; the happy and sad; the big and small; those wilting under the heat of life's pressure and those blooming in the sunshine of life; the healers and hurt; the non-communicative and the communicative; the thinkers and feelers. People influence, often with stories.

Cordell loved to meet people. He always seemed to have a knack for researching their stories and delivering the news of people's lives. If you will live joyfully, two necessary relationships lay a happy foundation—a relationship with the Person of Christ: relationships with people. Cordell himself spoke of people—his father in the grocery business; Irene and Kippy; Mrs. Hall, his teacher in high school; Jack, whom he worked for in his younger years in the funeral business; his friend Michael; and colleagues like Jane. The circle of life surrounds by a circus of joy when relationships with Christ and people form an unbreakable bond. Did Cordell learn about those bonds in a rock house?

E-Encouragement. Encouragement, of all qualities, is the one thing that everybody needs. Cordell's booming voice (for, after all, he was a communicator himself) asked two questions; "What can I do for you today?" and, "Can I pray for you?" P.T.

Forsyth once noted: "Prayer is the highest use to which speech can be put. It is the highest meaning that can be put into words." Cordell constantly inquired about my wife, Judy, during her tumultuous bout with cancer. His "today" question and his prayerful spirit in the circle of life's stories remind me of two vital keys to genuine communication—care and prayer. Richard Foster once said, "intercession is a way of loving others." Before his death, Cordell shared with his good friend Michael that he was going to retire and intercede daily for others. That was Dr. Parker, an encourager in the stories of life.

E-Education. Cordell graduated from *Denton High School* and *North Texas State University*, and he loved education, students, and speech communication. He once threatened to quit school in the real pressures of education, its costs, and challenges. He relented, though, "I promise I'll finish," he told his mother. He did finish his doctorate in education and surrendered his life, not to his beloved interest in mortuary science but to education. Life takes unexpected twists and turns. Stories wind and bend with surprise.

One lady called him a "giant of a man." He won awards for teaching in 2001—the prestigious Chancellor's Exemplary Teaching Award, the Gold Apple Award, and the Humanities Distinguished Award. I was privileged to introduce him when he won the Gold Apple Award. Afterward, he thanked me, adding, "Thanks for taking the time to drive this far to introduce me. I never knew that speech class meant that much." He once told me, based on my speech class experience, that he thought I would be a man of letters (an educator) but not a public speaker. We laughed about that. Who knows what God will do to shape and surprise in the story of life?

C-Communication. I hear an echo in my ear. "You have verbal and non-verbal communication." If you will have a happy marriage, a successful business, or serve as a good employee, you need good communication skills. If you walk through life's valleys or stand on life's mountains, you will need to communicate to endure or celebrate. If you raise kids or raise corn, you will need communication. If you live life with laughter, love, and abundant life, communication will serve as your most basic tool. I wonder what Aunt Essie communicated on the day Cordell was born in that rock house?

H-Hope. Cordell loved gospel music, especially the Florida Boys. He researched stories of people and church and Christ at home in the heart. As a boy, he sold newspapers. I like to think he liked the news but loved the Good News of Jesus even more. I see him in my imagination—throwing newspapers at dawn; sitting on a riding lawnmower on a hot summer's day at the funeral home; making a body run with the funeral home director; driving an ambulance through a busy street; standing in a church parking lot; laughing, side-splitting laughter, while standing beside a splashy pool; standing in front of a speech class talking; giving a speech; smiling as he receives an award; promising his mother; sitting in church while I preach ("A-," he said that day); loading his office in a box; telling stories, and crying in a rock house while Aunt Essie holds him close to her chest in love.

Most of us never get too far from where life begins—its education, values, and spiritual roots in places like a rock house. Jesus asks us not to get too far from him. He tells us about life and death, the stories, and the story: "Let not your heart be troubled; you believe in God, believe also in me. In my Father's house are many mansions, and I go to prepare a place for you." I am here under the old oak tree pondering a rock house in heaven and a wooden porch where a guy in a cowboy hat sits in a rocking chair near a pond in a circle of people. By the way, if you listen really close, he's telling stories.

I Dress for Success

I'm sitting here under the old oak tree, watching the early morning sunrise, preparing for the day ahead, and longing for Cambridge, England.

Just this morning, I biked on a golf course near the lake. The ducks waddled and paddled along. Birds chirped, fluttering effortlessly into the morning air. Workers mowed the grass, trimming and cutting the golf greens in preparation for a day of bogeys, sand traps, and "fore!" I stopped on a wooden bridge near the golf course and watched an orange sun slowly rise to greet the day.

The old Apostle Paul told the Romans that creation groans like a woman in childbirth (Romans 8:22). Creation grunts, grinds, and groans with the pain and excitement of the birth of a precious child. On this day, though, creation does not groan. It hums. It sings. It makes a joyous melody that starts the day with freshness. The sun births a chorus of praise to the Almighty. God conducts the choir of creation.

While the sun rises, I am perspiring and thinking about "next." Next week has come. The next thing to do must be done. The next project lay ahead. Life is full of "next." On this morning, I watch the sun, and my mind rolls toward "next." I must get home, shower, and dress for the day to come.

Paul held the importance of clothes and dressing for each new day in his mind. Paul knew all too well that the Roman garb of veils, head coverings, mantles, tunics, togas, and togas with identifiable purple stripes. The Romans never left home without the right clothing. After all, the purple stripers wanted everyone to know their status and importance in the Roman world. Graceful, bald headed Paul urged Christians to "put on

Christ" each new day (Romans 13:12). Don't leave home without him!

On a cold January day in 1996, men stood in line for five hours to purchase San Francisco Mayor Willie Brown's old clothes. The mayor donated eight Italian suits, an Italian tuxedo, eight designer jackets, a slew of silk ties, 18 dress shirts, a vest, and 12 pairs of slacks, one of which was black leather. Guys waited in line to buy the mayor's clothes. One man quipped, speaking of the mayor: "He's a wonderful, self-made man. I'm proud to be a Willie Brown clothes horse association member." One guy spent $379 on Brown's old clothes. I guess that guy wished to dress for each new day like the dapper mayor.

I never hear the words "clothes horse" without thinking of Trudy, who, in her nineties, once told me as she lay in a nursing home bed: "I'm a clothes horse. I buy all my clothes at *Goodwill*." Amazing how different we all are: One guy rises with the sun to put on an Italian suit, and one woman rises with the sun to dress for success with clothes from the *Goodwill* rack. The sun still rises, but remember, God looks at the heart.

I once heard a preacher ask, "Do clothes make the man, or does a man make the clothes?" I think he was trying to say that life is more than clothes and that God looks past clothes and straight into the heart.

We, preachers, say stuff that is not always what we mean. The day that preacher asked the question, I figured he forgot about all the women who listened. Should he not have asked, "Do clothes make the woman, or does a woman make the clothes?" All I could think of is that clothes are made in factories by people with sewing needles and machines with foot pedals. The preacher, though, recovered and got me back into understanding when he used a cliché. He thundered after his question, "The clothes don't make the man; the man makes the clothes!" Hallelujah! God looks right past Italian suits and

Goodwill dresses and locks his eyes on hearts. I think that's what the preacher was trying to say. So, dress up your heart.

Tom Wolfe writes long books. An interviewer once asked him about his clothes. He replied: "I don't drink, I don't smoke, I don't even drink coffee. I don't play tennis; I don't even play golf. I found when I was working at the Herald-Tribune making $135 a week that as long as you don't do those other things, I had enough money for fancy clothes." I do not know Tom Wolfe. Still, he would make a good Baptist because Baptists like "don'ts" quite a lot. I would like to ask him about his "do" list, not to be confused about your "to do" list. Tom Wolfe, please tell me what you do. Do you smile? Do you sing happy songs? Do you buy your clothes at *Goodwill*? Do you dress your heart with Jesus? Old Paul again suffices, "Put on the armor of Light." I hope Tom Wolfe's "do" list includes dressing for each new day with the Light.

So, here I am, sitting near the old oak tree, thinking "next." The sun rises in a panorama of color. A fish swirls in the water below the bridge. A turtle pops its head from beneath the water's surface. A blackbird perches near the bridge. And I must dress for the new day. What will I wear? How will it look? What color shall I choose? Will the colors match?

Old Paul keeps whispering, "Put on Christ." Old Cambridge scholar C.S. Lewis understands my morning clothes dilemma. He whispers, "That is very much like the problem with all of us: to dress our souls not for the electric lights of the present world but for the daylight of the next."

John D. Duncan

The Swarm of Bees

I'm sitting here under the old oak tree, thinking of bees. Bees bumble and buzz in these hazy, lazy days of summer. Yellowjackets have built a nest on my front porch. Studying their flight, work, and movements caused me to think of bees.

When I was a boy visiting my grandmother in the mountains of North Carolina, we attended an after-church picnic. The picnics were a kind to love because you could eat all the fried chicken and homemade food you desired.

You would also meet all the relatives you never knew and many whose names you will never remember. I loved it when my aunt would say, "She's your cousin on your grandmother's side, once removed." I loved the picnics, the people, the pizzaz.

That evening, the guys went back to the church to play basketball. After we finished hoops, a bee buzzed—a hornet zoomed from the eave of the fellowship hall roof, made a nosedive for me, and stung me behind my ear. Ouch! I cried the tears of a little boy stung by the pain of life. Have you ever been attacked by a zooming bee?

Just the other day at my house, I saw something I had never seen before—a swarm of bees. The bees moved in concert while buzzing in harmony like a big see-through beach ball. The wind carried them past my mailbox, through the driveway, up over the trees, and into the field behind my house. Not one stray bee left the symphony abuzz. I guess bees understand the joy of teamwork.

Recently, I read a book by Sue Monk Kidd titled *The Secret Life of Bees*. She talks about bees building a nest in her home as a child, her relationship with her mother, and the sting of a painful life. She uses fabulous quotes like, "There is nothing perfect; there is only life." Kidd has a great quote about bees: "When a bee flies, a soul will rise." I am unsure what the quote means, but it rolls easily off the tongue and sounds good.

Then I found myself thinking about the Apostle Paul. Was he ever stung behind the ear by a nose-diving hornet? Did he ever battle a swarm of bees? Did his soul rise when a bee would fly? I am not sure, but he gave young Timothy sound advice for ministry and life, "Therefore, my son, be strong in the grace that is in Christ Jesus" (II Timothy 2:1).

That's what's buzzing in my brain today. Be strong. Be strong in God's grace. Be strong in the grace that is in Christ Jesus.

John D. Duncan

The One that Got Away

I'm sitting here under the old oak tree, thinking about fishing. Jesus called fishermen to follow him.

The orange sun rose over the bay in Key West, Fla. The humidity of the morning and the coming day excited me. I watched the sunrise while the glassy waters mirrored the life of the sun. I ate breakfast, a feast of watermelon, sausage, scrambled eggs, and orange juice. I walked off the ramp of the cruise ship on that summer morning and boarded a smaller vessel for fishing on the Florida Gulf Coast. The Duncan men—my father, George Sr.; my brother, George Jr.; my nephew, Graham; and I greeted that morning as we ventured on a fishing expedition. Sal and Brian, the crew of the ship, greeted us. Brian explained where the ice water was, where we were going, and our task for the day—to catch fish.

He exuded confidence that we, the Duncan men, would, no doubt, catch fish. Captain Brian opined along the way: "Fish with the best and not the rest."

I am a disciple of Jesus. He loved fishermen. He loves me. I am no fisherman, but I do like to fish occasionally. Does that make sense? We rode out to our fishing spot on the boat named "Bullbuster." I could not help but think of Key West, Ernest Hemingway, and his books *The Sun Also Rises* about bullfights in Spain and *The Old Man and the Sea*. In Hemingway's book about the old man and the sea, he tells the story of an old man battling a shark on a fishing excursion.

Hemingway describes the fish with great lines: "Then the fish came alive, with his death in him, and rose high out of the water, showing all his great length and width and all his power and beauty. He seemed to hang in the air above the old man in the skiff. Then he fell into the water with a crash that sent spray over the old man and over all of the skiff."

Would today be the day when I would battle a fish and splash of the ocean would spray mist on my face?

Brian drove us in the "Bullbuster" 10 miles out into the Gulf of Mexico. We fished over a World War II vessel named "Alexander." Sailors guided the vessel in WW II, but later it became a target for bombers practicing air raids. I guess the sunken ship "Alexander" was named after Alexander the Great, Aristotelian pupil, military general, 4th century B.C. military strategist, and the great one who once tamed a defiant colt. The sunken "Alexander" was our fishing spot. Would today be the day to tame a wild fish? Brian instructed us that we were fishing for "yellow snapper." I asked Sal, whose cackling laugh kept me entertained if it helped to talk, "Does it help to talk to the fish?"

"Yeah, oh, yeah," he cackled and laughed and laughed and cackled.

The Duncan men caught yellow snapper, enjoyed the Gulf, and bonded in the life of the sun and the spraying mist of the ocean waters. Then it happened.

As I reeled in hook, line, and sinker, a small yellow snapper, a larger fish, zoomed quickly across the top of the water. "What do I do?" I asked Sal. "Leave it there," he instructed me.

Before I could say, "Howdy," or whatever a Texan fishing in Florida would say, a kingfish grabbed the yellow snapper, the hook, and took my fishing line fast and furious a hundred yards into the Gulf. Laughing and crying out, I said to Brian and Sal: "What do I do? What do I do? Tell me, what do I do?"

Anne Lamott, in her book *Traveling Mercies*, speaks of the two best prayers she knows: "Help me, help me," and "Thank you, thank you, thank you." I cried out help me with the words, "What do I do?" Just hang on," Sal said as he cackled, "he'll get tired,"

The fish tired. Sal and Brian explained to me how to reel in the kingfish. I struggled and battled and fought for 20 minutes. My hand felt tremendous pain, but I kept reeling.

Hemingway has a couple of sentences about pain: "I must hold his pain where it is, he thought. Mine does not matter. I can control mine. But his pain could drive him mad."

The pain in my hand did matter. Was the pain of a hook in the kingfish driving him mad?

The fish and I fought and struggled, struggled and fought until I had the fish within 10 feet of the boat.

Then suddenly, with a spin on top of the water, the fish whipped his tail like a sword and cut the line. It is my fisherman's story of the big one that got away.

So here I am under the old oak tree, thinking. Life is cackling laughter and struggle and days where men bond together in the sun's life and the ocean's spray mist.

Abundant life is about being a disciple of Jesus, a fisherman whom Jesus loves. It is about saying to our Lord God in Jesus Christ, "Help me, help me, help me!" and "Thank you, thank you, thank you." Life is about the story: fishing, the big one that got away, and the gospel story of Jesus' love. Feel the sun. Feel the mist of ocean spray. Feel the love - of Jesus. "Come unto me all you who are heavy laden and I will give you rest" (Matthew 11:28).

Of Marathons and Truth

I'm sitting here under the old oak tree, thinking about the *Olympics* in Athens, Greece.

The *Olympics* buzz with prospects for heroic feats by well-trained athletes. The United States team—the swimmers, the runners, the sand volleyballers, the basketballers, the divers, the shot putters, and the like—have prepared themselves for their respective events.

I cannot watch the *Olympics* without thinking of two things—the marathon and the Apostle Paul.

The marathon is so named because the Greeks defeated the Persians in the Battle of Marathon in 490 B.C. A Greek general dispatched a messenger, who ran to Athens to announce the victory. His name was Pheidippides. He ran a distance of 26 miles from the plains of Marathon, by the coast, through the foothills to Athens. When he arrived, he announced, "Rejoice, we conquer!" After his brief victorious announcement, he died. If it's your time, your swan song, I can't think of a better way than going out on a winning note.

The *Olympics* also remind me of the Apostle Paul.

In Athens, he visited a place called the "Areopagus," also known as the "council of court." On a rocky hill between the Acropolis and the agora or marketplace (think of *Wal-Mart*), the Areopagus is the place where Paul debated the philosophers and Sophists of his day. They worshipped an unknown God. Paul announced God could be known in Jesus. Down here in Texas, we proclaim a God who changes lives in Jesus. Wow!

During the *Olympics*, television photographers shoot videos of Athens and scan the Acropolis. It houses an infamous structure called "The Parthenon." Known to the Greeks as the "place of virgins," it was a pagan temple in Paul's day. It has also housed a mosque, a Christian church in the sixth century, and other pagan temples through the years. The more things change, the more they stay the same.

All this brings me back to Marathon and the Apostle Paul. We, as Christians, all run a marathon in life, running in the victory of Christ. And in a world of paganism and the offering of many gods, Paul's word of truth in the resurrection power of Jesus, who can be known, is still the important message of the day.

The *Olympic* motto is "faster, stronger, higher." In ancient Greece, the *Olympics* included processions, sacrifices, and banquets. The victors were crowned with a garland of wild olive twigs. A lot has changed through the years—from olive-leaved crowns to gold medals. All this reminds us that we live in a changing world, a world that runs marathons, celebrates with banquets, and honors gold-medal winners. Still, it is a world where Paul's message of gospel truth forms a rock-solid foundation stronger than the Parthenon.

By the way, this old oak tree has added another year, another ring around its trunk. Maybe I should travel to Athens.

The Presence of Christ

I'm sitting here under the old oak tree, thinking about the presence of Christ. Jesus said, "I am telling you what I have seen in the Father's presence, and you do what you have heard from your father" (John 8:38).

The poet Gerard Manley Hopkins details Christ's presence in his poem *As Kingfishers Catch Fire*:

As kingfishers catch fire, dragonflies draw flame;
As tumbled over rim in roundy wells
Stones ring; like each tucked string tells, each hung bell's
Bow swung finds tongue to fling out broad its name;
Each mortal thing does one thing and the same:
Deals out that being indoors each one dwells;
Selves-goes itself; myself it speaks and spells,
Crying, "What I do is me: for that I came."
I say more: the just man justices;
Keeps grace: that keeps all his goings graces;
Acts in God's eye what in God's eye he is—Christ.
For Christ plays in ten thousand places,
Lovely in limbs, and lovely in eyes not his
To the Father through the features of men's faces.

He speaks of Christ who, in his presence, "plays in ten thousand places."

Christ in his presence shows up in hospital rooms, in back alleys where indigents dig for scrap food in dumpsters, in the eyes of a father whose tears trickle down the cheek at graduation exercises, at funerals where widowers weep, in birthday celebrations, at church, in prayer meetings, but, mostly, Christ shows up in the human heart. Christ plays in the ten thousand places, but he plays a melody of joy when he resides in the human heart.

The other day, I heard a lady describe her airplane ride to another city. She got up out of her chair and went to the back of the airplane to the bathroom. While waiting in line, she looked through the window.

A man wearing a large cross around his neck saw her and asked, "Are you looking for someone?"

"No," she replied, "I am simply looking at the stars."

"Look closely, and you'll see angels," the cross-bearing man responded.

"All I see is stars," the lady again replied.

"Look really close, and you can see Christ on the wing," he chimed.

The whole discussion led them to talk about their common faith and witness to the living presence of Christ.

So, here I am on this hot Texas summer day, thinking about Christ's presence.

Somehow, my mind drifted to North Carolina, where my grandmother lived in the mountains. She eases into the room on a cool night while the mountain winds blow the curtains. A car passes by. The stars shine brightly. A cricket chirps. A firefly glows. The floor creaks. And then my grandmother whispers in the quietness,

Now I lay me down to sleep
I pray the Lord my soul to keep
If I should die before I wake
I pray the Lord my soul to take.

As the breezes blew and while my grandmother whispered her prayer, I sensed God's presence. "Be still and know that he is God" (Psalm 46:10). Christ plays in ten thousand places; he makes a melody in the soul.

I believe in God's presence. And next time I fly on an airplane, I'll think of the cross, glance out the window for the stars, and look for Christ on the wing.

John D. Duncan

A World of Contrasts

I'm sitting here under the old oak tree, wondering about a world of contrasts.

In London. grief reigns in the aftermath of terror while innocent children play cricket in open fields and streets. Hurricanes rip through the Gulf of Mexico, but daily cruise ships sail the seas with carefree travelers. In Granbury, a trip to *Wal-Mart* to purchase the necessities of life is contrasted with the fact that American consumers waste money every year on things they do not need or never will use.

Contrasts, they swirl around us—up and down; good and bad; happy and sad; tall and short; light and dark; mountains and valleys; winners and losers; and fast and slow.

Contrasts appear in the Bible, too.

Take, for example, Jesus' visit to the temple after his triumphal entry into Jerusalem via a gate. The next day, Jesus went to the temple. Contrasts abound—the holy presence of God in the Holy of Holies with the priests and the prideful money changers who barter doves on a table in the temple courtyard; the anger of Jesus and the casualness of the money changers; the inner turmoil of plotting among the scribes and the outer peace of Jesus; the hostility of Jesus' enemies and the blissful amazement of the crowd; the unrighteousness of religious leaders and the righteousness of Jesus; the flying coins and the doves sitting in cages; the house of prayer and the den of thieves. Contrasts multiply.

Still, when I think of the temple, I think of the veil of the temple torn in two when Jesus died on the cross—one Christ, two pieces of cloth severed at the center; one holy Jesus, an unholy world; light on the cross, darkness around. Add lightning and thunder and midnight at midday, and you have the makings of high drama. Or, as one of our children said in Vacation Bible School when he heard the story of Jesus: "Oh, that! I saw the movie!" Welcome to a world of contrasts—the real drama of Jesus' sacrificial life placed as Hollywood theater to a 21st century 10-year-old.

All this leads me back to where I started—the contrast between a world of terror, London, and a world of peace, Jesus. So much discussion continues about safety, protection against terrorists on trains, religious extremists, and a bomb on a bus. Lord Byron says sarcastically in one of his poems, "I say—the future is a serious matter." The future is a serious matter.

In the confusion of terror at King's Cross. one survivor described the scene as shards of broken glass, trails of blood, and the feeling like she was in a fish tank watching others fight for their lives. A teenage girl collapsed in tears and had a tissue with the word "life" printed on it.

I do not know much about terror, although I sense it every time I go through security at the airport for a trip. I do not know much about King's Cross, although it is my travel point of connection twice a year on the way to Cambridge. I always say, "Seven million people in London, and they were all on the train today." I do not know much about that fish-tank feeling, but I know we live in an ocean of people as diverse as the fish in the seas.

As for contrasts, I am reminded of one necessary constant: Jesus. He is the same yesterday, today and forever (Hebrews 13:8). In a world of contrasts, the King's Cross anchors the soul. And this message is a simple yet essential one today: In Jesus, you have abundant life.

John D. Duncan

Dreams

I'm sitting here under the old oak tree, pondering the dog days of summer. Recently, I heard of a man who had a dog named Dreams. Family members uttered with a wry smile the dog's name and how much the man loved his dog. After all, a dog is a man's best friend, so it goes.

The whole thought of dreams left me wondering, was the man's dog named for dreams, you know, "dreams," the hopes, plans, visions, and future wishes that with hard work or dumb luck or sheer charisma might come true? Or was the man thinking of bleary-eyed video reels in the brain that awakens you in your sleep then causes you to smile or create restless, heart-pounding nights by scaring you out of your pajamas?

In the 21st century, leaders on every corner talk about the concept of a dream. They will say glorious words about vision statements, mission statements, the importance of a clearly defined purpose or what you seek to accomplish, or your stated goals for the company, the school, the church, or even your life. The Lord knows we have heard the words "purpose-driven" until our eyes pop out of our heads like the annoying sound of a false fire alarm that rattles your brain, heightens your senses, but cannot be shut off. Purpose, I suppose, is necessary as a fire alarm, but like a fire alarm, at some point, you have to move on, get out of the building, find out what happened, put out the fire, and actively and safely move on with life. A dream, vision, and mission are only good when an action results.

Since this is a cyber column for church leaders, I should add that every church needs a dream, a vision, a mission, and purpose statements. Rick Warren was right. We need purpose-driven churches and purpose-driven lives. Long before Rick Warren, whom I respect, the wisdom writer of Proverbs spun his front-porch wisdom, "Where there is no vision, the people perish" (Proverbs 29:18). The Hebrew idea is that no vision leads to "no restraint," chaos, pandemonium, and stuff out of control, like destructive winds during a storm. Lord knows we understand chaos. Lord knows we have enough chaos in our churches. That is why dreams, vision, mission, and purpose are good for churches.

Christian leaders, though, must realize that trying to define purpose all the time and not getting your feet moving in action kills a church. As a Christian, the Christ of Philippians 2:5-11 serves as a good model to help you live in God's purpose. Since Christ is our vision, or dream if you will, then most of the people I know, beginning with me, have a way to go. You can name Matthew 28:19-20 as your church's dream for reaching a lost world, but at some point, you have to go into the world to talk to them and engage them. That is action. Everybody needs a dream that spurs meaningful, spiritual action that touches the kingdom of God and other people.

Where there is vision, the people flourish. Live your dreams, as they say. Go for your dreams. So, the dog's name was Dreams, the best friend a man could own, a prize dog on the journey of life, a dog fit for a king, or at least one that made his owner feel like one. Who knows but what the man thought that dog was the dog of any man's dreams, faithful to lick him when he came home from work, friendly when no one else would say one word to him, and always present at his feet in those down-and-out times, responsible like a bird dog is for the hunter when it comes time to fetch the prey.

Then I thought, maybe the man who named his dog Dreams pondered his own dreams. I guess we do this sometimes. I do not dream often. But recently, I dreamed I was driving a car backward and into a body of water. The dream did not scare me because I made it to land on a sunny day before I woke up. If an interpreter showed up, he probably would say it was stress in my life or that I would soon be traveling to England over a large body of water where they drive cars on the wrong side of the road, and things seem backward. I know, the interpretation does not make sense but humor me here. Life can get confusing.

Imagine how wonderful the Bible is in its divine word, imaginative spark, and purpose-driven-God-talk truth that we all need. The Bible, of all books, speaks of dreams and the interpretation of dreams. Joseph, in prison, mind you, before he became second in command in the politics of Egypt, had a dream that his brothers would all bow down to him. Joseph also interpreted dreams for a butcher, a baker but no candlestick maker. Actually, a butler, not a butcher, but the butler was restored to his former glory while the baker was beheaded. Either way, all of Joseph's dreams came true: His brothers bowed down to him, the butler smiled again while answering a knock on the door, and the baker was butchered, hanged, never to smile again. So much for dreams.

You can check this out in your Bible, Abimelech dreamed, Laban dreamed, Jacob did, too, of ladders, Joseph dreamed in shock before the birth of Jesus, and you could argue that Paul dreamed when he was caught up in the third heaven. Young men, the Bible says, have visions; old men dream dreams. Maybe my dream means I am getting older.

I've said all this to say that a man named his dog, Dreams. May your life be blessed with purpose. Live your dreams. Put God in your dreams. Who knows—you might one day be second in command in a kingdom or be restored to previous honor or write a book about a life of purpose or sing on American Idol or ride a victorious bike down the streets of Paris or graduate from college or tour Europe. Dream big, but do not forget God in your dreams.

That goes for you, me, churches, businesses, the high school football team, and the *Lion's Club*. And beware: A day comes for all when dreams die and can no longer be lived, a day of reckoning, hopefully, unlike the butchered baker whose dream came true.

For such a time, make sure that you know God because whether you drive backward into a body of water or build a big business or church or live your dreams or all your dreams come true, you still have to deal with God in the end. I always figured it's best to make sure it is his light lighting the way in your dreams. And if none of this works, just get you a dog. Dreams might not be a bad name! Sweet dreams!

John D. Duncan

Twenty Years in One Place

I'm sitting here under the old oak tree, thumbing through an old Bible. It is a wide-margin brown calf-skin Cambridge Bible. Old, yellowed tape lines the Bible with notes, quotes, and a date written in the front on a leafy page—July 1984. I bought it as a seminary student and paid $70 for it when I worked at a Christian bookstore.

For years when I used that Bible to read, study, and preach, I would write notes in the margin, tape quotes, and pen notes in the front and back.

In the margin of James 1:4 ("But let patience have her perfect work"), I scribbled in green ink *upomone*, a Greek word meaning that in Christ we can joyfully "stay under the load" of life. In the back, I wrote a list of 30 traits of human nature, from worry to restlessness to anger to loneliness to pride. Human nature clothes us all. Walt Whitman poetically penned, "Agonies are one of my changes of garments." In another, I jotted down a thought: "The melody in our hearts often speaks of the master of our lives."

Interesting quotes are taped inside the Bible: Of visitation, George Buttrick said there are three rules, "You've got to do it; you've got to do it; you've got to do it." Of speech, the Greek sage Publius once said, "I have often regretted my speech but never my silence." Of life, George Truett once said, "We are to learn that life is a school with many teachers." Numerous quotes fill the pages, but one I often refer to is by Dietrich Bonhoeffer. A preacher, long since gone on to be with the Lord, handed pages to me one day with a mysterious, wry smile. "Make sure you read this," he garbled. What does the quote say? The quote is long but ends with these words: "The more thankfully we daily receive what is given to us, the more surely and steadily will fellowship increase and grow from day to day as God pleases." I knew the man, a pastor, preacher, who wanted to send me two messages: (1) be thankful for what God gives, his church, his people, his blessings, his hardships; (2) Grace prompts gratitude and increases fellowship with God in light and in the shadows of life.

I have for exactly 20 years, by the time you read this, been privileged to serve and pastor the same church, Lakeside Baptist Church in Granbury, Texas. I have lived through the normal stuff—the joy of baptisms and weddings and good church reports and people joining the church and laughter and of people inviting Christ into their lives against all hope and the thrill of a roller coaster ride of church growth and its celebrative moments as well as the exhaustion of euphoria in its midst. Laughter has not been absent from our church, nor joy. After all, one child announced that he just knew I was THE real John the Baptist. Another sketched a picture of me preaching one Sunday. I held the Bible in one hand, gesturing with another, smiling while my hair waved in the wind. The pulpit seemed small, and my eyes looked big. The little girl showed it to her mother after church one Sunday. She pointed to me and to the caption beneath, exclaiming, "This is what Brother John does!" The caption read, "Blah, blah, BLAH, blah, blah, BLAH!" Laughter has arrived in chariots of fire with joy chained to the parade behind.

I have also had loads dumped on me, felt the pressure of such, and dumped stuff myself. In the first country church I pastored, white, wooden with no air conditioner on a hot Texas summer, and an outhouse to boot, I preached my 19-year-old heart out one Sunday, ranting and raving on Romans 12. My first sermon was, low and behold, all of 12 minutes. On this day, though, I brought home the preaching bacon at a boiling, fire-breathing 45 minutes, nearly ruining my voice along the way. Only eight people showed up, but I gave it to them good, probably because the other four regulars had not shown up. Mr. Parks, an eighty-something farmer-rancher who liked to chew on toothpicks while smiling, said afterward, "Preacher, when just a few cows show up, I don't dump the whole load." We laughed, but I thought about what he said all the way home and for days. I decided he loved his pastor, and he was being funny, not rude. But along the way, I have experienced the deep and dark because of words not spoken in love and harsh things that sometimes people say around the church. Almost 20 years ago, one guy told me I would never make it in the ministry because I was too soft, whatever that means. Another told me I could not preach. And a few have given me, as one lady said, "a piece of my mind," and it left me reeling to pick up the pieces, whatever that means.

At times, it seems that I have been in the belly of a whale like Jonah, twisted in seaweed and vomit, have wept like Jeremiah on days when no converts came, have asked God to touch my tongue with Isaiah's fire, have longed for Malachi's refiner's fire to zap a few people, have sloshed water out of the boat in the storm with Jesus' disciples, stood at the Mountain of Transfiguration-joy and celebrated God's work, rejoiced at the Jordan River during baptisms, cried like a baby at Lazarus-like funerals full of emotion and family dynamics ("Lord, if you had been here my brother would not have died!"). I have waited anxiously for God's miraculous work in hospital rooms after snake bites, shipwrecks, and Roman beatings, not to mention cancer, heart surgeries, and broken arms. Life is never dull. And I believe that the gospel has always been good news amid all the bad news. It's what keeps me going and what I look forward to every day, the good news of the gospel of Jesus Christ.

Anyway, here I am 20 years later, thumbing through my old Bible, simply giving thanks to the Lord for his blessing of 20 years in one place, the mercy and misery of it, the happiness and struggle of it, and the peace and chaos of it, with mercy and happiness and peace in the grace of it all far outweighing the rest, and God's light overpowering the shadows.

I thank the Lord and the people of Lakeside for the privilege of serving as pastor and for the blessing of God. I see faces—like the elderly, long-departed Dorothy, church member, and neighbor who lived next door in those cracker-box-sized apartments, who in the darkness of the early years had the vision to hold my hand and look to the heavens and declare, "God is going to do something great in that church!" I did not feel great but believed her, and together we believed in God. I see Ruth, who modeled "the music of our hearts often speaks of the master of our lives" and played the organ, a melodious song, one Sunday night, *Set My Soul Afire, Lord!* when the organ caught on fire. Watch what you sing for, but know that encouragement moves mountains, and Ruth delivered it like a song, making a huge difference in a person's life. I see Riley, a charter member and a godly deacon who served on the pulpit committee 20 years ago, now an octogenarian in and out of the hospital and residing mostly in a nursing home; I see his faithfulness to the Lord that inspires me to this day. I see Sam and Jerry, quiet as church mice, reserved but full of wisdom, and the ones who helped me achieve my dream of further education in Cambridge, England. I see a host of other faces, young and old, with stories and words too numerous to be printed here, people to whom I am eternally grateful. And I see the face of Christ, glowing like the radiant sun, dripping with the thorn-crowned brow of love and pouring out his grace on me daily like a Texas rain shower that waters the bluebonnets and makes them rich in color and lovely in their Texas dwelling places.

Thanks, Lakeside Baptist Church, for 20 years of serving Christ together. I anticipate God's future work in the vision, the faithfulness, and the dream of serving the Lord. I also thank staff members, friends, family, and a cloud of numerous witnesses.

And so, here I am, 20 years later. What have I learned? Trust in the Lord with all your heart. Pray long. Work hard. Honor the word. Love Jesus. Care for people. Watch what you sing for. Keep the good news good. Take care of the things the Lord asks you to take care of and let him take care of you. Look to Christ. Be thankful, always. Try not to dump the whole load on people all at once! Find the grace of God on the journey of life. Or, to quote Henri Nouwen, taped in my Bible, "Lord, give me the courage to be a dove in a world so full of serpents."

Hope Radiates

I'm sitting here under the old oak tree in July, pondering past events and thinking of our nation at grief in America—grieving families in the loss of soldiers, grieving church members who have lost loved ones, and still feeling the grief of long-forgotten, at least by most, of the Virginia Tech tragedy of last spring. How soon we forget, but grief never forgets.

Really, though, I find myself thinking about the power of the teacher-student relationship. My mind cannot even fathom the events of Virginia Tech—the horror, the funerals with sad songs, or the grief that, like an ocean wave, will not, for some, go away. It will roll in waves ceaselessly. Walt Whitman wrote two magnificent lines in his poem, Memories of President Lincoln: "With the countless torches lit, with the silent sea of faces and unbared heads."

On this hot summer day, I find myself looking out beyond the old oak tree. The bluebonnets have sung their glory as spring has passed. Not too far from here, new roads, construction, and the yellow flashing lights of construction blink and signal progress. And school is out for most, but summer school is in (my daughters are attending summer school): teachers teach students the basics, reading, writing, and arithmetic. Socrates, Plato, and Joseph T. McClain would be proud.

I have thought about the terrible tragedy of Virginia Tech—the blood, the pictures, the anger, the death, the vigils with countless torches lit, and the sea of faces, those who unnecessarily lost their lives, the grieving families on the journey of long lament and even the family of the killer who will live with a mark of the beast the rest of their lives. I think of pastors speaking at funerals trying to explain the unexplainable with comforting words from the Shepherd's Psalm with images in fields of green and stories of how Christ lost his Son in a bloodbath and how life takes a sudden turn. You do not know where to turn, and so Christ turns to you in the sacred silence and mysterious mess of life unpredictable. What do people do without God? Christ? The Holy Spirit who hovers as a comforter? I hear the voices of pastors, "God was there. He is here now. The Lord is my Shepherd, valleys and a rod and staff and light in the dark and countless torches lit amid a sea of faces." In the sea of faces, mothers, fathers, students, they still weep, the countless torches reflecting glistening tears on running cheeks in the shadows of death unplanned.

I also hear the voices of skeptics: Where was your God? I agree with C. S. Lewis, "Atheism turns out to be too simple. If the whole universe has no meaning, we should never have found out that it has no meaning: just as if there were no light in the universe and therefore no creatures with eyes, we should never know it was dark. Dark would be a word without meaning." I know I do not always understand C. S. Lewis either, but he is right: If there is no God and no meaning, how would you know there were no God, and no meaning since part of the meaning we gather in life comes from the contrasts: dark, light; atheist, Christian; death, life; student, teacher; wicks on candles snuffed out, glowing candles in the wind, with countless torches lit in the sea of faces. If only the skeptics would look into the sea of faces. If only skeptics would peer into the torches lit and find light.

One, I am thankful for the Shepherd in a moment like this time in history on planet earth. I believe in God more than ever. I need the grace of the Shepherd's care in valleys deep and utter gratitude for the Shepherd's love on the mountain. Two, I keep thinking of the students and teachers and the teacher-student relationship, especially the one student who lost her professor in the rampage and uttered, "I will miss my brilliant professor."

I even wonder what she is doing this summer. Summer school? Camp? Weeping with willows on long summer nights?

For all we like to take credit for, we are products of the teacher-student relationship: parent to child, boss to employer, trainer to trainee, teacher to student. Of all the crazy things I am thinking about, words bouncing back and forth in my mind like a ping pong ball, are those words, "I will miss my brilliant professor!"

I once had a professor who has since passed on whom I miss. His name was Dr. Joseph T. McClain. He taught Greek and Bible at Howard Payne University. He loved running and sports, especially any team from Oklahoma, boomer sooner, and the pride of an Okie from Muskogee and all that. He also pastored a church in Shelby, North Carolina, wrote me letters, and said things like, "Don't get any tar on your heels." He had strong opinions about politics, school, education, and even my life. He once told me emphatically, "Don't graduate from college in three years! Don't do it!" I did it anyway and thought later that maybe he was right. He once sent me on a mission trip to Wyoming and to the hardest church, a new church start to preach a revival where I preached to three people on the first Sunday. The pastor apologized because only he, his wife, and son showed up. He admitted later that his other son stayed home and slept.

Dr. McClain said he sent me there "To see what you're made of." He loved Bible verses like, "He who humbles himself shall be exalted. He who exalts himself shall be humbled." He longed to teach me the way of Christ, the way of discipleship, and the way of Biblical study in the Greek language, which like a farmer, he aimed to plant as seeds in my heart. His teaching seeds bore fruit, and now some 25 years later, I still hear his voice deep in my soul.

All told, he taught me Greek and how to interpret the Bible, and he loved A. T. Robertson's commentaries full of word pictures, and he gave me books from his library, always signed, "To my Faithful and Most Able Co-Worker with Love, Joseph T. McClain 12/25/81." A good teacher will guide students through a maze of discovery, like walking a corridor and opening doors and windows full of new adventures. A good teacher makes learning electric, pulsating with lightning and thunder and heightening the senses like the warning from an approaching storm. A good teacher invokes discipline. "Study a little every day," McClain would say. A good teacher helps you see what you often do not see in your inner self and calls out that self to be shared, and cheers you to grand heights. A good Christian teacher offers insight into the way of Christ and into the way of developing the mind of Christ.

I miss my brilliant professor. Oh, how I miss him. He did all of that for me.

Matthew (8:19-27, NIV) records an exchange between teacher and student-disciple: "Then a teacher of the law came to him and said, "Teacher, I will follow you wherever you go." Jesus replied, "Foxes have holes and birds of the air have nests, but the Son of Man has no place to lay his head." Another disciple said to him, "Lord, first let me go and bury my father." But Jesus told him, "Follow me, and let the dead bury their own dead." Then he got into the boat and his disciples followed him. Without warning, a furious storm came up on the lake, so that the waves swept over the boat.

"But Jesus was sleeping. The disciples went and woke him, saying, "Lord, save us! We're going to drown!" He replied, "You of little faith, why are you so afraid?" Then he got up and rebuked the winds and the waves, and it was completely calm. The men were amazed and asked, "What kind of man is this? Even the winds and the waves obey him!"

Here I am under this old oak tree. Summer sizzles. Fields of green offer praise. Countless torches glow in the sea of faces. And I am thinking of the most vital teacher-student relationship:

Jesus to his disciples, Jesus to his followers, Jesus to people in the twenty-first century like me. So here is what I think: If we took more seriously the relationship between teacher-student and as disciples of Jesus allowed Christ to teach us as his students, maybe, just maybe, there would be less violence, more peace; less darkness, more light; less wandering, more meaning; less hopelessness, more hope; less sadness, more joy.

Jesus had a rag-tag group of followers, sons of thunder and fishermen and women and bad people gone good under the grace of God and good apples made better under the glory of God's goodness. Transformation took place one on one, face to face, heart to heart, soul to soul. I pray for the grieving and pray for the church of Jesus to cling to the heart of Christ, discipleship, reclaiming, in the words of Dallas Willard, a church culture of discipleship because the church of America tends toward churches full of "undiscipled disciples."

Once in a children's musical in our church, the recurring theme in the musical was, *Stop! Look! Listen for Christmas!* My prayer is that in more recent events, we will stop, look and listen for Christ, that we will see 'the countless torches lit and the sea of faces" and look into Christ's face to hear, in the words of Matt Redman in his book *Facedown*, "the intimate whispers of God." Under this tree, the wind rustles the leaves. A cool breeze blows. An ant crawls nearby. A bird catches the upward current of the wind.

And hope radiates, a Torch brighter than torches lit, and one Face stands out amid the sea of faces, the Shepherd who stands in a field of green with arms open wide, speaking in an intimate whisper, "Come unto me all you who are weary and heavy laden and I will give you rest." I stand. I speak. I move toward the Shepherd and say, "I am coming, Lord. I am coming." I see beyond the Shepherd, torches lit, and the sea of faces, and I fall facedown in awe. I weep. And I look up; Christ weeps and

John D. Duncan

grieves for the sea of faces. And the wind blows. And the wind blows. And the wind keeps blowing.

Above, Where Christ Is

I'm sitting here under the old oak tree, wondering where the summer has gone. Here in Texas, August beckons. Gerard Manley Hopkins, the poet, once quipped, "Mine, O thou lord of life, send my roots rain." I have been away from the church for a sabbatical of sorts, resting, finding pleasure in reading and writing, and resting and longing to return to my post as pastor to be with the people of God. The Lord is sending my dry roots rain. I feel refreshed.

I find myself thinking of the future, climbing Jacob's ladder to peer into what God has in store; gazing at Jeremiah's future and a hope; scoping Paul's letter to the Colossians (3:1) from prison where from the deep and dark, he declares, "Keep seeking those things above, where Christ is...." I think of the future, one with no land phones and digital, of green cars in an eco-friendly society and HDTV where at least we yearn to see the Dallas Cowboys or Dallas Mavericks in multi-color championships on crystal-clear screens. I think of the future, cancer walks, cancer research, and cancer cures on the horizon. I think of the future, political speeches winding down and electronic election polls minus the chads; of hyped cars with powerhouse engines advertised with mega "horsepower"; of outsourcing in business and televised conference calls on HDTV with a clear sound like talking to the neighbor next door; and of churches with digitized sound and big screens and bands like the Beatles echoing praise choruses and rhythmically blasting hymns high to the heavens. The future is widescreen and wide open. Yes, keep seeking the things above, where Christ is.

Still, my mind drifts to the gospel. Despite all the technological wizardry, the gospel still impacts people one person at a time by riversides, in the marketplace, over coffee or a meal, at gravesites, and in homes where people pray for the light to shine in dark places. Henri Nouwen once declared of "Christian leadership in the future," "It is not a leadership of power and control, but a leadership of powerlessness and humility in which the suffering servant of God, Jesus, is made manifest." Nouwen invites leaders to humble themselves as Christ to be servant leaders.

All told, humility is a difficult thing. C.S. Lewis once noted that his "school life was a life almost totally dominated by the social struggle, to get on, to arrive, or, having reached the top, to remain there, was the absorbing preoccupation." Come to think of it, the climb to the top in business or an organization to which you belong or, dare I say it, in the church, as often happens, and the drive to get ahead, control, and dominate, seems to me, to be one of life's ongoing struggles. We never really outgrow school life—the jockeying for position, the jokes, the jealousy, the envy, the bullying that goes on, and the cliques. Still, getting to the top and a preoccupation with "the top" is different from "Keep seeking the things above, where Christ is."

Getting to the top might find you preoccupied but prideful. After all, Lewis adds, "Pride leads to every other vice ... and is an anti-God state of mind." Now I doubt that any of us ever think of ourselves as anti-God in any state of mind. On the other hand, though, I guess most of us have demonstrated pride toward a co-worker, a spouse, or even a church member. This, of course, is why we seek the things above, where Christ is so that it rids us of pride and leads us to serve Christ in our present and future. Still, we must first fall down before Christ in humility to seek the things above.

It is complex in principle, but maybe a picture helps. I am thinking under this old oak tree on this hot Texas summer day of two people. Last spring, on the same Saturday, I was privileged to preach both their funerals. They were different but alike,

Under the Old Oak Tree

saints on the journey of struggle but humble in their hearts to the core and to the end.

First, there was Phyllis. Phyllis worked at the local *Texaco* gas station. That is where I first met her, paying the fare, discussing rising gas prices, and taking her prayer requests as she offered them because she knew I was a pastor. She lived from 1939 to 2007 and lived in California, Arkansas, Tennessee, and Granbury, Texas. She lived a quiet, humble life with her cats and a dog named Stormy. She liked to listen to Elvis, who, by the way, does not live in Granbury and has never appeared here as far as I know, but Granbury once had an Elvis impersonator named Care who sang at a hangout on the local town square, "the man of a thousand voices," who could sing to the rafters like Elvis and look like him and shake his leg the way Elvis did. Phyllis liked listening to Elvis, and at her funeral, Elvis sang *Amazing Grace*, music from one of his old albums, of course.

Phyllis had humble beginnings, born to sharecroppers in a shack in Earle, Ark., loved to watch western movies, and spent most of her days scanning gas credit cards, discussing the price of gas, stocking gas station shelves with sugary sodas, and talking to Stormy when she got home from work.

Phyllis assured me she knew Christ, a "recovering Methodist," as I think she once named herself. She never came to our church because she worked on Sundays but always requested prayer and accepted her simple plight in life without complaint or desired fanfare. She lived humbly in the shadows of life and the sunshine. And the Light of her life was Christ. She quietly kept seeking the things above, where Christ is.

Then there was Raymond. Phyllis died at 67 years of age. Raymond died after 93 years. Raymond was born in 1913 in Arcadia, La. President Franklin D. Roosevelt proclaimed a "new deal" for the American people back in the 1930s and formed the WPA (Worker's Progress Administration), and Raymond's grandfather, brother-in-law, and father-in-law all worked for the

WPA for $1.50 an hour. Raymond's first job was in the *Ringgold Sawmill* for 15 cents an hour. He later moved to Shreveport, then to Fort Worth, where he enrolled in the seminary. Raymond worked a full-time job and attended seminary for three years until his health deteriorated. His family physician instructed him to quit seminary, but Raymond never stopped serving Christ nor seeking the things above. He served in small churches and as a deacon at Travis Avenue Baptist Church in Fort Worth and a deacon here in Granbury at Lakeside Baptist for 14 years.

Brother Raymond lived in the same house on James Avenue for 43 years and drove the same car for 28 years, a 1948 Chevrolet. Who lives in the same house and drives a car that long anymore? Raymond worked for *Bell Helicopter* until 1978 and then retired. He never retired from serving, preaching, teaching, and praying. I loved to hear Raymond pray. He prayed with a southern drawl, his voice deep and resonating as a man who knew God personally. He prayed one-syllable words with two syllables, words like "our" and "God" with a humming intonation, "Our-a God-a." He prayed sweet prayers, deep ones, from the depths of his soul, calling out light to Light, begging for Light to penetrate the darkness and for the peace of God's wondrous grace to sweeten the soul of a world in chaos. For all his long life, Raymond sought the things above, where Christ is.

P.T Forsythe once spoke of shutting the chamber door, praying quietly, audibly, humbly to the Lord. "Write prayers and burn them," he wrote in 1913. Brother Raymond's prayers intimately rattled heaven's throne and touched the heart of God, and his prayers burned in his heart as though the only two people present were him and God. He kept seeking the things above, where Christ is.

Oh, humility is challenging. However, those who possess it know God and understand themselves and serve quietly, humbly, find a way to be salt and light in the world that is dull and dark, and simply go about living life seeking Christ daily.

So here I am under this old oak tree, feeling refreshed, longing for the future, and enjoying Christ's grace in the present. James, the half-brother of our Lord, once wrote (James 4:10), "He who humbles himself will be lifted up." He sounded exactly like Jesus, who once said in Luke 4:11, "He who humbles himself shall be exalted and he who exalts himself will be humbled." I am praying, "Mine, Oh Lord, send my roots more rain. Lord, send my roots more of your reign." And I am watching, praying, ever aiming to walk humbly in the glow of his grace and anticipating the future that stands widescreen and wide open to the possibility of God's glorious and humble future work. I keep seeking the things above, where Christ is.

John D. Duncan

Forgiveness

I'm sitting here under the old oak tree, looking for a quote. We live in the age of the sound bite, the dazzling quote, the striking quotation. We are a shorthand society that wants life minimized, shrunk down, and sometimes summarized in a few short words or sentences. For these reasons. a quote helps once in a while. And I find myself looking for quotes.

I guess I could quote Hank Aaron, who, after Barry Bonds hit his record-breaking home run, said, "My hope today… is that the achievement of this record will inspire others to chase their dreams." Chase your dreams! Or I could quote a Crandall Canyon, Utah, miner who felt guilty and wondered if he should have turned back to help his fellow miners: "I think I did everything I could. It was like having your brights on in a fog." Or I could quote C. S. Lewis. After all, I just returned from Cambridge, England, where he once taught English. He said, "It is astonishing that sometimes we believe that we believe what, really, in our heart we do not believe." He spoke of forgiveness and stated that for a long time he believed in forgiveness but did not really believe it until he practiced forgiveness, finally forgiving a cruel schoolteacher from his youth.

The old oak tree here has lived through storms and hard Texas summers and winters, days when limbs have been chopped off, and days when the storms put stress on the tree's roots, days when life under this old tree delivers pain in the form of broken relationships and small sins under the seismic universe that grow into big battles. C.S. Lewis states the obvious: to live, heal, grow, and enjoy the joy of life and Christ; forgiveness in its simplest form requires surrender and humility, two of our most difficult human traits. Philip Yancey calls forgiveness a most "unnatural act."

My very first preaching assignment was in a nursing home. I arrived on my first Sunday, a sermon in hand, the gospel ready to be delivered in the context of the world as I knew it in 1979. Billy Graham once said something like, "When you prepare to preach, prepare with the Bible in one hand and the newspaper in the other." John Stott said that the preacher delivers the gospel "between two worlds," so we must learn to know God's word and the times we live. Billy Graham aside and John Stott aside, I had my ready, aim, fire sermon ready to launch. I arrived, led the wheel-chaired crowd in a few hymns, and launched my rocket of a sermon in their direction, a sermon from the Bible fitting for the times and the news of that day. It was my first encounter with preaching realities—people falling asleep, people looking around, faces smiling as if tuned in, and eyebrows furled as if to communicate, "I am not too sure I agree with this." I cut my sermon short. My sermon on the gospel and the forgiveness of the cross seemed too heavy. I had not considered the preacher's first rule of order—to consider the audience to whom you will speak. I launched a rocket when the nursing home captives needed the water of mercy, bandages to sustain life's weariness, and comforting words for the lifelong battle most of them had lived.

After realizing my mistake and finishing the sermon, I walked around and greeted the people. One lady latched to my arm and pleaded. Her gray hair and weather-wrinkled-face gloomily looked up at me from her wheelchair. She gritted her teeth and begged: "Will God forgive me? Will God forgive me? Will God forgive me?"

"Yes, God will forgive you," I told her as she asked the question in repetitious rhythm. Each time I went to the nursing home, no matter what I preached, she asked me the same question after the short sermon. I can hear the echo of her words in my ear to this very day. I wondered if maybe, sometime, somewhere in her life, if maybe her subconscious had remembered a sin and the guilt associated with it and kept recalling it in association with the preaching of God's word, triggering the repetitious words, "Will God forgive me?"

It took me years to realize she probably had a case of dementia. Still, I have often wondered if unforgiveness had hardened her heart or if some event, sin, or broken relationship had never joined hands with the healing balm of Christ's forgiveness.

While in Cambridge, I walked into the city. While walking, I passed Queen's College by the River Cam. I walked over that bridge many times with no excitement, just the usual picture takers, the boaters below the bridge in the river, and the bikers whizzing by. On this day, a crowd had stopped, and all eyes were fixed on a bicycle and a potential rider atop the bridge's five-inch rail. A college student challenged his buddy: "Come on! Ride!"

"I am not sure I can," the scared teenager replied while the crowd looked on. Had the young man been a bike rider on the bridge's rail? He risked falling onto the stone street or falling headfirst into the river 15 feet below.

"OK, chicken, get down," the challenger yelled. He took the bike from the fearful teenager, climbed aboard, held his hands up for the crowd, placed his hands on the handlebars, and proudly and promptly rode the bike across the thin rail. He did not fall and made it to the other side of the bridge, still balanced with the bike's pedals. The cheering crowd applauded as he jumped down to the pavement. He took the bike back to the other end of the rail, looked at the fearful teenage rider, and exclaimed again, "Now ride!"

I left the scene unwilling to watch the fearful rider lest he fall. The metaphor for forgiveness here conjures up the same emotions—fear, risk, and a longing to get past the present moment and to the other side. Genuine forgiveness may incite fear ("Why should I forgive? They do not deserve this!" Or "He will have to come to me crawling before I forgive him!") but, ultimately, requires the risk of waltzing a thin rail called the cross of grace if we are to bridge the gap between friends and between God.

If you are looking for another metaphor, the Apostle Paul says that the preaching of the cross is foolishness to some, but to those of us who are being saved it is the power of God (1 Corinthians 1:18). The gospel, to some, may seem as foolish as riding a bike across a rail, but it has the power to transform those who live under the glory of the cross and practice forgiveness in their daily lives.

The cross of Jesus honors forgiveness. Practicing it may be hard but necessary and vital to life in a relationship with God, your spouse, or your enemy.

Jesus cried on the cross, "Father, forgive them for they know not what they do." Paul charged the church at Ephesus to forgive even as Christ has forgiven you (Ephesians 4:32). And forgiveness hails as the one redeeming quality in us that cleanses us inside-out while replacing tears with smiles and the dark agony of sin with the glorious light of joy.

So here I am under the old oak tree. Chase your dreams and beware of earth-shattering events that blind you like lights on in the fog and circumstances that shock you on life's journey. But to walk across life's bridge of peace and joy and reconciliation and happiness, life's most unnatural act, forgiveness, requires life's most supernatural act, Christ's forgiveness in you forgiving others as Christ has forgiven you.

After carrying the bitterness and a grudge for years, C.S. Lewis recalls the day he forgave his old teacher: "But this time I feel it (forgiveness) is the real thing. And (like learning to swim or ride a bike) the moment it (forgiveness) does happen it seems so easy, and you wonder why on earth you didn't do it years ago." Forgiveness sets us free. It frees us to swim in the joy, to glory in the peace of Jesus Christ, and to ride triumphantly on the thin rail of grace.

Autumn

John D. Duncan

Autumn Song

Now the leaves are falling fast,
Nurse's flowers will not last,
Nurses to their graves are gone
But the prams go rolling on.

Whispering neighbors left and right
Daunt us from our true delight,
Able hands are forced to freeze
Derelict on lonely knees.

Close behind us on our track,
Dead in hundreds cry Alack,
Arms raised stiffly to reprove
In false attitudes of love.

Scrawny through a plundered woods,
Trolls run scolding for their food,
Owl and nightingale are dumb,
And the angel will not come.

Clear, unscalable, ahead
Rise the Mountains of Instead,
From whose cold cascading streams
None my drink except in dreams.

W. H. Auden

A Garden of Good Cheer

I'm sitting here under the old oak tree. thinking of cheer. I hear the echo of Jesus' words in my ear, "In the world, you will have tribulation; but be of good cheer, I have overcome the world."

Long before the drive-through window at *McDonald's*, Internet hook-ups, cable television, and *Who Wants to Be a Millionaire?* trouble showed up in North Fort Worth.

The year was 1931 when the Depression settled like dust on the Texas plains. It was the age of *The Grapes of Wrath* when life crushed the grapes of optimism. In that year, 12 13-year-old girls banded together at the Rosen Heights Baptist Church. Although the stock market failed, these girls joined together to study God's word and practice that love never fails (I Corinthians 13:8). Wilma began as the first teacher of The Good Cheer Class.

Walk down the hall of the first floor of the Rosen Heights Baptist Church on any Sunday some 69 years later, and you'll find a wise group of elderly ladies still spreading good cheer. Today if you join the class and miss one Sunday, you're guaranteed a card in the mail saying, "We missed you last Sunday."

In 1933, Liz joined the class. "Those were the days of the Depression, and none of us had much," Liz shared as she reminisced about the Dust Bowl days. "We all graduated from North Side High School and started getting married. But we still scraped together money to help," she added with joy in her voice.

The first deed of cheer carried the ladies from the north side to the east side of Fort Worth to a sanitarium. In a quarantined cottage, Maedell, a woman whose lungs rattled with tuberculosis, struggled. Each week, the women of good cheer eased her struggle by supplying her with food and smiles. Maedell's faith lives on in the memory of these ladies.

The second act of kindness spread cheer to a widow, Velma. Poverty weighed down her heart, her household, and her five children. The ladies lifted her burdens by taking her to dinner each weekend. Although the ladies of cheer themselves were poor, they still collected $40 to purchase a mangle to assist Velma with her piles of ironing.

When Ouida's older son, Bill, contemplated quitting school to help his mother support the family financially, again, the ladies cheered her. The ladies chipped in a few dollars each week. Bill stayed in school and graduated, later becoming a professor of entomology at a Florida university.

These acts of cheer blossomed like a garden of flowers coloring the landscape. The ladies remembered their hard times and aimed to sow seeds of cheer to individuals and families who fell upon hard times.

"We brought our sowing machines to church and sewed dresses for the little girls at *Buckner's" Children's Home*, Liz recalled. One receives the impression that the ladies cherished time together and the enjoyment of ministering to others.

The garden of good cheer multiplied through the years--assistance for underprivileged children; gifts for battered women; scholarships for young people; help for mission projects; food baskets for needy families at Thanksgiving and Christmas; charity gifts in memorial for choir robes, church furniture and construction for church growth. The women also cooked meals for families walking through the valley of the shadow of death and workers who remodeled the church.

Through the years, the ladies mixed a recipe of good cheer, producing cookbooks to finance their acts of help for times of trouble. The *Good Cheer Cookbooks* started in 1940 with no recipes using cake mixes. The 1950 cookbook displayed a blue cover. The 1967 *Happiness is Good Cheer Cookbook* spotlighted

"Peanuts" on the cover. Connoisseurs still remember the recipes with frozen strawberries and lemon *Jell-O.*

A picture of the church filled the cover of the 1985 *Favorite Recipes Cookbook.* In 69 years, the class has had only two teachers, Criner and Jerry. Periodically, the ladies gather for coffee and tea, chatty talk, and plan for other ways to announce good cheer. The ladies gather in hats and flower-print dresses and share a meal together. Some carry home doggie bags reminiscent of the penny-wise and frugal ways learned in the dark days of the depression.

As the ladies leave, they step into the 21st century and modern tribulation. But Jesus cheers their souls. As they wave goodbye to each other, they await the 70th reunion of The Good Cheer Class, getting out the gospel of good cheer until they meet again.

And so here I am under this huge oak tree, knowing that seeds of cheer develop deep roots of faith which sprout branches of love which produce the fruit of hope. If only every church had a The Good Cheer Class.

John D. Duncan

Pillars of Granite and Crystal

I'm sitting here under the old oak tree. thinking about pillars. Pillars stand strong with Christ as their foundation to support the church of our Lord Jesus. So today, I'm reminiscing about a couple I pastored in college.

Not too long ago, T. Earl and Emma S. died. They lived long lives--he a spry 92, and she an energetic 85, just days short of her 86th birthday. I was pastor of Locker Baptist Church from October 1980 until September 1982. Earl and Emma served as what you might call pillars of the church. He was granite, a rock-solid saint faithful to Christ. She was crystal, a sparkle in the granite, ever aglow with the glory of God.

Earl was born on July 18, 1904, the son of Gertrude and James. He ranched in San Saba County in Central Texas his whole life. Earl loved his Lord, loved his church, and loved his pastor. And he had a great sense of humor. One Sunday, our attendance dipped to a grand total of five. It really wasn't that big of a deal; we averaged 12 a Sunday, but attendance peaked at an all-time high of 28 one Sunday when the Boy Scouts showed up. Boy, was I in high cotton on that day!

I was in low cotton, though, on that five-in-attendance Sunday. When you're new in the ministry, you kind of feel like it's your fault when attendance isn't so good. Needless to say, I unloaded my whole sermon on all five, 45 minutes of Jacob and Joseph, Job and Jonah, John the Baptist and Jesus--all in one holy breath! Since I majored in Greek in college, I threw in a few Greek words to let them know that this city boy wasn't so dumb after all!

Then Earl, boots spit-shined, blue jeans starched stiff, cracked a smile right smack-dab after the closing prayer. He quickly moved to the front and shared this little bit of homespun wisdom. "Preacher, when a few cows show up for feeding time, I just want you to know, I don't dump the whole load at once!"

That was Earl, full of laughs, quietly mentoring a green preacher on what it meant to serve the Lord. I sat with Earl through surgery, visited him in the hospital, and went out to eat at old Underwood's barbecue in Brownwood. T. Earl Parks ministered to me more than I ever ministered to him. That's Earl, granite with a rock-solid faith in a world crumbling at its very foundations. For Earl, the Rock was Christ.

Now Emma was born to Osha and Thomas in Coryell County on Nov. 19, 1910. In those days, you weren't born in a hospital with video cameras, epidurals, and doctors on stand-by with beepers on their belts. You were born, well, at home, with hot rags and lots of painful grunts and groans, loud oohs and ahs. A pretty girl she was to her proud mama and daddy!

Earl and Emma married in Rising Star on the last day of 1941. What a way to end one year, riding with your new bride into a new year!

Emma became a home economics teacher in Richland Springs, not far from downtown Locker, which in those days was nothing more than a corner store, a white-frame church, peanut farms, and lots of cattle. Boy could Emma teach--cooking, sewing, and home economics. Many a San Saba County girl learned at the feet of Mrs. Emma.

Emma dressed quite nicely--lace cut just right, flowery prints, hand-made, home-made, buttoned in prim and proper fashion. She wasn't stuffy, just manicured properly. Legend has it she arrived at church one Sunday in a new dress. She looked down to pray, only to notice her new dress was wrong side out. She quietly slipped out after the prayer, out to the outhouse, that is. She changed that dress right side out. That was Emma, a woman who wanted things to look just right. She clothed herself fine, so fine. But she knew God looked beneath the exterior to the heart. Oh, did Emma have a heart--a heart for God!

Emma loved to sing *Make Me a Channel of Blessing*. It was my job to lead the singing. Back then, the church asked, "Do you want to sing and/or preach?" Long before Deion Sanders made it popular, all I could say was, "Both." I preached and led the singing and told Mrs. Emma, "I've never even heard this song." But we sang it, nonetheless, and every time I hear it, I think of her. She was crystal, a life shining in a world full of dark shadows, radiating as a channel of blessing to everyone who saw her. And the Light was Christ.

Put Earl and Emma together, and you have marble, smooth as silk; transparent as clear glass. That's just the way they were, beautiful saints serving Jesus happily.

Earl had not been in the best of health, but the lawn mower had been repaired and needed to be picked up. After all, his grandson would be over in a few days to mow the lawn. So, on Wednesday, Sept. 25, 1996, Earl and Emma got in their pick-up truck and drove to San Saba, about 20 minutes from the Locker community, to load the riding lawn mower. They never made it home. I never got the details, but somebody smashed their truck, and Earl and Emma entered heaven, he that day, she days later. A double funeral set them to rest; their caskets were placed six feet under in the sandy soil of Locker Cemetery next to their lineage. Ah, but their souls, they rest in heaven, in a cleft beneath the Rock, in the sunshine of washed Light. I guess they made it home after all, huh?

I'm here to tell you, you cannot build a church without pillars, without Rock and Light, without granite and crystal, without good folks like Earl and Emma. Old Earl, he's smiling really big for sure. Bet that's some ranch he's got now!

And Emma? I think I hear her singing, "Out in the highways and byways of life, Many are weary and sad; Carry the sunshine where darkness is rife, Making the sorrowing glad. Make me a blessing, Make me a blessing, Out of my Life. May Jesus shine; Make me a blessing, O Savior, I pray, Make me a blessing to someone today." Oh, that Emma. She's dressed fine now, oh so fine.

Make me a channel of blessing.

John D. Duncan

'Just Right'
Thanksgiving

I'm sitting here under the old oak tree, remembering Thanksgiving. To claim the words of poet Gerard Manly Hopkins, "thoughts against thoughts in groans grind." My grinding thoughts carry me to Thanksgiving 1993 as I reflect on the life of my once-upon-a-time senior adult friend.

Thanksgiving in 1993 passed with its usual routine. The first blast of winter's chill frosted the earth. Leaves tumbled from trees to form messy piles in the yard. Families gathered, stuffing themselves with turkey and dressing, cranberries, and pecan pie. And a church fed the less fortunate in our community. Thanksgiving bustle swirled.

But over on Elizabeth Street, a house stood empty. The homeowner, Gladys, was gone. Did she travel to visit her only sister? No. Did she leave Hood County to visit the big city to get a jump on her Christmas shopping? Gladys didn't like to shop. Where would she find extra money to spend anyway? She liked to stay home and write letters to missionaries in foreign lands.

But silence stilled her house this Thanksgiving, except for the rustling of her dog, Fluffy, who shifted his body to find a comfortable position in which to lay, moaning from sadness because Gladys was not at home.

It was that weekend of 1993 that I learned the meaning of Thanksgiving.

I returned to Granbury from visiting friends and family. A message alerted me that Gladys had fallen. An emergency crew carried her to the hospital. Injuries prevented her from caring for herself. So, Gladys was sent to the nursing home for Thanksgiving.

You had to know Gladys. She liked things just right—food placed in the pantry just right; clothes hung on the hanger just right; trees trimmed to her specifications. But on this day, things were not just right.

"Pastor," she said as I greeted her at the nursing home, "can you help me? Could you tell the cook how to fix me a grilled-cheese sandwich?"

She instructed me, and I instructed the cook on how to cook a cheese sandwich to Gladys' liking.

Glady's life was withering like a tree after the heat of summer. Her life faded, an 84-year-old whose leaves had fallen, a tree which was decaying, a life near death, that time when the limbs are nimble and break off easily. And all was not just right for Gladys.

Gladys once lived in full bloom, a blossoming tree sprouting flowers of joy and happiness. She taught school. She loved God. She loved people. She loved her church. And she wrote those letters of encouragement to God's servants all over the world. I called it *The Gospel According to Gladys*.

And so it was that her last Thanksgiving passed. And the nurse brought her a cheese sandwich cooked just right. And together, we thanked God for it. And Gladys looked at me and said: "I've got a lot to be thankful for. God has been so good to me."

And I left the nursing home pondering Thanksgiving—of snow and the Plymouth Colony; of pilgrims and Indians on the first Thanksgiving; of sliced turkey and juicy dressing; of the noise of guests celebrating the holiday; of Fluffy and quietness on Elizabeth Street; of a cheese sandwich and grateful words. And I knew everything was just right, for the blessing of Thanksgiving comes in simplicity; Words of thanks lifted to Almighty God for breath and life, for each day with loved ones and friends. Oh, give thanks to the Lord!

John D. Duncan

Holy Fire

I'm sitting here under the old oak tree, thinking about holy fire. In Cambridge, England, I recently noticed a peculiar plaque on a church wall that stirred my soul.

Nestled quietly in the center of Cambridge sits a small church. The church lay silent, dwarfed by larger stone buildings of antiquity. Like an old piece of petrified wood in a forest of towering trees, the church relishes its glorified history. The Church of Saint Edmund King and Martyr signifies the storied past of God's servants during the Reformation.

Early one Sunday, I attended services at the church. A small group of no less than ten people showed up. Most came early to pray and to share in Holy Communion. I attended by virtue of an invitation. A friend preached from the Gospel of Matthew about the woman whose faith blossomed. She wished to simply take in breadcrumbs from the Master's table. The woman pleaded with Jesus for her daughter's health. Her faith and Jesus' power intersected in a moment of truth. The daughter was healed at once (Matthew 15:21-28). Jesus' crumbs yielded a joyous blessing.

"Crumb's from the Master's table" raced through my mind as I exited, glancing to my left. My eyes fixed on a round, gray stone plaque screwed to the wall. My eyes froze on the names of martyrs. One recognizable name stood out--Thomas Cranmer.

Sir Thomas Cranmer studied Bible in Cambridge, had a deep love for Jesus and his word, was deeply influenced by Luther's Reformation in the 1520s, and assisted in the production of an English Bible. He died in 1556, having been deposed and burned at the stake for his belief in Reformation principles.

The church plaque honored Sir Thomas by acknowledging he died by the "violence of holy fire." Not much happened on that Sunday morning. Things have sure calmed since Cranmer, and his boys helped reform the church.

"Holy fire," now that's intimidating. We once experienced what seemed like holy fire one Wednesday night at church. Angie, Vicki, and my wife, Judy, cooked the Wednesday evening meal. Judy splashed frozen French fries into a pot of bubbling grease. Presto, a holy fire appeared, a flash of orange flames leaping straight toward the ceiling. Judy screamed so loud I heard her from down the hall. I raced to the kitchen, grabbed the fire extinguisher, and put out the fire. People still talk about the time the preacher's wife almost burned down the church. Holy fire fizzled on Wednesday night, although for a moment, I wished for the revival of Moses' burning bush at mealtime in a pot of flaming grease.

"Holy fire"--what could that possibly mean? The prophet Jeremiah claimed, "fire in my bones." Blaise Paschal (1623-1623), the French mathematician and religious philosopher, once described his encounter with God in one word, "Fire." Thomas Cranmer was consumed by it.

Holy fire yearns for the Light of God to come and stay, a fire that burns bright to warm your soul and others, a fire willing to sacrifice because of Jesus' death and resurrection that lit the fires of eternity.

Elizabeth Barrett Browning says it best:

Earth's crammed with heaven,
And every common bush afire with God.
But only he who sees takes off his shoes,
The rest sit around it and pluck blackberries.

"Holy fire." It sounds serious. Ask Angie, Vicki and Judy who, by the way, were not hurt by the fire in the church kitchen. Ask Blaise Pascal. Ask Thomas Cranmer, whose love for Jesus stretched his life to the limits.

John D. Duncan

    Cranmer, that boy, he stirs my soul to a deeper devotion to Jesus. And me? I'm under this tree now, seeing, ready to take off my shoes. Why would I want to sit around and pluck blackberries?

In Our Town

I'm sitting here under the old oak tree, musing about the madness of the world and watching the world go by. In our town, life leaps.

In our town recently, CNN became the channel of choice as terror struck like lightning. Eyes were riveted to television sets from the local school administration office to the high school, from the local car wash to homes near the lake. A small airplane made an attempt to fly, only to be greeted and grounded by two F-16s in a matter of minutes. A little girl climbed into her bed that night and announced, "I'm scared."

Life forever changed but soon began to roll again like the slow turn of a water wheel. *Pam's Coffee Shop* resumed its service by offering the $2.99 special of eggs over-easy and fluffy homemade biscuits. On the soccer field, 7-year-old Caleb scored a goal. His dad never said much, but his mother leaped in excitement and spilled her soft drink on nearby fans. Wal-Mart's business picked up, with customers stocking up on dry goods and staple goods sure to survive in a crisis. The local funeral home had a long morning procession or mourning, if you prefer. It seems one of the saints in a nursing home died quietly, somewhere between a Presidential speech and a report on the Taliban.

In our town, the high school prepares for an enthusiastic week of homecoming. Prospective queens drove to the big city to purchase dresses and high heels fit for a queen. The homecoming parade left much to be desired, but the fireworks display afterward illuminated the starlit sky. Hopes still blossoms, and maybe the football team can win a homecoming game for a change.

John D. Duncan

In our town, a friend lost his job with American Airlines. A mother e-mailed and said, "Pray for my son." Seems her son sent her an e-mail detailing his cherished love for her while at the same time declaring love for his country and penning succinctly that his family would not hear from him "for a long time." His ship set sail for deep seas loaded with missiles, guns, and cat-quick jet fighters anxious to zip across enemy skies. A mother shed a tear.

In our town, gas prices are down with the stock market, but United States flags are up--everywhere. One neighborhood lined its streets with American flags. The neighborhood network sent out a warning to bring the flags in at night because flag thieves roamed clandestinely. Flags are up, and so is church attendance. One church reported a record-breaking attendance on a recent Sunday. Rumor had it that locals flocked to churches like swarms of bees. Rumor also had it that preachers delivered sermons full of good news and that it was refreshing like the sweet scent of pollen from a flower. One lady admitted, "I ain't been to church in years, but I just couldn't stay way after the mess." Most everyone understood "the mess." An elderly man shared with his pastor, "The worship service made me cry." Grown men haven't dripped tears from their eyes in church in years. Women know how to cry, but men are learning. The local shrink says that tears are "therapeutic," whatever that means.

In our town, a parent confessed a broken heart over Ground Zero, dust-covered streets in New York, the horror of devastation in Washington, D.C., and threats to national security. Another shared relief, discussing over chips and hot sauce at the local *Chili's* his phone conversation with a loved one who survived "just 150 yards from the plane crash at the Pentagon." I'm finding that a national crisis makes the big world a small place.

In our town, progress keeps rolling. *Home Depot* raised its big, thick concrete walls, stirring enough dust to slow down traffic on the main highway. Speaking of highways, traffic's been slow anyway because road construction continues, and just about everywhere you go, some guy in a hard hat and an orange vest holds a sign that says either "Slow" or "Stop." A church made progress, too, by pouring its new foundation and hoisting the steel beams. The preacher talked about the progress on the community's cable channel, saying, "And the foundation is Christ."

Speaking of Christ, in our town, two people, a forty-something man and woman purchase cheap poster board and make signs with magic markers. They stand beside the main highway and flash these colorful homemade signs. One says, "Jesus is coming soon." Another praises, "Give glory to God." And another, "God loves you!" One guy stops to offer money, but they refuse. "This is our ministry," they mutter. They don't have much, but they know they've got Jesus, which ain't too bad considering the way things have been going in our town.

In our town, life meanders. *Down at Your Image*, hair stylists crank out haircuts, and manicurists have been painting lots of fingernails. Rumor has it that the chatty hair salon talk is way up. Tension is up too. Worry is up. Fear is up. And it was exciting to see metal birds called airplanes up in the sky again. What's up with you?

I guess you could say that in our town, awareness of people is up too. One local man took the day off to spend time with his kids. A local physician decided he'd take a little more time with each patient. And the guy who changes oil at the gas station smiled at customers and acted like he really loved his job. Even his boss appeared surprised. A contagious smile pushes back clouds of darkness.

In our town, I guess it would be safe to say we're noticing things we haven't noticed before. We're looking at the stars and thanking God for buzzing airplanes. We're cheering for our kids again on soccer fields and thanking God for snotty noses and Saturday full of kids zigzagging on fields of green. We're singing *God Bless America* and praying on courthouse lawns and thanking God for freedom of worship. We're hugging the kids tighter, letting go of petty pride, and scratching and clawing to hang on to all we've got: a foundation of faith. "And the foundation is Christ," at least that's what I heard the preacher sputter on the local cable channel.

Darkness hovered for a while, but we're starting to scratch out some light and joy. As the poet William Blake once said, "But he who kisses joy as it flies, Lives in eternity's sunrise." Yes, that's what we're doing in our town. We're kissing joy again. We're applauding sunrise. After all, the joy of the Lord is our strength. His light rises.

"And the foundation is Christ.' Maybe that cable channel preacher is right. A fierce wind whipped into our lives several weeks ago, but the Foundation still stands. A storm showed up, but joy conquered. Light pierced the darkness.

So kiss the kids. Pick up the phone and call your relatives across the country to say, "I love you." Slow down and visit with friends in *Wal-Mart*. Look up in the sparkling sky and give thanks. Fall down on your knees and pray to Jesus. Kiss joy. Watch the sunrise. Then remember, "But the Lord is in his holy temple, let all the earth keep silence before him" (Habakkuk 2:20). Didn't I hear that on the local cable channel? And what on God's green earth did we ever do before we got local cable channels?

"Let all the earth keep silence before him."

The Great Separation

I'm sitting here under the old oak tree, pondering the great separation. Tragic events of more recent days send my mind swirling about eternal destinies and the last days.

"Preacher, do you think we're in the last days?" one saint recently asked. CNN may say no. Jerry Jenkins and Tim LaHaye say yes. Jesus said he did not know the hour when the end would come.

"It's hard to tell," I replied, adding, "A lot of people thought the end had come when Hitler was on the march during World War II."

C.S. Lewis talks about the great separation as the "great divorce," that longstanding gap between heaven and hell that began when the angel Lucifer fell like a star from heaven. Lewis is too philosophical for me when he says, and rightly so, "There is but one good; that is God. Everything else looks good when it looks to him and bad when it turns from him." That C.S. Lewis. He always had a way with words.

I tend to think more practically—Jesus in heaven; Lucifer and his cohorts in hell; and the last days when comes the "great separation," the division between the sheep and goats.

Then my mind drifts to that November Saturday when the sun rose high over the Locker community, some 30 miles from Brownwood, Texas. On Saturdays, I visited the saints of Locker Baptist Church, where I was privileged to be pastor.

The little box of a church painted white with wooden slats had a steeple, wooden pews and floors, and an outhouse to boot. On my first Sunday, this nervous preacher requested to use the restroom. Now, I grew up in the city. The control for the cooling and heating was mounted on a wall. Windows were for looking through and keeping thieves out, not for opening.

Plumbing lay beneath the foundation, indoor stuff with all modern conveniences. Merle, on that day, gave directions, "Go outside, take a left, and you'll find the restroom behind the church, right next to the cows."

"Oh my, outdoor restroom! Outhouse!" My nerves tightened, but I made way to the outhouse and cautiously took care of business.

Locker Baptist Church, what memories. We averaged 12 a Sunday. High attendance thrived on a Sunday we had 28, only because the *Boy Scouts* showed up. Thank the Lord for *Boy Scouts*! I don't think I ever preached a sermon on the "great separation," but a dog entered the church and walked the aisle one Sunday before the invitation. Have you ever tried to talk to a dog while the whole church stared?

One Saturday, I experienced an eyewitness view of the "great separation."

I stopped by to visit Merle. His wife directed me to the back, where he was weaning animals. I walked to the back, peered through the fence, and watched him separate the babies from their mothers.

Searching desperately for pastoral words of conversation and encouragement, I said, "Mr. Merle, I like your sheep." Life sometimes sends us on a mission, and in the quest for the right words, we observe and open our mouths. After all, Jesus said, "Out of the abundance of the heart, the mouth speaks." So, I spoke, "I like your sheep."

Merle lassoed a wide smile as he glanced at me while sending a whining baby into a fenced pen, "Preacher, them's goats!"

He chuckled and kept right on working the great separation. We never discussed it again, not baby goats being weaned from their mothers, not the difference between sheep and goats, not the great separation.

So, is it the end? I cannot tell you. A wall plaque that I saw recently assumes it. It featured painted words hung on a house door: "When I die, bury me at *Wal-Mart.*" Two bumper stickers predict it. One said, "If the rapture occurs, this car will be unmanned." It threw me for a loop because a woman was driving. Why not "unwomanned"? The other bumper sticker commanded: "Jesus is coming soon! Look busy!" And so the question, "Preacher, is this the end?" I don't know. But I am talking to Jesus and praying and believing in him and serving him with all my heart. And I do understand that when the end comes, Jesus can tell the difference between the sheep and the goats, and at the "great separation," he will separate the sheep from the goats. Trust me, when that day comes, being a sheep is what you want to be, a sheep under the Shepherd's care.

And me? Come to think of it; I am looking "real busy." And it has taken me a long time, but I am starting to tell the difference between the sheep and the goats, believe me.

"All I can say is, when the end comes, you better be ready!" I pontificated to the lovely saint.

So if the end comes, you better get ready. Until then, watch out for goats. Make friends with sheep. And, by all means, get to know the Shepherd.

You'll be glad you did when the "great separation!" comes.

John D. Duncan

Tumbling Turtles

I'm sitting here under the old tree oak, musing about the day the world came tumbling down. I think of the horror, the pain, and the questions. Country singer Alan Jackson wrote a song about it: *Where were you when the world stopped turning on that September day?* Businesswoman Sara Strunk was there and lived to tell about it with questions like "Why?" and "What's next?" Todd Beamer entered heaven's glory because of it. We look at life through a different window now.

Dr. Seuss once wrote about tumbling turtles in *Yertle the Turtle*. He told the story of a turtle on the "faraway island of Sala-ma-Sond, Yertle the Turtle was king of the pond."

Yertle was the turtle on top of the heap, turtle upon turtle stacked, with Yertle at the top. Yertle once proclaimed, "I'm Yertle the Turtle, oh marvelous me, For I am the ruler of all that I see!" Yertle stayed on top of the other turtles until the turtle at the bottom of the heap, Mack, burped. The burp sent Yertle tumbling down and into the mud with a "plunk." I am not suggesting that our great nation has been prideful or "on top of the heap," but that Sept. 11, 2001, sent all of our worlds tumbling down with a "plunk." Sept. 11, 2001, was the day the world went "plunk."

Where do people turn when the world goes "plunk"? We turn to God. Of course, in some circles, God appears as a debatable issue. The wall bangers cry foul, "One nation under God?" The cautious warn, "Be careful not to pray in public places such as schools much or mention the Jesus thing on government property." The Satanists spray-paint churches with words, "We hate God." Hate makes no friends. Hate knows no limits. Hate works long hours plotting revenge. Hate annihilates. Witness New York. Pray tell, though, the day the world went plunk, prayer to the Almighty resurfaced amid flames and smoke streams of terror. Even on government property, politicians gathered in unity to sing, *God bless America*. And, come to think of it, God still blesses America. Have you thanked God for his blessing lately?

The day the world came tumbling down like turtles still reminds me of one certainty about the uncertainty in our world surrounding Sept. 11, 2001. I find myself thinking of Yertle the Turtle lying in the mud. The day the world stopped turning reminds me of one simple truth: Humanity has fallen from grace and finds itself stained with sin. The poet Burns called it "man's inhumanity to man." John Calvin called destruction one of life's surest sources when people obey only themselves. Theologians named it original sin. Sin, at its best, distorts life and, at its worst, destroys life.

So, what about the world? Where do we turn in a world where all the turtles tumble into mud? Martin Luther, early in his ministry, tried to reform people. "You're too inexperienced to reform rascals," his friends declared. Luther learned of God's merciful and gracious work in people to reform them through the combination of gospel truth and the Holy Spirit's empowering grace. Luther applauded the person who accepted God's trilogy of genuine spiritual reform—repentance, faith, and forgiveness of sins. Luther confessed that the Apostle Paul offered a mercy seat for the mudders in sin (Romans 3:25). He said, "It will serve as a strong protection and defense for me. My heart and conscience will crawl under it and be safe." God, after all, still has a way of reforming rascal sinners and washing mud-stained tumblers with the wonder of his grace. All Christ asks us to do is to crawl under his mercy seat.

So here I am, sitting under the old oak tree. A light mist of rain falls across my face. In the distance, a real-live turtle eases through lake waters. And, of course, Dr. Seuss enlivens the world with talk of tumbling turtles. And on Sept. 11, 2001, the world went plunk. Fierce warriors went to great lengths to spread hate. Jesus went to great lengths to spread love. And here I am, sitting in the mud, learning to crawl under God's mercy seat, albeit praying in a world of tumbling turtles and mud-stained sinners for all people everywhere to crawl under his mercy seat to experience the safety of God's mercy and grace.

Daniel in the Lion's Den

I'm sitting here under the old oak tree, pondering Daniel in the lions' den. I am not musing over Daniel in the Old Testament. I do rejoice in God's glorious work in closing the mouth of the lion and setting him free. On this day, I remember another Daniel.

Daniel called me on a crisp day at the church, much like we enjoy on these October days in Texas. "Preacher," he muttered, "I need to see you right now!" Daniel emphasized, "Right now!" and I quickly gathered my things, walked to my car, fired up the engine, and drove less than two miles to Daniel's house.

According to Brennan Manning in *Ragamuffin Gospel*, Eugene Kennedy writes, "The devil dwells in urge to control rather than liberate the human soul." I arrived at Daniel's house knowing that the devil worked overtime to keep Daniel fenced in and under his control. He had a long history of bondage to sin, a lifestyle contrary to Christ's, and an alcohol addiction.

One late Christmas Eve, my wife baked cookies, and I took them to Daniel, where he lived in a one-room kitchen at work. The loneliness of Christmas Eve consumed him, and in tears he drank alcohol until he could no longer clearly recite the words "Christmas" or Eve." When I knocked on the glass door while breathing the cold chill of winter's air, Daniel slowly lifted himself off the couch, stumbled to the door, opened it, and tried to lean on me so I could hold him up. I handed him the cookies, announced "Merry Christmas," and scrambled because at that moment, I could not hold Daniel up and because Daniel tended toward displays of anger when inebriated. Tears flowed as I exited. The devil dwells in urge to control.

Enough of Christmas Eve, now back to the cool, crisp day when Daniel phoned me. I arrived at his house, greeted by his growling, white-fanged dog, a pit bull chained to an oak tree. The pit bull circled the tree, chipping the bark like a carver shaving a piece of wood for the next masterpiece. I slowly eased from the car. The dog approached me quickly with the chain's reach jerking the dog backward ferociously. Daniel watched from the door.

"He won't hurcha!" he yelled while simultaneously screaming at the snarling, barking dog. "Shut up, mutt."

Relief washed over me as I entered the house. Could this be the day that liberation set Daniel free? That Christ the liberator removed him from the clutches of Satan's urge? That Daniel might find a way out of the Lions' den?

"Sit down, Preacher," Daniel softly spoke as his steely eyes glared through me. He lit up a cigarette and talked, somewhat half punch drunk, and half brain scattered while looking at the ground.

My eyes scanned the room. I stopped long enough to examine the helpless man who, in tears, talked and, with the weary lines on his face, appeared depressed. Suddenly the softness and tears turned to rage like a lightning bolt from the sky on a clear day, and Daniel rose, stumbled, ripped off his shirt, and hollered, "Look! Look here!" He pointed to his side. "Look, Preacher!"

I do not need to tell you, but I will that if the pit bull caused my heart to race, now ever faster it raced. I looked at the door. Could I make a run for it? Would the chain on the dog break if I made it outside? What have I gotten myself into? Who's in a den of lions now?

King David prayed from caves, "Lord, help me." Thugs lowered the prophet Jeremiah into a dark, mush cistern. He begged, "Lord, save me." A thief hung on a cross next to Jesus and moaned, "Lord, remember me!" The Apostle Paul fell to his feet in blindness on the Damascus Road, uttering, "Lord, make me see." Paul once remarked, "From now on, let no one trouble me, for I bear in my body marks of the Lord Jesus" (Galatians 6:17). Caves? Cisterns? Blindness? Pit Bulls? Cigarettes? Buttons popping off a shirt and falling on the floor? Marks? "Look, Preacher!"

Jesus, with Paul, I pray, "Let no one trouble me!"

Daniel pointed to his side again. A mark, a scar lay raised over his bony ribs. The scar marked his body as a trophy of some fight, a stabbing when he worked with the Mafia in Miami.

I sat, shocked. His ex-wife later said that it was all a lie. Was it? Is it? All I know is that I listened with wide ears and wide eyes at that moment. Would this be my dying day? Would this be Daniel's day of liberation? Does the devil prance and roar like a lion? Does the devil have an urge?

Finally, my heart bouncing against my chest, I shared the gospel with Daniel. I shared in desperation. I shared in hopes of liberation. I needed to get out of the house. He dropped to his knees and, with slurred speech, invited Jesus into his heart. Tears streamed down his face. Tears leap out of the soul and the eyes in agonizing moments of desperation. Jesus calmed him. I prayed with him, and I quickly exited the house. His ex-wife said that he invited Jesus into his heart all the time. "It was a game." She said, "Only God knows if his decision was genuine. Only God knows anyway, everything, anyhow."

I baptized Daniel. He came to church a few times. Then he disappeared. Stick around the church long enough, and people will disappear. It serves as one of the great mysteries of ministry. Where do they go?

The last time I saw Daniel, he was getting in his car at a convenience store. He saw me, and I saw him. My mind drifted back to Christmas Eve and homemade cookies, pit bulls and Mafia mandates, and buttons falling and marks on the body. Oh yes, the devil has an urge.

"Hey Preacher, old Daniel's in the lions' den again; pray for me." He drawled. I told him I would, and he left with a brown paper bag full of who knows what. As he left, he repeated to himself, "Old Da-a-a-n-n-i-e-lis-s-s-szzzz in-n-n in the lions' den."

Oh, by the way, his ex-wife said he was in Nevada. Daniel himself told me he might go back to Miami, where he received his mark on the body. Scars tell stories.

And so here I am, sitting under the old oak tree praying for Daniel, wondering, "Daniel, where are you?" And, thinking, there are a lot of Daniels in the world in their own lions' dens. Only Jesus' liberation can set the captive free. And the ministry is the most exciting, liberating, adrenaline-pumping place a person can be. I see pit bulls; I see scars. I see my heart bouncing against the wall of my chest. And Jesus dwells in urge to liberate every human soul.

That's what I wanted to say. That's it: Jesus dwells in urge to liberate your soul.

Goings-On at Church

I'm sitting here under the old oak tree, giving thanks. For one, I have a new red oak tree in my backyard courtesy of Jody, Carla, and Paul. Thanks for the tree. I can sit under it on sunshine and dripping rain days and muse deep thoughts about bizarre things. I can mull over life and the ministry, over faith and God, wondering into the night about how people make it without God or how God makes it with us. Anyway, thanks so much. Or, in the words of the psalmist, "I will give thanks to God with my whole heart" (Psalm 9:1).

Other than a season of thanks, there's not much going on near the old oak tree. There is however, a lot of stuff happening around the church. Erma lost her lens out of her eyeglasses last Sunday but found it Monday, still on the seat where she sat. Life delivers wondrous discoveries. "I can't see without my glasses these days," she announced. I'll call it Erma's wisdom. She might not be able to see without her eyeglasses, but with or without glasses, she sees life with wisdom because of her faith. Erma sees more than most of us. Erma keeps us "seeing" around the church. Every church needs an Erma.

Here around the church, we had a wedding. The preacher united in marriage Ryan and Crystal. The girls wore beautiful blue dresses, and the guys wore black tuxedos. Glitter sparkled on the dresses, and the guys looked dazzling with bow ties. The flower girl stole the show, dropping white rose pedals to clear a rose-speckled path for the bride. Parents shed tears, and everybody smiled for the guy taking pictures. Weddings glitter the earth with joy. I pray their marriage dances with joy. They will move to Maryland. Do we not live in the age of mobility?

Here around the church, we have had funerals. C.E. died. He announced to me 13 years ago, at the age of 63, that God called him to preach when he was in his forties. "Preacher, I just gotta tell ya," he would always start his sentences with those words, "I felt called to preach 20 years ago." I did not know how to handle such a statement, so I prayed, and we prayed and asked God to help C.E. start a church. He started Brazos River Baptist Church. The little church grew, and C.E. was never happier. He died at 75 years of age. Life goes smoother and brings cheer when you follow God's call. I will miss C.E.

Then Linda's mother died. Her name was Ann. She contracted pancreatic cancer. Doctors poked and prodded and did one of those expensive tests and then made her wait anxiously for a few days. She returned to the doctor to receive the test results. The doctor put his hand on her shoulder, pursed his lips, and delivered the news: "Mrs. Ann, I don't have good news for you. You have pancreatic cancer." He explained what that meant and then comforted her. She understood his message and knew she would soon die.

"How long is it gonna take?" she quizzed, asking how long before death comes. Or eternal life begins.

"Well," the doctor replied, "it won't be today, and it won't be tomorrow, but the good Lord is fluffing your pillow."

"I'm ready," she said, "I've got a lot of people I've got to see." She whispered of heaven. C.S. Lewis once whispered of heaven, "Heaven will solve our problems, but not, I think, by showing us subtle reconciliations between all our apparently contradictory notions. The notions will be knocked under our feet. We shall see that there never was a problem."

God fluffed her pillow and prepared a mansion for her (John 14:1-6) and called her home and that because of heaven, there never was a problem. She left a note saying: "When God takes me home, which I hope is a long time from today, I want to be in the cemetery next to Willie (father of my children). Bury me in my pajamas selected from the blue suitcase. Open casket or closed (your choice). All my love goes ...."

Ann never signed her name. Why sign it when the people you love know all your love goes to them?

We buried her in a cemetery next to Willie in Mexia. The cemetery holds the tombs of numerous Civil War heroes. Dicky Flatt of the famed politician Phil Gramm's "Dicky Flatt Test" (How will this political decision affect a guy like Dickie Flatt?) showed up for the funeral. He runs a print shop in Mexia. One local instructed me to drive by the local fried chicken outfit because Anna Nicole Smith used to work there. I even drove by Ann's home place for most of her life—a white frame house with a green roof on 910 Hunt Street, where a playground for the grandkids still stands in the backyard. We buried Ann in her pajamas in a casket on a fluffy pillow. Her love still goes.

And finally, here around the church not too far on Sunflower Street, Pearlie sits in her recliner. She, too, has cancer, and a tube pokes a hole in her throat. She talks with a rasp. Doctors tell us it will not be long now before cancer takes her. "Welcome, Pearlie, to the pearly gates," Saint Peter soon will say. She's ready; she's ready. She told me so after we prayed just the other day. I think God is fluffing her pillow even now.

There's not much else going on around the church except children on the playground and the printing of the church newsletter and plans for weddings and funerals. Erma's down the hall volunteering to fold the newsletters and spinning wisdom. I sure am glad she found her glass lens. I need to call and check on Jane and Linda and see how they're doing in the shadows of grief. I need to get the tires changed on my car. And God fluffs a few pillows. The sun shines today, and life drops many a feather that tickles the nose and softens the heart.

John D. Duncan

The Bridge

I'm sitting here under the old oak tree, wondering about a bridge. The musical duo Simon and Garfunkel used to sing "Bridge Over Troubled Waters." Early this morning, while biking, I stopped on the bridge near the lake, not too far from the old oak tree. But the bridge I am thinking of is in Cambridge, England.

If you travel to Cambridge, you will discover a center point in the middle of the city. The "city center," as the locals call it, swirls with activity. Near the city's center, you will find a *GAP*, a *Marks and Spencer* store for groceries, and a market square where you can purchase fresh flowers, a T-shirt for approximately $18, and Doc Martin's sandals for half the price you buy them in *America*. *Walk* a short distance, and you will find *Borders*, *Starbucks*, and *McDonald's*. The world shrinks, and suddenly everything starts looking the same, no matter where you travel. The college students gather at *McDonald's* for lunch, so if you are hungry, you will want to beat the rush by arriving before 11:30.

Walk past *McDonald's* and stand on Trinity Street. Look to your left, and you will find one of the world's most recognizable architectural wonders—King's College. If you toured King's College with a guide, you would hear about the chapel and the mischievous stories of college students who climbed the spires like rock climbers and placed umbrellas at the highest point, some 100 feet in the air.

Walk to your right, and you will journey toward Trinity College. The neatly manicured Great Court fascinates. The field looks like a beautiful carpet of green. Spend two British pounds on the brochure that explains the buildings, history, and the grandeur of all that is Trinity College. You will be interested in knowing movie producers filmed portions of *Chariots of Fire* in the courtyard. The running scene where the two runners sprint around the courtyard enlivens the movie. When I traveled to Cambridge with my family last spring, we rented the movie. Why not rent the movie? I love that great line in the movie, Eric pleading with his sister about his dual call of missionary work and running *Olympic* races. He says: "God made me fast. And when I run, I feel his (God's) pleasure." Take Cambridge slow. Find something in life to feel God's pleasure.

Trinity College houses numerous treasures in the Wren Library—an eighth-century copy of the epistles of Paul and an original manuscript of *Winnie the Pooh*. Walk beyond the library and the New Court and over the bridge where, beneath, lies the River Cam. Remember, we speak of a bridge, and Cambridge displays many bridges over the River Cam, including the historical Mathematical Bridge, originally built with only wood and a flawless design. Across the bridge, you will find an ice cream truck. By all means, buy an ice cream cone. It sure tastes good!

Exit Trinity College and walk down Trinity Street to Saint John's College. Saint John's holds three courts. Architectural professionals refer to the Gothic design of the buildings as the "Wedding Cake." Walk through the tree courts, and you will again stand on a bridge. Across the bridge and over the River Cam, you will find what the locals call the Backs, a beautiful floral walking path that produces breathtaking postcards from behind the colleges.

As you view the Backs, look below the bridge, and you will see students and tourists punting. No, punting is not football but rather a journey on the River Cam in a canoe-like boat.

Stand on the bridge and note the Kitchen Bridge and the infamous Bridge of Sighs, a bridge modeled after one in Venice, Italy. Turn around, and you will see the River Cam and bridge after bridge, stone bridges made in symmetrical form near perfection. The bridges have withstood walkers, bikers, rain, storms, and the test of time. How can you cross the River Cam without a bridge?

Study the center point of each bridge. You will find a triangular stone called a "keystone." The keystone locks the bridge into place. It holds the bridge together. Remove the keystone, and the bridge will crumble.

Today I am sitting here under the old oak tree, thinking of a bridge with its keystone, Jesus Christ. He locks my life into place, creating stability when a river of turmoil swirls in the world below. Jesus holds my life together. Jesus keeps my life from crumbling. In him, I can cross over one day into that glorious land with streets of gold and fields with carpets of green. Ah, the King will be there. And I can walk in the glory of all that is in the King's domain. Peace fills my soul.

I think of Jesus, the Bridge, and I recall Jesus' words, "My peace I give to you. Let not your heart be troubled, neither let it be afraid" (Matthew 14:27).

Suddenly old Augustine's prayer comes to mind: "O Lord God, grant us peace, for all that we have is your gift. Grant us the peace of repose, the peace of the Sabbath, the peace which has no evening."

Oh, did I tell you the sun shone high in Cambridge? Did I mention it was the middle of the day? Do you think we taste delicious ice cream in heaven? Have you stood on a bridge? Is the Bridge in you?

Good News

I'm sitting here under the old oak tree, wondering about good news. The Romans spoke of good news as glad tidings. Jesus came preaching the good news. Everybody likes to hear good news.

The year was 1967. Good news was hard to find. The U.S. State Department announced that 5,008 Americans were killed in 1966 during the Vietnam War. Protesters marched the streets for peace. Lyndon Johnson served as president while trying to work through the upheaval of Vietnam on the American psyche. Families anguished as loved ones were missing in action. A fire broke out in Apollo 1, killing three men. Racial segregation and prejudice caused a whirlpool stir in society at large. The Cold War froze international politics. The poet Langston Hughes died in 1967, too, forever leaving an imprint of dreams for good news as wishful thinking in his own thoughts: "What happens to a dream deferred? Does it dry up like a raisin in the sun?"

Good news faded in 1967, but the news kept coming. The Beatles sang *Penny Lane* on the radio. Katherine Hepburn had Hollywood abuzz in *Guess Who's Coming to Dinner?* Vince Lombardi's Green Bay Packers won the first *Super Bowl*. Mickey Mantle hit his 500th home run. A gallon of milk cost $1.15; bread, 22 cents; gas, 28 cents; and a postage stamp, 5 cents. Christian Barnard performed the first heart transplant in Cape Town, South Africa. *Andy Griffith* and *I Love Lucy* greeted the television airwaves as two popular shows. Oh, for the return of Mayberry and laughter.

In churches and camps across the South, good news of a different sort suddenly began to spread. Bob Oldenburg and friends from *Broadman Press* began to write music from an office in Nashville, Tenn. The times begged for good news. The times called for action. The tumultuous times invited Christian action. The times called for *Good News*, one of the first youth musicals written for young people and for the church.

Words began to flow from a ready writer, Bob Oldenburg, the writer and composer of many songs: "Good News is the way of living, Good news is the way of giving. Good news says come on, get with it; Good news says wake up and live it!" The musical score followed, and the theme of God's good news began to take shape in musical pizzazz: We're Gonna Change This Land!

Just the other day, I sat with Bob Oldenburg on his back porch. He sat in his wheelchair. I rocked in a curved rocking chair. I looked beyond the porch on the hill in Granbury, where his house sits overlooking the picturesque lake. I listened as Bob shared with me how he wrote the words in 1967 and how young people sang *Good News* in 1968.

Bob's gleaming eyes peered at me, then drifted at a distance as if he were watching a video clip of yesterday in his cinema mind. He looked at me again and talked.

"The music had a beat, youth music with a beat, and the young people loved it," Bob shared with excitement. Never wanting to take any credit for himself or away from another, Bob explained how the music was "led by the Lord and God's own hand."

Bob wove stories of how the kids loved the music, how the good news spread, and how a group of young people sang with guitars at Glorieta, N.M., and in churches on Sunday nights.

"The music struck a chord with kids, but with adults, the music was controversial, "Bob added, almost as if he were hearing the rhythm of the music in his head.

On another occasion, I had heard Bob say that one pastor said, "We'll have none of this music in our church!" He stopped the good news. In another church, a deacon unplugged the guitar. Controversy swirled in Baptist circles long before Amy Grant was singing *My Father's Eyes* and long before the Michael

W. Smith worship music was played in churches as it is today with keyboards, electric guitars, and electronic drums.

Good news upsets the apple cart at times.

Good news upset the Pharisees so much in Jesus' day that they wanted Jesus killed.

Death in 1967 had been in the news because of the Vietnam War, and, to my knowledge, no death threats were made against Bob Oldenburg's life for writing *Good News* and bringing controversy to the church of that day. However, real, genuine, life-changing good news touched the hearts of many who both sang and heard the good news of Jesus' gospel set to electrifying music.

These were not hymns and anthems for choral production, but rather Elvis' cousin had come to the church in the form of a church musical with rock-n-roll, or at least, news about Jesus the Rock with a little roll.

Bob's eyes moistened as he talked about salvation. "One college student explained how Christ came into his heart after the singing of 'Good News.'"

"Come Alive," one song shouted. The young man came alive with Christ. Jesus made him a new creature. The scene repeated itself countless times as young people invited Christ into their hearts. Who knows what might have happened in the church where the pastor stopped the music or where the deacon unplugged the guitar?

I asked Bob, "What did you feel and think as you wrote *Good News*?"

He quickly responded, "The only life worth living is the Christ-life." He then quoted Galatians 2:20, "I am crucified with Christ, nevertheless not I, but Christ lives in me."

I looked beyond the porch. The wind rippled Lake Granbury. The sun made the lake sparkle. Leaves flowed green, yellow, and red on trees surrounding the lake. I looked at Bob, sitting in his wheelchair, eyes watery, body frail as a board easy to bend because of cancer's merciless decay, and saw that gleam in his eye.

Today, as Bob whispers about final things in the grand finale of his life and recalls yesterday, and struggles through each day while anticipating the pain and joy of tomorrow, I know Bob's heart overflows with good news. He longs for home.

In my mind, I hear the Apostle Paul as I see Bob, "Therefore, we do not lose heart, but though our outer man is decaying, yet our inner man is being renewed day by day" (2 Corinthians 4:16). I hear Paul, but suddenly a tune, a *Good News* tune with words, Bob's own words, begins to rattle in my brain:

"I have a home with love all around, mine it will always be, There mother love and sweet tender care come as a blessing rare;

> "Dad always gives the help that I need, but what of it all,
> "If it is not getting through?
> "This is my land with freedom for all, mine it will always be,
> Here liberty and justice for all comes as a blessing rare;
> "Mine to enjoy and mine to protect, but what of it all,
> "If it is not getting through?
> "He is my Lord, my Master and King, mine He will always be, Freedom from guilt and freedom from death come as my blessings now;
> "Unending joy and abundant life, but what of it all,
> "If it is not getting through?"

For Bob Oldenburg, soulful saint of the good news and faithful servant of the living Christ, the gospel has gotten through to him. His life stands as a testimony of faith. As one wise sage once said, "No test, no testimony."

Bob faces the test of life and death yet smiles in the joy of Christ's abundance as he awaits his home with love all around.

His faith lives on! His testimony sings! God's Good News echoes into eternity.

And so, this is life: Cold wars and dreams that dry up like raisins in the sun and *Penny Lane* and *Guess Who's Coming to Dinner?* and *I Love Lucy* and guitars and leaves changing fall colors and a wind ripple in the lake and laughter and dripping tears—and a smile full of good news!

John D. Duncan

Rain Must Fall

I'm sitting here under the old oak tree, remembering drops of rain dripping on my head. Recently I stood under a tree while making a pastoral visit. The picturesque scene might well have been painted on a postcard.

Clouds looked down. Rain dripped. Like a ball of fire, the orange sun peeked behind the clouds and over the horizon as it set. The grass beneath my feet glowed green. Conversation ensued.

The poet Longfellow once spoke of rain: "Be still, sad heart! and cease repining; / Behind the clouds is the sun still shining; / Thy fate is the common fate of all, / Into each life, some rain must fall,"

Grief ensued as part of the discussion. Grief grabs the gut, the heart, the emotions and spins a tangled web in life. Henri Nouwen says, "We can only keep it together when we believe that God holds us together."

I visited with Lance, standing in his yard as the rain dripped. I watched and listened as he shared with me how grief was spinning a web around his life. Lance drives a white truck. He lives in a house in an open space. He proudly smiles because he has a new baby. His 26-year-old wife teaches school. She also has cancer for the third time—breast cancer, then spinal, now brain. We can only keep it together when we believe God holds us together. Lance and his wife, Amy, aim to keep it together as God holds them together.

Rain dripped on my head while Lance shared his pain, grief, hopes, and tears.

Grief makes friends, like the bond of friendship formed in the foxholes of war or crises of despair. My mind drifted back to two years ago as I listened to Lance. My wife had cancer. After surgery, a double mastectomy, four rounds of chemotherapy poured like poison into her body and put her on the road to a long recovery. I sensed Lance's grief, misery, and agony. Grief takes no prisoners. Grief sends in swarms of uncertainty. Grief happens.

Before I left that day, I prayed with Lance. Rain dripped on my hand. Into each life, some rain must fall.

I drove down the muddy road thinking of Lance, cancer, and Zoe. Just days earlier, a mother and father buried their 28-day-old baby. Born prematurely, the parents named her Zoe Grace, "Zoe" for abundant life and "Grace" for God's gracious hand that catches tears that push up from grief-stricken hearts to eyes so that eyes like waterfalls pour forth tears.

Zoe's mother spoke at the funeral. Zoe survived for days on life-support equipment; a child kept alive by machines even when little Zoe had no inkling of life, not even the remotest brain wave. Zoe's mother spoke of the family's decision to let go of Zoe. She spoke with tears. Into each life, some rain must fall.

At the funeral, the mother eloquently spoke: "I know today God understands. He had to let go of his Child (Son) like I had to let go of Zoe. He watched his Child die. But now Zoe is in heaven with God."

As I drove out onto the main road, I pondered life in its mystery and grief. The poet Tennyson says, "I am a part of all that I have met." Frederick Buchner says, "Grace is something you can never get but can only be given." Jesus says, "Let not your heart be troubled; you believe in God, believe also in me" (John 14:6).

So now here I am under the old oak tree, remembering. God gives "zoe," an abundance of life to those who embrace him. His grace, like rain, drips as pain, happiness, and grief and forms us to him to make us whole. He stills the troubled heart. He sees all. He knows. He cares. He understands. Into each life, some rain must fall.

John D. Duncan

    As I think back to the dripping rain under the tree with Lance, I know. I know the dripping rain fell from the heart of God, God's heart pushing up tears like rain that fell from his eyes to help us know that in grief, we do not weep alone. God weeps with us. He sheds tears that drip a waterfall of compassion. When he weeps with us, we experience hope in the shadows, "zoe" in death, and grace in all its parts.

    Into each life, God's rain must fall.

Blessed Rest

I'm sitting here under the old oak tree, thinking of rest. Augustine once said, "Our hearts are restless until they rest in God." I wonder if Augustine needed rest when he wrote those words.

As a pastor, I hear the words "I'm tired" as much as I have ever heard them. I am beginning to wonder if a persistent weariness circulates mysteriously like a virus, silently encircling the earth.

Baptists notoriously know how to fill up a calendar with "busyness." Baptists schedule enough stuff to make them feel like marathon runners near the end of a race.

In *Painted House*, author John Grisham affirms the Baptist reputation for busy schedules and saintly weariness. He writes: "Nobody met as much as us Baptists. We took great pride in constant worship. Pearl Watson, my favorite Methodist, said she'd like to be Baptist, but she just wasn't physically able."

Here, under the old oak tree, I think about rest. What does the Bible say?

Joseph desired to rest and be buried with his fathers (Genesis 47:30). Exodus spoke of a Sabbath rest when all work ceased (Exodus 34:21). God told the people of Israel, "My presence will go with you and give you rest." (Exodus 34:20). After a hard-fought war, God gave rest from enemies, a long, hard nap on a pillow (Deuteronomy 25:19). Even the land deserved rest from war (Joshua 14:15). Such rest called for praise to God from his people (1 Kings 8:56). Job lamented, much like many people today, "I have no peace; no quietness; I have no rest, only turmoil." Was Job trying to put three toddlers down for a midday nap?

The psalmist acknowledged, "My soul finds rest in God alone" (Psalm 62:1). He picturesquely described God as a bird spreading her wings over her young to protect, "He who dwells in the shelter of the Most High will rest in the shadow of the Almighty" (Psalm 91:1).

Isaiah thundered, "In repentance and rest is your salvation, in quietness and trust is your strength" (Isaiah 30:16). Jeremiah spoke of a battle and a sword, asking, "How long till you rest?" (Jeremiah 47:6). Ezekiel gently wafted a verbal blessing, "May a blessing rest on your household" (Ezekiel 44:30).

Jesus rested on a pillow in a boat dead center in the Sea of Galilee during a storm. The winds and waves seemed not to bother him. The disciples, though, that was another story. They panicked, immediately woke up Jesus, and pondered their possible deaths in wide-eyed fear. "Peace be still," Jesus spoke, ending the chaos and calming the storm. Jesus gives rest. That is what he does best. He later invited us into his rest, "Come to me, all you who are weary and burdened and I will give you rest" (Matthew 11:30).

So, here I am under the old oak tree. All this "rest" talk makes me weary. I think I'll clean the acorns and lay my head on a few leaves and take a nap. Hey, maybe, I will live to the ripe old age of 100. Recently I read where 100-year-old B.C. Watts, a man who voted in 19 presidential elections, said the key to his long life was his nap every afternoon.

As for you, Robert Frost puts it best: "It's rest I want—there, I have said it out—/From cooking meals for hungry hired men/ And washing dishes after them—from doing/Things over and over that just won't stay done."

The undone creates restlessness.

While thinking of the injustice in the world, the poet Langston Hughes appropriately lamented, "Jesus, ain't you tired yet?"

All in all, our Lord never faints nor is weary. He gives rest (Isaiah 40:31). For this, I am eternally grateful. Thanksgiving blessings of rest to each of you.

John D. Duncan

Seasons of Change

I'm sitting here under the old oak tree, wondering about the seasons of change. Fall arrives with the splendor of change. The few trees that dot the landscape will turn from green to yellow, brown, and red in our town. Change will color the world afresh.

I'm sitting here pondering the change that surrounds me. Our middle child left for Baylor University. Baylor is a good school. After all, the women's basketball team won the national championship, the campus appeals wonderfully to the human eye, and the Baylor tradition lives forever, but for me, it represents change. The cell phone generation means I can keep in touch almost daily, but life in our home finds an empty room and a strange quietness.

Change happens in our town, too. *Home Depot* arrived, and *Lowe's* followed suit. There is a new *El Chico's* on the main drag, and *Cotton Patch* just opened so that the locals have new options for lunch. Traffic here has picked up, so traveling across town and over the bridge where the lake waters glisten on a sunshiny day takes longer. Waiting on the new array of traffic lights and appropriately placed stop signs is not unusual. Our simple little town finds itself battling an occasional road rager. I guess the stress of change shortens the fuse of some drivers. Change taxes the emotions.

In the wider world, change comes daily. Is the Gaza strip preparing the world for Armageddon? Has London train terror so zapped the psyche of our world that the loudest pop causes heads to turn and faces to wince? Has genetic testing provided scientific breakthroughs or created dilemmas for a society already confused? Change abounds.

The space shuttle lands in California, football season rolls around, and scientists research a species of frogs whose tongues, if touched, will dispense poison. The scientists say the poison is caused by the frog's diet of ants and termites, which causes alkaloids to build up in the digestive system and can poison you. Scientists say the poison of this species of frog can kill. Has the ecosystem changed so much that weather patterns have changed, and frogs can poison people with whom they make contact? Can we really clone sheep? Change swirls.

In the church, things change—the music, meeting times, people, and expectations. Can anyone keep up with Joel Osteen? The television generation raises the expectation of church life all the more. In our town, church starts abound, the saints are always looking for the latest thing when the latest thing turns out to be the same old thing, and people drift back to the church of their first choice. The impartial God loves all people and the church of your choice of any size. Things change but stay the same.

And here in Texas, a hot summer soon ends, and the Texas Rangers baseball season will end in disaster, and the Dallas Cowboys will wish for a winning season, and Christ will still reign on his throne, not as an absent landlord or a landlord collecting the rent once a month, but an ever-present God-in-Christ-by-the-Spirit involved in the intricate details of your life.

I witness change daily. Just the other day, I delivered news to 95-year-old Ruth. The once upon a time church organist who played for our church for ten years, including the Sunday night we sang *Set My Soul Afire, Lord,* and the church organ caught on fire, received news from me that her daughter is dying of cancer. Is this kind of change supposed to take place, a daughter entering glory before her mother? And then I had to give the news to Riley, while family members listened in the wings, that his forty-something daughter had died from an infection, suddenly, unexpectedly, sadly, leaving two children without a mother. Change came swiftly. Was anyone ready for it?

When I shared the terrible news with Riley, a charter member of our church now residing in a nursing home, cried out, shed tears, and wept, saying, "Has God put too much on us to handle?"

I did not know what to say, except after a long silence, "Sometimes, Riley, we cannot explain life, and that's why we need abundant life." He stared at me and cried, tears falling from his face like raindrops.

All in all, I can only view this change by looking up to the face of God. Three things, I guess, are certain in life-death, taxes, and change. Still, in the world of Crawford, Texas, prayer vigils where a mother carries a cross and waits to see the president, a world where astronauts joyously return to mother earth in high tension and drama, a world where boys and girls enter school with backpacks and lunch boxes, a world where the fall arrives in an array of color, and a world where change is as constant as a faucet dripping water, in this kind of world, Jesus Christ is the same yesterday, today and forever.

I guess Oxford scholar C. S. Lewis was right when he said: "Send a saint up in a spaceship, and he'll find God in space as he found God on earth. Much depends on the seeing eye."

Things change, and all I can think of is opening your eyes in a changing world and looking to the one constant that anchors the soul in the winds of change. Look closely, and you'll find strength, grace, hope, and abundant life because change is life, and life is change, and it's why we need abundant life in Christ. Yes, Jesus Christ is the same yesterday, today, and forever.

The Light of the World

I'm sitting here under the old oak tree pondering light. Like an orange basketball, the sun greeted the crisp October morning with light. Last night the stars filled the sky with twinkling dots of light against a dark blue backdrop. Then, of all things, I walked into my dark house and reached for the switch on the wall and flipped it, and then, presto, a light bulb flashed like a camera flash and burnt. Thankfully several more light bulbs helped me find my way around the house. Light illumines.

I love this time of year because the rotation of the earth on its axis makes the nights longer, the cold waves of arctic air march south, the nights sparkle with the stars and moon, and the constellations dance in the heavenlies. In the second century, the ancient Ptolemies compiled star catalogues detailing the brilliance of the stars in their movement and position. I am not sure if it's true, but supposedly Julius Caesar once declared that he was as constant as the northern star. Scientists discovered last year that the star Polaris is increasing in light by 250 percent. One scientist said that such an increasing brightness should not be happening, adding, "It's kinda scary." Light intrigues.

As a boy growing up, my family would visit the mountains of North Carolina. One of my favorite things to do was ride up the mountain in an open-air jeep just as the sun set. The lights on the jeep guided us through the rugged, mountainous terrain. We stopped, jumped out of the jeep, climbed into a cave through a hole that we could barely squeeze our bodies into, and walked gingerly through the cave with dripping water, cool air, and the echo of a voice spoken.

One wise guy holding the flashlight led us through the cave and then turned off the flashlight creating an eerie dark-like scene out of a Halloween movie, one with strange sounds and bats buzzing and a heart-pounding so hard that you feared it might just leap out of your chest. How relieved I was when the small bulb on the flashlight popped on, and we stepped our way cautiously back to the hole and out of the cave, and back into the jeep. My heart slowed its rhythm, and calm prevailed. Light delivers peace.

Annie Dillard writes of wonderful things in her childhood: of snowflakes like stars falling on the day she and her friends ran for their lives after hitting a car with a snowball; of a white house with five bedrooms and stairwells and a green lawn with stones; of reading books and checking them out from the library; listening to the radio and watching movies and boys and girls and baseball and bikes and streetcars with headlights and lamp posts on the streets, streetlights that cause snow to twinkle like glitter when the light shines on it just right.

Annie Dillard tells one day of a storm that blew through the town of her childhood. It shut down the power and created an eerie dark like the one I experienced in the cave in the mountains of North Carolina, except for a small, dimly lit light bulb that lit the room and stayed on mysteriously while the rest of the street stood pitch black. Light faintly arrests the darkness.

So here I am under the old oak tree. For many people in the world today, darkness looms: homeless victims of Tasmanian hurricanes and victims of angry car bombers and victims of cancer cells eating away at the body and victims of drugs and alcohol and victims of sin that darkens the soul and victims of teenage rebellion and financial troubles where the checkbook runs bone dry and victims of life itself in the unplanned, the unwelcome and the un-asked-for events that send clouds pouring over life. Yet in the stillness of a star-lit night, I am reminded of the Light, light like a star twinkling, like a light penetrating a dark cave, like a light intercepting a storm on a pitch-black street. And the light is Christ.

Jesus said, "I am the Light of the world." He illumines life. He intrigues. He delivers peace. He arrests the darkness. He comes in splendor and grace to fill us with his light. One light shines. One light keeps getting brighter. One light eases our fears. And the light is Christ.

C. S. Lewis put it best, the challenge we face in life involves this: "to dress our souls not for the electric lights of the present world but for the daylight of the next." The apostle Paul invites us to live in the glory of God's light, to shine like stars. I leave you with this poetic prayer by London pastor/poet John Donne, "And burn me, O Lord, with a fiery zeal." Fill souls with your Light.

John D. Duncan

Life of a Pastor

I'm sitting here under the old oak tree, musing with laughter over the life of a pastor. The poet Langston Hughes has a line in one of his poems about the "circus of civilization." From time to time, I refer to myself as the ringmaster of the circus. As a pastor, I find myself in situations that God must deem painful, laughable, or, at the least, enjoyable.

My mind drifts to the past—one July day years ago, when a teenager fell through the roof of a boat dock and splashed in the water, and his body lodged beneath a rock, and he drowned. His mother's sadness as she held him in the ambulance still haunts my memory. The blood and the grief and the collision of "shoulda, coulda, woulda," or at worst, "if only I had ...." In grief, people think of everything that might have changed the situation that led to death. The horror of the boy's death, the wailing of the mother, and the flashing red light of the ambulance still reverberate in my mind.

The bizarre funeral that took me to New Mexico seemed eerie and humorous—eerie because family members would not speak to each other and humorous because the minister with whom I shared the memorial service mistakenly announced at the beginning, "We are here today to remember J.D. Duncan." Needless to say, I grabbed my arm to make sure I was alive. Was I dead or alive?

The ride to the funeral had been a whirlwind trip to West Texas, where a man whom I had never met before picked me up at the airport and took me to his house, where I slept in his bed (even though he admitted he had no clean bedsheets). Oh my!

The next morning, we left early for the funeral, a 150-mile drive through West Texas dust and oil wells and summer heat, with the sun's rays pounding your forehead and telling you it never rains here! Needless to say, the guy drove me to New Mexico in his Cadillac convertible. Before you think I rode in style, consider that the car's air conditioning was broken, so we rode with the top down, him smiling and me wearing a black suit and tie that blew with my hair in the wind.

After the funeral, we rode back to that West Texas town the way we went—the roof down and my hair blowing in the wind. It was 106 degrees, the sun pounded our foreheads, and I said, flippantly, "What would cap off this day would be a rainstorm." About that time on this Texas summer day of heat, we drove through one dark cloud. Around the cloud, the baby blue sky shone, and heat showered rays of sunshine that burned your exposed skin. But low and behold, that one cloud moved over the Cadillac convertible and dumped rain, a "gulley-washer," whatever that is. We had no time to raise the convertible roof, so for a few short minutes, I knew what Noah felt like standing on the deck of the ark as rain fell from the heavens. As my driver smiled and we laughed, all I could think of was, "God causes the rain to fall on the just and unjust," or at least, "into each person's life, a little rain must fall." And it does.

All this actually leads me to another, more recent experience—a backyard wedding on a ranch where, as the bride described it, "We're having a redneck wedding." The groom talked on his cell phone, explaining directions while he stood in front of the crowd in his black tuxedo with tails. She came waltzing down the aisle with a big grin. The bride and groom stood while the wind popped the plastic decorations and while the crowd could not hear one word I spoke. Cows moved. A dog barked. And the sound of the music, Nora Jones singing Elvis' old song, "Love me tender," sounded muffled. I offered vows, and before I finished, he grabbed her, kissed her, and shouted. I introduced them as husband and wife, watched them dance down the aisle, heard the bride's father yell, "Now everyone, move your chairs," had my picture made with a digital camera, and left. I did sign the wedding certificate. I did not stay for barbecue.

All told, I find myself as a pastor between birth and death, between funerals and weddings, sandwiched between heaven and earth, pouring out the good news of Jesus Christ. Sometimes I cry. Sometimes I laugh. Sometimes God cries. Sometimes God laughs. Sometimes the sun shines. Sometimes the rain falls. Sometimes the wind blows. And sometimes you skip the barbecue. Still, God gets his work done. Amazing grace, that's what I'll call it.

The circus of civilization keeps moving, and God is not just in the shadows but often in the sun and rain and wind and in the hearts of the people he loves. Amazing grace, that's what I call it.

Thinking of Carolina

I'm sitting here under the old oak tree, thinking of the mountains of North Carolina. My family roots are there from way back, and I just visited two aunts in their eighties. I love the mountains and North Carolina, and on some days, I may suddenly break out in James Taylor's song *Carolina in My Mind*.

Today I have Carolina in my mind. My grandfather served as a foreman in the mining industry. I imagine the business is much today like it was, with dump trucks and tractors with huge front-end loaders and conveyor belts and blasting techniques, with dynamite and guys wearing hard hats and taking lunches to work in steel pales, and dust, grit, and grime. My grandfather, best I can tell, was a man of the earth. He also lived as a man of heaven: Sunday school superintendent at Pine Branch Baptist Church in Spruce Pine, N.C.

My grandmother, Ruth, passed away on July 7, 1997. Her middle name was Easter, and if your middle name is Easter, because she was born on Easter in 1904, then you can pretty well decide that she was a spiritual person. She drank Christ's living water and began drinking it, like most of us do, early on. Legend has it that her mother, Ibbie, prayed every night in a house with the window open while the curtains blew in the cool mountain breeze. I never met her, but my great-grandmother prayed the devil out of things. From all I can tell, she took the Apostle Paul's admonition to pray without ceasing seriously.

Alfred Lord Tennyson once wrote about prayer: "I will not cease to grasp the hope I hold of saintdom, and to clamor, mourn and sob, battering the gates of heaven with the storms of prayer, have mercy, Lord and take away my sin." They say Ibbie prayed by the window, and you could hear her praying in the meadow below. She battered heaven with storms of prayer. I pray you have some dear soul in your life who prays and one dear soul who prays for you.

On my recent trip to North Carolina, I visited Pine Branch Baptist Church and its adjoining graveyard, a place where the relatives of yesterday have been given a place of rest.

I love the church, not just Pine Branch, but any church where the cross is lifted up, and Jesus is glorified. Eugene Peterson once commented that what he liked about church was "the mess," a conglomeration of people serving Christ that only Christ could make clean. Barbara Brown Taylor says the church, people, "need each other, to save us from self-righteousness," and "we also need each other to keep us in shape for God." We cannot go at it alone! We need God and each other. Frederick Buechner says the "visible church is all the people who get together from time to time in God's name." I think church is the body of Christ, alive, vibrant, human, divine, messy, and clean all at the same time. Christ and his name form the common bond. Christ is the super glue.

I picture that mountain church like the church used to be, the center of God's work, the center of the action, the focus of the gathering of people, the ones who smoked on the steps before church, and the babies who cried when the preacher screamed and the teenagers passing notes and shooting spit wads on the back row and the saints praying and amening and shouting and singing *Amazing Grace* and *Give Me that Old Time Religion* and *Kum Ba Yah*. I know church used to be where the community gathered and prayed and laughed over fried chicken and homemade biscuits and mashed potatoes and corn and green beans out of the garden at the annual church homecoming picnic while the children played. Problem is, that's all changed, the Internet and all and Palm pilots and day planners and busy schedules and restaurants open on Sunday and cable TV and people working on Sundays to make a living and people finding rest in the graveyard near the front door of the church and mobility, and things aren't the way they used to be anyway. Life changes, and I am not saying it is bad because I must admit, I like my iPod, and I like to eat out on Sunday after church, but it's just the way things go sometimes.

Oh, as I was saying, there was a time when the church used to be the center of community and God, for that matter, but now it's the workplace and money at the center of most communities.

With Carolina in my mind, that red-brick mountain church and manicured graveyard brought back memories—of Preacher Joe, who foamed at the mouth when he spoke, took long gasping breaths, and yelled when he preached the word of God because it's the only way he knew to preach and yet people still talk about him like he's a saint because he loved his flock like kids love candy; of Adam, who led the music one arm at a time and checked on our relatives and took them popcorn some nights and opened the church and closed it for years, so much so that when he died of cancer, it left a big hole in the church; of other relatives and folks, too, people you called aunt and uncle even if you never knew how you were related to them. Then there was "Uncle" Faye.

I should tell you Faye was not really my uncle. Nor was Faye, my aunt. She was a relative, for sure, and a woman who always came to visit when we arrived in the mountains. She had a dog, liked to sit on her porch and watch the TV with the volume on "loud," talked of prayer, and had this unique ability to blow on the wounds of life. Once I skinned my knee playing baseball or jumping over the boxwood bushes in the front yard of the house my grandfather built in the '30s, I am not really sure. I cried. I moaned. I held my knee. I sat on the porch, and Faye calmed me and blew on the wound. If I were preaching, it makes for a great illustration, you know, something like "Comfort ye, comfort ye my people" from Isaiah 40:1 or Hebrews 4:12, where it says that Jesus is our high priest whom we can trust and call on to find grace and mercy just in the nick of time. If I were preaching, I would tell that story of my Uncle Faye, who was not really my uncle, and say that Jesus is like that; he blows on the wound and soothes our broken hearts. He heals. But since I am not preaching, I must tell you that my Uncle Faye could blow on a wound and heal like nobody's business. You are fortunate if you have a healer who blows on the wounds of your life. And you are blessed beyond measure if you let Jesus blow on the wounds of your life, too.

So here I am under the old oak tree. The space shuttle has launched. Scientists talk about an explosion of light. The Friday night lights, Texas football on Friday nights, have started up again, the parents cheering, the teenagers hanging out, and stars being born on fields of green. Church is in full swing. Fall is in the air. And Carolina is in my mind. And Jesus, well, he has you on his mind.

Thanksgiving List

I'm sitting here under the old oak tree, pondering life as I know it on this rainy day. Another Sunday has folded its page on the calendar, and Thanksgiving soon arrives. I love the Lord, Sundays, the church, and I have so much for which to give thanks.

Actually, I was thinking about that first Thanksgiving. Thanksgiving has its roots in the harvest home celebrations that took place in England before the Pilgrims ever arrived on the sand and shores of America. Thirty-eight English settlers docked the shores of the James River at the Berkley plantation in what is today known as Charles City, Va. The settlers declared a "Day of thanksgiving to God" after their torturous ride across the Atlantic. Later, another group of Pilgrims arrived at Plymouth Rock on Dec. 11, 1620, and then further south at Cape Cod, Mass. I can only imagine that first harsh winter in New England. The snow, the questions, the death as they lost about half their settlers, the grief, the misery, the agony, the anger, the longing for home, the joy, and even the adventure of the new land.

In the spring of 1621, the Indians, led by Samoset of the Wampanoag tribe and Squanto of the Patuxtet tribe, taught the pilgrims to plant corn or "maize" to harvest alewives of the herring family and to fertilize for crops like peas, wheat, barley, and pumpkins. The following autumn, Gov. William Bradford and the Pilgrims organized a harvest festival in appreciation for the help of the Indians. About 90 or so, Pilgrims and Indians gathered and celebrated a time of thanksgiving amid a feast of vegetables and wildfowl like geese in the spirit of thanksgiving. The first Thanksgiving was celebrated with no afternoon Dallas Cowboys football, no pecan pie, no family squabbles, and probably not even a turkey. Another thanksgiving celebration did not take place in New England for 55 years, "the silent years," as I call them.

Later, the governing council of Charleston, Mass., announced a thanksgiving proclamation on June 20, 1676, declaring a day of thanksgiving on June 29, 1676. The U.S. Continental Congress declared Thanksgiving Day on the 28th of November, a Thursday, in 1782, and celebrated with gratitude for the mercies of Almighty God. George Washington declared the day of thanks on the 26th of November, Thursday, in 1789, invoking "the great Lord and Ruler of the nations," along with appreciation for "the great degree of tranquility, union and plenty which we have enjoyed."

Finally, Abraham Lincoln's infamous words in 1863 highlight the "blessings of fruitful fields and healthful skies," along with gratitude for mines and population growth and with the "Almighty hand to heal the wounds of the nation and restore it," and with the "gracious gifts of the Most High God, who, while dealing with us in our anger for our sins, hath nevertheless remembered mercy." Lincoln invited all people in America and the world to share in a Day of Thanksgiving on the last Thursday of November with "praise to our beneficent father." Who talks like that? Who writes like that? I wish more people wrote like that. And who better to invoke thanksgiving than our 16th president? After all, America had weathered many a storm from that first blustery New England winter to politics, civil war, and the struggle for survival and the hope of economic growth.

One nice thing about American thanksgiving, long forgotten, is the staple and stable force of the church—churches that still today dot the New England landscape like pictures from a Norman Rockwell painting as a reminder of the blessing of God and the anchor of hope that to this very moment steeples point to (God) as they rise toward the heavens.

I'm sitting here thinking with romantic flair, say, of the renaissance, even idealistically, about that first Thanksgiving—

gentle snowflakes tumbling mid-air like cotton balls from the sky and pilgrims and Indians smiling at each other while they eat amazing maize and wild geese and talking about the weather because it was the only real thing to talk about and dreaming of new homes and peace on earth, goodwill toward men. I see children laughing and playing in the snow and hear a prayer of thanksgiving to Almighty God. As I dream of days past, reality hits, and I think about the joy along with the sadness of so many who died before that first Thanksgiving, the tension of new people in a new land or an old land, depending on which side of the fence you're on, and the enormous task ahead to gain consensus, build structure and make a nation, people united in the land so fresh. I think of suffering and gratitude to God as the twin pillars that provided a foundation for America as we know it.

I guess we've come a long way from the first thanksgiving to now. This Thanksgiving, people will eat turkey, not wild geese, and watch football and stay in out of the snow or the rain or the sunshine and be in need of a little tranquility and union and give thanks for the plenty we have enjoyed.

I guess not much has changed, has it? America is still where we weather many a storm, where politics divide, where wars rage, and where people struggle daily for survival and economic growth. The weather channel keeps us informed of the latest change in the temperature, barometric pressure, and dew points. Politics leap over red and blue in the red, white, and blue, with negative political ads, scandal, and dreams of a better tomorrow. Care packages are sent to soldiers on war duty in Iraq, while suicide bombers drive cars into buildings in Baghdad. Wars rage among nations, communities, in homes and hearts, even silent wars as gruesome as Iraq or Baghdad.

All in all, people struggle to make ends meet or pursue life, liberty, and the pursuit of happiness. Are you happy? And all in all, America is a land where economic survival for many is the challenge of finding daily bread for $2 a loaf and for trying to dig out of the hole of financial debt. It is a way of life in America for most.

Still, the steeple points to the heavens, to Almighty God and the ruler of nations and the Most High God. We all have much for which to be thankful, corn and pumpkins and cable TV and heating in the winter and *iPods* and *X-Box* and cars and *Starbucks* and *Home Depot* and *Blue Bell* ice cream from Brenham and family and churches with steeples and laughter and friendships and comfort in grief and light in the darkness and God's blessing abundant. Make your own list and truly give thanks.

It is, sometimes, a crazy world. We have the actual weekly accounts of a police log printed in the local newspaper in our town. It goes like this: A woman stepped outside of her house and heard two shots fired; five horses are out and getting into their neighbor's house; neighbors took a dead dog to the end of the street and dropped it off; a man called 911 and complained he was kicked out of a bar and wants to get back in; a Comanche Cove man reported his chain saw and weed eater stolen but found it in the pawn shop. Or consider an anonymous poem once written about thanksgiving: "Tell me, Mr. Turkey, Don't you feel afraid When you hear us talking 'Bout the plans we've made?" America, sometimes, it is a crazy and wild and bizarre place.

Several years ago, a man handed me a book by Dietrich Bonhoeffer. He was a pastor, old and used up, tired but wise. He handed me the book and told me to pay special attention to certain pages. I copied the section, cut it out, and taped it in front of my Bible. What was Bonhoeffer's message to me through the man? "How can God entrust great things to one who will not thankfully receive from him little things? ... A pastor should never complain about this congregation, certainly not to other people, but also not to God. Let him do what he is committed to do and thank God. The more thankfully we daily receive what is given to us, the more surely and steadily will fellowship increase and grow from day to day."

Lamentations puts it best, "It is of the Lord's mercies that we are not consumed because his compassions fail not" (Lamentations 3:22). "Oh give thanks unto the Lord, for he is good; his mercy endures forever!" (Psalm 107:1).

So here I am under this old tree and thankful for it. I'm hoping for snow, waiting for Thanksgiving, remembering our nation, praising God for his mercy, and giving thanks. Please pass the turkey. And know that my list of all I am thankful for never ends.

Happy Thanksgiving!

John D. Duncan

Thinking Baseball

I'm sitting here under the old tree, thinking baseball of all things. John Grisham, in his book about baseball, Bleachers, says: "Football was king and that would never change. It brought the glory and paid the bills." I am under this old oak tree, thinking of baseball at the start of football season and realizing that Friday night lights and football is king in Texas while thinking baseball and the game of life. Or, in the words of the poet Langston Hughes, "Jesus ain't you tired yet?"

My life as a pastor is a wonderful life. Never mind that preaching, as they say, is "between two worlds," the temporal and the spiritual, and on some Sundays, since I preach three times on Sunday morning, I hit a single, a double, a triple, or a home run. And, yes, while on some Sundays I strike out, at least I have the privilege of walking up to the preaching plate to take my swings again on the next Sunday.

My life as a pastor is a wonderful life. Not long ago, one of our church members asked me, "What do they call you around here?" I replied, "Call me whatever: pastor, preacher; hey you—and call me to dinner anytime!" The man looked at me rather seriously and said, "No, really, what do they call you?" I searched for the right words and tried to figure out simultaneously as my mind churned like a computer who "they" was and said, "I guess if I have to be called something, I prefer 'pastor.'" He replied, "Well, son, all that education, I think you deserve respect and a little formality. They should call you doctor." I smiled as we shook hands, and about that time because God's timing is always perfect, a 7-year-old church member, a boy who was also my neighbor, yelled, "Hi John!" Ah, first base laughter after a Texas League single.

Under the Old Oak Tree

My life as a pastor is a wonderful life. One guy called the church one day and asked the receptionist a question. I love the questions and have a few for the Lord when I get to heaven, like, "Why could the Dallas Cowboys not keep Coach Tom Landry longer? Why did the Mavericks not win a championship? And, in baseball, Lord, why could the Texas Rangers not climb out of the cellar most seasons? Why did you not give them Nolan Ryan from the start?" The guy calls the church with the question, "Is it OK if I jog when the pastor preaches?" Now "preaches" rhymes with "peaches," and if I were from Georgia, I would eat a peach every time people called with questions, but that was one question I had never been asked nor have heard since.

"Jog?" I asked. "Yes," the receptionist said. "He says that he likes a church that inspires him, and when he gets inspired by the preaching, he fills with the Holy Spirit and likes to jog around the worship center while the pastor preaches." Football is king in Texas, and I told the receptionist to tell him he is welcome, but please do not jog. I told the staff, football is king in Texas; if he jogs, tackle him, pray with him, but by all means, no jogging while I preach. The guy never showed up, and I do not like peaches, but the ministry is an interesting place, and you can see and hear a lot on second base.

My life as a pastor is a wonderful life. I must tell you, I am never bored, and ministry is the most exhilarating, creative, energizing, and exhausting place a person could ever be. I find people who live with pain and uncertainty and anxiety and misery and happiness and joy and laughter and sadness all thrown into the same heart and put on a smile like a clown when the inside feels a frown. Czeslaw Milosz once said, "There are days when people seem to be a festival of marionettes dancing at the edge of nothingness." There is hopelessness out there, and in my life as a pastor, I encourage them to run to Jesus and find hope in him and keep running amid their marionette lives of clown and frown and find meaning, not in the madness of it all, but in the mercy and Master of all. I am at third base. Jesus, ain't you tired yet? Will we make it home?

My life as a pastor is a wonderful life, but sometimes you enter into the unknown and the cloud of the unknowing. You gasp for breath and ask the Lord for Holy Spirit inspiration that will keep you jogging, and you pray like mad that he does not forget your name. The Lord longs for you to call him by name, and you do, and you realize how much you need God and Christ and the Holy Spirit to jog your heart and how important life, in its spirituality and simplicity, really is. Are you following me? We're talking baseball, life, and making it home.

Josh lived in our community, and I served as his pastor. He played baseball in our town, wore number 19 on his jersey, and died of a heat stroke at 18. Yes, he wore 19 and died at 18. I love being a pastor, but when a young person dies, you double the grief and silence the tongue on explanations. God's grace is sufficient, and the Presbyterian preacher George Buttrick was right, "Life is essentially a series of events to be borne and lived through, rather than a series of intellectual riddles to be played with and solved." When Josh passed away, life hurt, events seemed like a blur, and I wanted to solve riddles: Why this? Why now? Why? Why? Why?

C.S. Lewis says in *A Grief Observed* that he wanted to escape the pain of grief. "If I knew any way to escape, I would crawl through the sewers to find it." I have discovered in life's riddles and in life's grief that the only thing a person can really do is live through it and hang onto Jesus like a rock climber might cling to a rope.

Oh, Josh wore number 19, lived to be 18, and loved baseball. He had a good sense of humor and, from all I can tell, followed Jesus and tried to get others to turn to him. Life, when it ends, can be summed up as time, place, and people. He lived from 1989 to 2007, spent time on the baseball diamond, and had a 90 mile an hour fastball, so I am told, and he touched people's lives. At Josh's funeral, his fellow teammates wore their baseball jerseys, and many of the people who attended the funeral wore white wristbands with the purple number 19 printed on them. Pictures and a video of Josh told stories—at birthdays, by the pond at his house, with friends, at baseball games, and one at his high school graduation. It's the text message generation, so I am sure students in the crowd had pictures of Josh on their cell phones and memories of Josh in their hearts. He was 18 and wore the number 19, and if I knew any way to erase the pain, I would crawl through the sewers to find it. I guess we can all be thankful that Jesus ain't tired yet and that he never sleeps nor slumbers nor faints nor is weary and that in the exhaustion of grief, his love and comfort are real and refreshing, and his grace is sufficient even when our words are not.

One picture stands out when I remember Josh—a home-plate celebration after an exciting victory. Life is like baseball—strikeouts and home runs, errors and game-saving catches, the agony of defeat and the euphoria of victory. Still, the point is to make it home, to home plate where Jesus lives. On the first base of life, look in, look out, and look up to God because life is short. On second base, make the most of every single day. On the third base belongs the things that matter in life—love and forgiveness and kindness and friendship and encouragement. Ultimately though, we can only find our way home by knowing Christ and playing the game of life for an audience of one: Jesus Christ.

So here I am under his old oak tree, knowing football is king and thinking baseball. The crisp fall air has arrived and reminds me that Jesus is king and that my life as a pastor is a wonderful life. Life hurts. Riddles come. And even as the shadows lean dark and dreary over life like shadows on the field of a baseball stadium, still hope springs eternal, and Jesus never wearies of loving us in the pain or greeting us when we make it home. Or,

John D. Duncan

in the words of Jesus, "Come unto me all you who are weary and heavy hearted."

A Sea of Change

I'm sitting here under the old oak tree, musing about change. To me, three things in life appear constant—death, taxes, and change. I look around Granbury and see change over the last 20 years, from *Wal-Mart* to *Home Depot*, to new schools and restaurants, to the roads once narrow now wide, to new people who bless my life.

I look at Lakeside Baptist Church and see a sea of change. The people have changed through the years, and so have I. We used to have pot-luck dinners, and now we must have stuff catered. Change arrives in many venues, but as good Baptists, we still eat the same thing—friend chicken and biscuits, of course. Some things change, but some do not. I love change. It challenges all of us!

Lindy at *Your Image* here in Granbury has cut my hair for a long time. Just the other day, she was cutting my hair and talking to her shop mates. The discussion turned to change. More specifically, the television show *Trick My Truck*. All these years, I thought I was in touch with the world—terror, Al Qaeda, Dallas Cowboys' last-minute heroics, presidential speeches, Larry King on *CNN*, pot pie salmonella outbreaks, Britney Spears losing her kids, the *Weather Channel*, college game day, and O.J. Simpson on the run again. All this time, I figured I was in touch with the world when, in fact, I had never watched *CSI* or *Trick My Truck*. Lindy and her co-workers explained *Trick My Truck* as a show where a gang takes an 18-wheel truck and totally refurbishes it. Now I am in touch with the world and realize that change is about to touch me.

For more than 20 years, it has been my privilege to pastor at Lakeside Baptist Church in Granbury. I arrived June 7, 1987. I survived my first two years by the grace of God and thrived in the glory of God's grace and the grace of his people for the next 18. C.S. Lewis once said, "But even the best Christian that ever lived is not acting on his own steam—he is only nourishing or protecting a life he could never have acquired by his own efforts." When I think of Lakeside, I think of what God has done through his people together, his steam carrying us up the river of life in the joy of service with the cargo of ministry. I think of what God has done—the great things he has done that we could never have acquired by our own efforts.

My youngest daughter, eight years old at the time, once asked me, "Daddy, are you the boss of the church?" "No, honey, I have two hundred bosses," I replied as I laughed, but then added, on a more serious note in her language, "No, God is the boss of the church." And he is. The church is the Lord's, and he gets his work done in and through and, sometimes, in spite of us. Anyway, after 20 years, I am soon to change—churches, locations, and walk through the sea of change begging for the steam of God as I cruise a new river of ministry. I will soon become pastor of First Baptist Church in Georgetown and the wonderful people there.

Lakeside has wonderful people, too, and I will miss them. I think of people with vision. I think of Riley, who told his wife before I arrived, "He's a good preacher, but he looks like Alfalfa!" I have not watched *Trick My Truck*, nor had I watched *The Little Rascals*, but the saints educated me on what that meant. Years later, I have laughed a thousand laughs over that comment. Yet no one ministered and had a vision for Christ, his church, and ministry like the legendary Riley Ro, as I will call him.

I think of Dorothy, long since gone to glory, a woman of great inspiration who always kept her Bible and The *Reader's Digest* handy. She was my neighbor when we both lived in tiny apartments. The prize my family shared with the elderly Dorothy, as we called her, was the laughter, the stories, and the joy of our common bond—Christ. She was a church member, and when the church was small, she held my hand, looked to the heavens, and declared: "God has great things in store! That's gonna be a big church one day." Her English was not so great, but her heart glittered with gold! Everybody needs someone to believe in you, and Dorothy believed in me and God's call on my life and the prize we shared was the prize of the mark of the high calling of God in Christ.

I think of John and Ruth. If they were a pie, he was the crust, and she was the whipped cream topping. He was opinionated and crusty and loud and boisterous, and she was the kind, gentle, sweet organ player in the church. They both grew up during the Depression. It hardened John yet made Ruth a sweet saint of gratitude for all she had. After I had been at Lakeside for one year, John said over lunch: "Bring me your resume. You don't deserve this! We're gonna find you another church!" I stayed another 19 years, and God blessed us both! Ruth once played the organ on a Sunday night, and I know I have told you this before, but she played *Set My Soul Afire*, Lord when the organ caught on fire. God showed up that night like Isaiah's tongue touched by fire, and when I think of John and Ruth, I think of the love they had for me and God's longing for his best in me, and I think of the fire of God that glowed in their souls and that, in life and ministry, it takes all kinds. And God uses all kinds of people to complete and accomplish his glorious work.

I think of Trudy, who in her 90s went home to be with Jesus, but right before she breathed her last breath, spoke words, her eyes bugging out her head with a sweet smile on her face: "I'm ready. I'll save a place for you." I find myself thinking this is what the Christian life is all about—Christ saving us a place and believing in him and working to make room for his people in churches, in heaven, most of all, and, not the least, in our hearts. Did not the Apostle Paul say of the Philippians, "I have you in my heart"? Lakeside, I say with Paul, "I have you in my heart." I love you and always will.

I have too much to say in terms of gratitude and thankfulness for the great years on my life journey. Anyway, *Trick My Truck* caused me to think of all the changes I will soon embrace. Actually, I am excited, a little nervous, but, all told, ready for the adventure. As change arrives, I will take the advice of a man who lived to be 100. He was asked, "What is the secret to your long life?" Today in this sophisticated 21st century, you would expect an answer like exercise, an apple a day, laughter, friends, broccoli at every meal, vitamins, working in my garden, or a job that I love. The man's simple response, "Keep breathing!"

So, here I am under this old oak tree, writing on the last days of my privilege of service to Christ as pastor of Lakeside Baptist Church. I am going to breathe in the day, the sunshine, the joy of Christ, the memory of yesterday, and the hope of tomorrow. I am going to remember and give thanks and keep plugging along and breathing in the grace of our Lord Jesus Christ in the glory of his future work in Granbury and Georgetown and, I guess, in my own refurbished, renewed, and remodeled life.

Change is in the air, but Jesus never changes. So, I am figuring that God's grace will carry me and the vision instilled by the saints of Lakeside Baptist. And I am figuring that, if nothing else, I will at least keep breathing to see what God has in store for the next 100 years!

Winter

John D. Duncan

Adonais

Ah, woe is me! Winter is come and gone,
But grief returns with the revolving year;
The airs and streams renew their joyous tone
The ants, the bees, the swallows reappear;
Fresh leaves and flowers deck the dead Seasons bier;
The amorous birds now pair in every brake,
And build their mossy homes in field and brere;
And the green lizard, and the golden snake,
Like unimprisoned flames, out of their trance awake.

Percy Bysshe Shelley

Under the Old Oak Tree

I'm sitting here under the old oak tree, thinking of a skunk I saw just the other day. You don't just see a skunk; you smell it. That day, I wasn't under the old oak tree long. I high-tailed it out of there. I hate it when foul-smelling animals force me from my lovable spot under the old oak tree.

Somehow my fast-footed journey into my house brought to remembrance old John.

John, where are you?

In the days of my pre-adolescence, it was John who lived out in the country in a big red-brick house with tall, white colonial columns. My old friend John played the drums, and I was with him in our band in the sixth-grade talent show. Never mind that we dished on *The Age of Aquarius*.

John's claim to fame was not his spread of land that made us all think he was rich, or his exquisite house with fine furniture, nor his razzle-dazzle drum skills, which, by the way, got him his own bedroom in the fixed-up garage. His parents put him there so that he could practice. Boy were those drums loud!

John's claim to fame was his foul smell. Near the end of our sixth-grade year, John came to school smelling like a skunk. You see, one day, a skunk maneuvered its way inside John's fixed-up-garage-of-a-really-cool room. The little critter inched its way into the room through a small opening. John stood on the bed, yelled, "Glory hallelujah!" and shouted for help. Since help was slow in coming, he begged for the Second Coming of Jesus!

Oh, what fun John and his parents had in ridding the red-brick house of an unwelcome guest. I never heard just quite how they caught the varmint. It must have been exciting to watch! But I'm sorry to say, everybody in the whole school knew John. We smelled him for the rest of the school year! And every time

John D. Duncan

I run from a skunk out here in these Texas hills or see a dead skunk in the road, I think of John.

And when I think of John, I often remember that the Apostle Paul said, "For we are a fragrance of Christ to God among those who are being saved and among those who are perishing" (II Corinthians 2:15).

So, put on the fragrance of Christ and steer clear of skunks. And be sure, if you turn your garage into a bedroom, fill in all the holes! Because you never know when a skunk might show up looking for a place to sleep!

Christmas Reminds Us of What's Really Important

I'm sitting here under the old oak tree, wishing for snow, anxious with wide-eyed wonder about the glory of Christmas, and wondering about Bethlehem's birth 2,000 years ago. Today Bethlehem is closed off because of Mideast tension. But long ago, God's Light burst into the darkness on a starlit night. I sit here under this naked tree and imagine that first Christmas long ago.

The weather report traveled through the villages of the Judean hills. An innkeeper shared the report with weary travelers checking into their rooms. Caesar Augustus declared a census. Thus, travelers went to their homelands to register for the tax. The law required it.

As the travelers entered one by one, the innkeeper asked each one who registered where he had come from and what the weather was like. He could then check the wind to know the weather report.

The weather report in Bethlehem included a biting chill of the north wind. To the north, among the cedars in Lebanon, snow. To the east, warm air for one more day. To the west, mild days with cold nights in the desert. And to the south, thunderstorms from the meeting of north and south in the fury of two opposite weather fronts. But in Bethlehem, the cold north wind whistled.

The innkeeper went about his duties late into the night. Weary travelers lugged their small sacks of clothing into their rooms. The talk was of the weariness, the weather, and a common lot of cursing Caesar for requiring a census.

"I guess there are two things we can be sure of with the Romans in charge," groaned a traveler as he spoke to the innkeeper. "We can be dead-set sure of death and taxes! Ugh!"

He carted off to his room. Another traveler came to register at the desk in the inn. "Need a big room for our family of seven," he requested. The innkeeper went through his usual list of words: "What's your name? What's your address? Sign your name. Pay the nightly rental. Place your animals in the stall. Breakfast will be in the lobby early in the morning. What's the weather like where you've come from?"

Responses appeared standard, common lot in the language of passage--small-time greetings, empty talk about nothing but room numbers, cold fronts, and tying the donkeys so they still could reach the hay. The talk remained insignificant until one guy blurted out in response to the usual list of words: "The weather ain't too bad, but I noticed an unusual star, the brightest thing I've ever seen. Crazy thing is, I could have sworn the star shone right over this little village. Anything happening around here of great importance?"

"Nah! No way. Boring, unless you consider that a young couple, Joseph and Mary, I think their names were, had a baby boy two nights ago. He's cute, but if you've seen one baby, you've seen 'em all. So, to answer your question, no, nothing of importance ever happens around here. All I do is collect the rent and give out the weather report!"

And so it was one night 2,000 years ago, the wind whistled, a star shone, and an innkeeper kept his routine, thinking all along that nothing of importance happened.

The wind, though, blew in a different way, God's Spirit bursting into the world through a babe. A star became neon for magi attending to the news of a baby born. The innkeeper registered his most famous guest unknowingly. And the baby became a sign for shepherds and wise men. And the sign became the Savior who came to bring peace on earth.

I fear we live in a world where people mutter, "Nothing of importance ever happens here." A world where the only news is bad news--court proceedings, drive-by-shootings, fourth-quarter losses, stock-market crashes, and heart-wrenched anxieties. A world covered by a blanket of darkness.

Christmas, though, shatters the darkness. God's wind blows. His star shines. His sign comes. And the angels sing glory!

At Christmas, the important announcement comes, good news casting light over the shadows, "For unto you is born this day in the city of David, a Savior who is Christ the Lord."

John D. Duncan

We Live in a Fantasy World

I'm sitting here under the old oak tree, watching the world go by. I'm remembering a cold January day not too long ago. I recall the words of Gerard Manley Hopkins in the shadows of grief: "Away grief's grasping, joyless days, dejection. / Across my foundering deck shone a beacon, an eternal beam."

Then I recall Grover, a man who lost his wife and was left alone.

I stood with my hand on Grover's shoulder. His aged body leaned from years that had weakened his knees. His eyes glazed from sleepless nights. Tears trickled down his cheeks as we stood by the casket of his deceased wife. I thought I smelled alcohol on his breath as he spoke.

I didn't really know Grover. The funeral home called me to preach his wife's funeral. "No church affiliation," the funeral home director uttered. I'm sure he had made the same call hundreds of times. The funeral home director explained how the family had no money but wanted a Baptist preacher to give the eulogy.

Grover looked at his wife, muttering something under his breath. Then he turned to me. Up to this point, I felt invisible, unnoticed, unseen as friends and family filed by the casket. At times preachers can feel like flowers at a funeral--background scenery that people look past.

I took my hand off his shoulder as Grover spoke: "We live in a fantasy world, but when reality hits, it's hard."

We said our goodbyes. We departed--he into his world; me into mine. But I could not shake Grover's words in a moment of grief.

"We live in a fantasy world." Walt Disney created an entire entertainment market with fantasy. He delivered into our homes such classics as *Mary Poppins, Peter Pan, Cinderella, 101 Dalmatians, Beauty and the Beast, Lion King,* and *Gordy.* Fantasy abounds.

These fertile fantasies unfold. Umbrellas create lift better than any helicopter. A man in green tights makes children fly into an imaginary world. A cleaning lady puts on a glass slipper and marries the prince. A family keeps 101 spotted dogs in their house. A beast becomes a beauty. A lion becomes king and saves the world from laughing hyenas. And a pig talks, eventually oinking his way into corporate success and fame. While we worry about fat grams and the ozone, pigs stake their claim on the world! Who can distinguish between fact and fiction, fantasy and truth?

Most of us live with harsh reality. Children don't fly. They throw Spaghetti on the carpet. They mess in their diapers. They scream for candy in the checkout line at Wal-Mart. Reality tests our nerves.

Cleaning ladies don't marry the prince. They dust. They clean the toilets. They mop. Their backs ache. Reality gets our hands dirty.

People don't keep 101 dogs in their house. At least they don't where I live. Can you imagine the smell? Who could afford that much Alpo? Besides, you'd die when 101 Dalmatians came to greet you and lick you when you came home after work. Reality is a wet lick across the face. Gross!

I should say, though, beasts do show up in our neighborhoods. This is the guy who dates your daughter. Lions interrupt quiet mornings, that grumpy roar you wish to send back to bed. And pigs have a way of making their presence known--in teenagers' bedrooms where clothes cover the floor; in politics where indiscretion embarrasses us; and in the entertainment industry where pigs stink up our culture. Reality sickens the soul.

Grover is right; reality is hard. Ask a mother whose child is manning a gun in Israel. Ask a child in Israel who awakens afraid in the morning. Ask a woman in labor. Ask a family who realizes the checkbook runs bone dry before the bills are paid. Ask a patient in a cancer ward. Ask Grover. His wife died.

Grover continued: "I don't handle reality well. This (death) makes you think about reality."

Funny how life works, isn't it? You can fantasize all day without a care on your mind. But reality jolts you, and you carry the weight of the world. You cannot get it off your back. It plagues your emotions.

Henry David Thoreau was wrong. He said, "Be it life or death, we crave only reality."

The 21st century is different. Computers can sound byte and gigabyte us into a world unlike our own. Movies cause us to wish for a make-believe life. Three-D sends us zooming into a world that looks real but is not. Be it life or death; we crave fantasy. Reality is hard. Reality is a cruel dancer that kicks its heel into your shin. Ouch!

Grover, old buddy, I remembered your parting words: "Why don't you talk on that sometime?" I took your advice. I'm talking on it.

You see, Grover, we who live in God's kingdom have a way of dealing with reality. His name is Jesus. He only asks that we follow him. As we get to know him, he invites us to look within ourselves. Pretty soon, we realize we're sinners. We learn to love God. We grow to love our neighbors, our enemies, even the boss at work. Jesus fills us with love, joy, peace, patience, gentleness, kindness, and a lot of other good stuff necessary for a joyful life. Sounds like fantasy, doesn't it? But it's not. It's real. Why? Because Jesus is real.

Now, what about reality? We face it every day, Grover. Even those of us who follow Jesus have to feel that painful kick of reality. The car won't start in the morning. The roof leaks. Robbers ransack the house. The washing machine floods the den and ruins the carpet. A doctor gives us bad news. The kids don't mind. The body won't get up and go like it used to. Death invades our lives.

Reality, though, whispers in our ears. Jesus reminds us: "I will never leave you or forsake you. Fear no evil. I am with you." And when he does, doubt gives way to faith. Pain surrenders to comfort. And death bows to life.

When life happens, the kind Jesus gives, we can handle reality. Jesus provides the strength to handle it. We don't crave reality. We don't crave fantasy. We crave Jesus. And when we do, Jesus eases the sting of reality's hard kick.

And, Grover, when you die, heaven's door opens. You enter a land with streets of gold, walls of jasper, crystal-clear rivers, and angels singing. "And God will wipe away every tear from their eyes; there shall be no more death, nor sorrow, nor crying. There shall be no more pain, for former things have passed away" (Revelation 21:4).

Until then, God shines his eternal beam. Now, that's no fantasy!

John D. Duncan

Letting Go of Great Treasure

I'm sitting here under the old tree, watching cars pass by. I'm remembering the car I wished I'd kept if only I'd been smart. Hear the story and think of all the things you wish you would have done because if you'd done them, you'd be rich or at least have an antique car to show to your friends. Or think of all the foolish things you've done in your lifetime while rattling your brain with that game called "If only ...."

The year was 1977. America inaugurated Jimmy Carter as its 39th president. Two 747 airplanes collided in an awful mid-air collision over the Canary Islands, killing 570 people. Human rights buzzed as the hot topic. "Roots" attracted more television viewers than ever for an entertainment program. Walter Cronkite gave the evening news. The Eagles toured America singing *Hotel California*. Elvis Presley died. *Close Encounters of the Third Kind* pleased wide-eyed movie-goers. And Roger Staubach and Tony Dorsett led the Dallas Cowboys on a *Super Bowl* run.

1977 was a monumental year, my sophomore year at L.D. Bell High School. I took driver's education, learned the finer points of city driving from my brother, and received the keys to a white one-owner heirloom passed down from my father--a 1966 white Ford mustang. While my mother's prayer life improved because she had two teenage boys driving, my father and I spent late 1977 and early 1978 refurbishing our white beauty.

We gave our car a major facelift, two non-mechanics plunging headlong into the trials and tribulations of replacing a leaky radiator. Task accomplished, we clothed the interior with new carpet, painted panels, and added an *Armor All* shine that made the seats glisten in the sun.

A fender-bender, courtesy of adolescent indecision on Bedford-Euless Road, caused a would-be follower to be a sure-to-be tailgater. I greeted my newly found friend, called the police, and exchanged the necessary insurance information to expedite repairs. The small collision injured no one but bruised my pride. The fender-bender forced me to add a fresh coat of paint to the white Mustang. My first car, now achieving the excellence I so desired, became my pride and joy, a treasure to cherish like fine china, a beauty to show off like dolls on display in the window of the local store.

Everywhere I traveled, that old white shining-like-new Ford Mustang caught the eye of many a car-lover. Once, while putting gas in my car at the station, a man offered me $1,500 for my car. In the words of a popular movie, was I foolish enough to say, "Show me the money! Show me the money"? Nope. I simply declined, claiming my father's hard work, good memories, and good gas mileage in the age of gas wars and gas rations. Besides, what would I drive if I sold my only mode of motor transportation? Worse yet, why hand over a family heirloom for a few pennies? Why give up a valued treasure?

Then, I hit my senior year. I went brain dead. I am not sure what caused this malfunction of mind. Was it falling in love with the girl of my dreams? Was it hitting my head in a high school basketball game? Was it "senioritis," that do-nothing, think-nothing, I-can't-wait-to-get-out-high-school-and-get-out-on-my-own attitude rising up ready to conquer the world?

I discussed with my father, of all things, getting a new car. I do not remember how our conversations went, except I said, "I'll take a new Mustang if it's OK." Agreement reached, I surrendered my 1966 white Mustang to the auction block and into the hands of a would-be Mustang-lover who purchased it. My father drove me down to *Helm-Lary Ford*, and I picked out a sparkling new, rust-colored 1979 (my graduation year) *Ford Mustang*. Glory to God and happy trails! After all, my teenage years neared an end; why not celebrate with something new?

Three years later, my 1979 Mustang was for sale, only a shadow of the old white Mustang I wish, to this day, I still owned. I learned a valuable lesson, "There is desirable treasure and oil in the dwelling of the wise, but a foolish man squanders it" (Proverbs 21:20). Only the brain dead give up their inheritance. Fools sell valued possessions. And a foolish son longs for what he does not possess while failing to hold and gratefully cherish what he does possess.

Jesus talked about laying up treasure in heaven, where moth and rust do not destroy (Matthew 6:19-20). Paul added: "See, then, that you walk, (should I say, drive, carefully), not as fools but as wise, redeeming the time because the days are evil" (Ephesians 5:15-16). And a man said, "I'll buy your Mustang." And a fool said, "Show me the money." And now I've learned a greater lesson: The brain-dead reject Christ's inheritance. Fools barter the kingdom of God. A foolish son craves stuff while missing out on the Stuff-of-Life.

And the wise? They lay up treasure in heaven. They redeem the time. They cherish close to their heart life's greatest treasure, Jesus Christ. And a wise man said, "Show me the Savior!"

Life Passes Quickly

I'm sitting here under the old tree, thinking of snow. I wish January would drop a blanket of snow on Texas. The cold wind blows, and the sun rises high here by the tree. Snow drifts through my mind.

I think of Trudy, the ninety-something sweetheart whose head was draped with gray. 'Your hair looks like snow,' a child once muttered to her grandmother. Trudy's snow depicted wisdom and laughter which flowed from her lips.

I first met Trudy at the XYZ club. XYZ stands for extra years of zest. The delightful Trudy, wearing a plaid shirt with a little bow, grinned and began her typical story or joke, "Preacher, did you hear the one about...." Trudy, never one to be shy, once announced, "I'm a clothes horse. I buy all the clothes I want at Goodwill." Ah, that Trudy!

She told stories like this:

Did you hear the one about the old man and woman who went to the restaurant? They sat down and ordered their food from the menu. The waitress took their order and returned later with their plates of food. She placed a plate of food in front of the woman and one in front of the man. The waitress returned to her station and watched, waiting to see if the couple would need tea refills and enjoy their tasty food. The man began to eat while the woman sat with her arms folded, staring at her husband.

The waitress watched the woman staring at her husband. She noticed the woman was not eating her food. The waitress walked to the table and spoke to the lady, "Is everything okay?"

" Sure," the elderly woman replied.

Again, the waitress returned to her station. She studied the woman as she continued to fold her arms and watch her husband eat while her food sat in front of her.

Finally, knowing the woman was not eating her food, the waitress marched over to the woman and pleaded, "Is something wrong with your food? I can take it back if something is wrong with the food."

"Ah, no," replied the elderly woman, "we've only got one set of dentures, and he gets to eat first!"

Oh Trudy, life of the party, always telling jokes, who several years ago invited me to her ninetieth birthday party where they could not find a cake big enough for all those candles! For Trudy, the joy of the Lord was her strength (Nehemiah 8:10). The strength of the Lord produced uproarious laughter. Like Peter and the first Christians at the nine o'clock in the morning hour in Jerusalem at Pentecost, Trudy possessed the joy that Pentecost critics once mocked, "They are full of new wine (Acts 2:13)." For Trudy, Jesus filled her with laughter.

Laughter subsided at the end of the year, on the last day of the year of our Lord, 2001. I visited Trudy one day. I grabbed a chair and sat down beside her bed. I quizzed, "Trudy, tell me what you're thinking."

Her face drawn up and radiant, her lips pursed yet trying to smile, she looked off at a distance as if she were looking at a picture on the wall. The glaze in her eyes lit up as she whispered through her raspy voice, the voice of a woman who was a true pioneer, the voice of a woman who had lived through the depression and lived to laugh about it, "I just want to go home."

Trudy went home at age 93. The woman who walked railroad tracks while wearing blue jean overalls in her youth, made tank parts for military equipment, repaired holes in pants into her dying days, went home to Jesus. And heaven was full of joy and laughter.

Trudy met Jesus, kissed him on the cheek, and bowed down. Her death, yet, day of eternal life, also became the day she met Allison, or Alli, as friends called her.

I echo the immortal words of Jesus in the shadow of death, "Let not your heart be troubled you believe in God believe also in me" (John 14:1). I hear the words of the Presbyterian preacher George Buttrick rattling in my ears, "Life is essentially a series of events to be borne and lived through, rather than a series of intellectual riddles to be played with and solved."

When Trudy met Alli, I choked down tears of sorrow and wailings of joy. Life cannot be solved, for death keeps stalking and arriving on the doorsteps of life. Philosophical riddles cannot be played with because abundant life keeps calling cards with names attached. Life can only be lived through a roller coaster of events and emotions, highs and lows, laughter and sorrow mixed in a bucket of tears.

On Dec. 16, 2001, an early morning phone call shocked me. A strained voice on the phone line muttered, 'John, Alli's been in a car wreck.' I do not remember the rest of the conversation, except a simple, "I'm on my way." Trauma erases the memory.

Life presents surprising contrasts. I found myself reflecting in the next forty-eight hours on strange things. Snow, not the white-capped top of an elderly woman longing to go home, but the snow of Wolf Creek Pass. A blizzard ensued for a few hours in the Spring of 1991. After the snowstorm calmed, Randall, Alli's father, and I were snow skiing in knee-deep powder, which provided an afternoon of delight. Randall and I fought the thick powder on high mountain trails. Randall followed me until suddenly he disappeared, falling into a hole of snow that covered him up. I sat in the snow, laughing and hearing his voice, climbing my way up about twenty feet to help dig Randall out of the snow.

We made it down the mountain that day and still laugh about the powder experience. Randall made me a wall plaque:

" "To Dr. J., The Black Powder & Tree Trail King of Wolf Creek Pass. --Waist Deep Wakeman"

I remembered Alli playing in a camper in their backyard. Frederick Buechner speaks of a room called "Remember" in our minds. I walked through that room. I remembered Carrie, Alli's mother, and the many times my wife Judy and my three girls shopped. I remembered little girls with bows in their hair playing on swing sets and the wooden fort in their backyard.

Life passes quickly. One day you're chewing a pacifier, and the next day you turn "Sweet Sixteen" while parading around a restaurant, the crowd singing "Happy Birthday." One day you learn to ride a bike, and the next day you learn to drive a car. One day your mother takes a bow and ties it in your hair and the next day the bathroom overloads with curling irons, blow dryers, lip gloss, make-up, and colorful hair bows. One day you wish for braces, and the next day your smile gleams with the glitter of silver. One day you cheer, and the next day you tear. Life races. And so, we must walk into a room called "Remember" and cherish life's basics: relationships and the people we love. Umberto Eco says, "Nothing exists that so fills and binds the heart as does love." The apostle Paul summarizes love, "Love never fails."

I reflected on life's rooms where Alli moved and lived: the youth room at church, the gymnastic room, the living room watching rented movies, the cheerleader's room, the schoolroom, the family room, the hospital room.

I arrived at the hospital that cold December night, greeting Randall and Carrie in a storm of uncertainty. A hopeless feeling washes over pastors in times of deep crisis. As I hugged Randall and Carrie, I sensed that feeling yet clung to the hope of Christ. As we went into the hospital room to see Alli, I knew that we were back in Wolf Creek Pass, knee-deep in a hole, waist-deep in the valley of the shadow. Love never fails.

Under the Old Oak Tree

For the next several hours, we prayed, watched, and waited. Alli passed from this life into the next. Alli entered heaven and kissed Jesus on the cheek. Heaven added a new smile; rooms raced through my mind, rooms with pictures: cheerleaders, four-year-old girls sliding down the slide at *Chuck-E-Cheese*, waxed-crayon-pictures on refrigerator doors, and hope of wedding dresses and wedding bells where I, Alli's pastor, would do the honors. Now, though, we're waist-deep in grief: Randall, Carrie, Andy, her brother, family, friends, my family (my three girls with so many rooms to remember), and our church family.

Oh, George Buttrick, solve the riddle: Why? Oh saint in the shadow of grief: Live through the series of events. Love never fails.

I'm here under the old oak tree. The sun shines high. I wish for snow. I am walking into a room called "Remember." Love never fails, but no one ever said love does not hurt. I'm sitting here in a shadow. Life hurts. Love hurts. I'm thinking of the day that Trudy met Alli. I'm laughing. Goodwill shirts draped with little bows.... and dentures! That Trudy! I'm crying.... hair bows and glittering braces! That Alli! I'm just a pastor, but I'm a wild roller coaster ride. I'm gripping the stabilizer bar, Jesus, in a world of riddles and events. My tears fall in a bucket. I am waist deep. Inspiration comes:

> *I tied a little a bow one morn,*
> *'I looked and said, 'Life starts today, rejoice, you're born.'*
> *I tied a little bow one day,*
> *I patted a blond head and said, 'Go play.'*
> *I tied a little bow at first,*
> *'It's off to school and a tear did burst.'*
> *I tied a little bow one eve,*
> *I said, 'Be cool, you see.*
> *Watch out for boys.*
> *Have fun. Enjoy!'*

John D. Duncan

> *I tied a little bow before,*
> *A birthday gift, I gave, Oh Lord,*
> *Oh to have seen,*
> *She was sweet sixteen.*
> *I tied a little bow at noon,*
> *I prayed, 'Dear God, it seems to soon*
> *To call your child home.*
> *But God whispered, 'Come.'*
> *And come she did.*
> *A girl waltzed into heaven with a big, bright smile-*
> *'Here's your bow, dear angel, tie it neatly*
> *And shine for a while!'*

A cool breeze blows here under the old oak tree. It's a world of bows and breezes, of laughter and tears, of sun and snow. When riddles cannot be solved and events cannot find answers, laugh, cry, and walk the room called remember: Love never fails. Jesus never fails. Jesus always loves.

Of Caves and Christmas

I'm sitting here under the old oak tree, thinking about caves. A perfect sunset hand-placed by God hangs on the western horizon. Magenta, orange, purple, and blue combine to form a picturesque sky as if hand-painted by the Master Artist himself. The sun sets low, and caves come to mind. Oh, and it's almost Christmas!

In the days of my youth, our family traveled to my father's homeplace in the mountains of North Carolina. One evening, as was our custom, we met Donald and his boys for a Jeep ride up the rugged mountains. We stopped at Chestnut Flat, a huge, cavernous hole in the side of a rock. We walked into the cave and felt mother earth sending a chill in the cool, musty cavern. A small pond sat back in the cave, where waters chilled a watermelon placed earlier in the day for our devouring at that moment. We sat around and picnicked. Of all the things I remember and forget, why do I remember this as if it happened yesterday? Cold watermelon in a chilled cave!

On another occasion, we trafficked the mountains and stopped at what appeared to be a hole in the ground just big enough to fit a body through. The Jeep stopped. Old Donald turned off the lights. He loved to scare my mother like "boo!" in the night. Darkness pierced the night. An eeriness hovered for a moment. Crickets chirped. June bugs buzzed. Some bug noised in the distance, a long, drawn-out whine in the darkness. Where was the light?

Donald turned on a flashlight, dropped us one by one into the cave, and led us by light through the cave. Might we get lost? Do you know the way out? Where are we? Where are you? Suddenly, with a chuckle, old Donald turned off the light. Darkness blackened the night. Who's there? Should I try to grab a hand? Whose hand? Can someone get me out of this dark, claustrophobic cave? The night clamored for light. Where was the light?

Old Donald turned on the light, and before long, we were out of the cave, back in the Jeep with the headlights on, driving down the steeply sloped mountain to home. Of all the things I remember and forget, why do I remember the steep slope? The Jeep headlights shining on the ground and the ground with stone shining like glitter on the kitchen floor? Why can I not forget the eeriness of darkness? Caves and dirt with glitter and flashlights turned off!

Oh, it's almost Christmas. Am I, like you, thinking of loved ones long since gone to glory? Those precious memories lingering in the brain, hanging around long enough to create a little nostalgia and cheer time memories in the middle years of life? After all, Christmas, for all its joy, pushes up old minds' meanderings of sadness and happiness like daisies popping up in an open field.

Oh, it's almost Christmas. Darkness pierces the night. In Afghanistan, soldier boys and girls huddle in cold tents waiting for what's next. Sophisticated high-technology tanks wired like Gameboys prepare for battle in the Middle East. Government security guards remind us of terror at airports in big cities like Dallas. How strange they peek in purses and backpacks for tweezers and fingernail clippers when scud missiles wait in the lurch. And in our town, a lady was found in her front yard, murdered, but no one seems to know why.

Life's question lingers: Why? Why does anybody anywhere die? Darkness drapes the world with an eeriness like flashlights turned off in a black cave beneath the earth's surface in the mountains. Why do mountain people always call it "the mountains?" Do these mountains have a name? Hey, do you need a hand in the darkness?

Oh, it's almost Christmas. In a cave in Bethlehem, also known as a stable in which stinky animals and camels and goats and sheep and hay and refuse and an awful smell like the one in your barn right now, in a cave, Jesus entered the world. C.S. Lewis called this birth of Jesus the "Grand Miracle." Fourth-century golden-mouthed preacher John Chrysostom called it "the mystery." Jesuit priest Alfred Delp called it "the shaking reality of Advent," speaking of golden threads connecting heaven and earth and a golden seed that should shake our lives up. German theologian Dietrich Bonhoeffer called it "the coming of Jesus in our midst," adding, "The coming of God is truly not only glad tidings, but first of all frightening news for everyone who has a conscience." That Bonhoeffer can scare you like a loud "boo!" in the dark, but he always got around to the good news and glad tidings of the gospel. He journeyed the darkness to get to the Light.

Oh, it's almost Christmas. A season of shopping and parties, bows and Christmas trees, and lights, like the ones people string on houses as they do on our street to get rid of the darkness.

And so, I am thinking of caves and Christmas, of watermelon and decorated Christmas cookies, of Jeep rides and house lights, of flashlights and a babe crying in a cave, of crickets chirping and pitch-black darkness, "the mountains" and Bethlehem, and for the life of me I cannot move my mind off of the glad tidings of Light.

The people who have walked in darkness have seen a great Light (Isaiah 9:2). And I'm glad to say to you right here and right now that for all Jesus' coming, he came to deliver Light and to give you a hand in the darkness. Oh, it's almost Christmas!

John D. Duncan

The Kingdom of Heaven

I'm sitting here under the old oak tree, pondering heaven. John in the Revelation heard a loud, mega voice from heaven. He saw a white horse when he peeked into heaven. He even described the New Jerusalem as a delightfully stunning city of splendor with precious stones and swinging gates and walls and numbers like 12 posted and a Lamb in its midst.

Jesus spoke fondly of the kingdom of heaven. He likened it to the grain of a mustard seed that grows and to leaven that quietly works its magic deep beneath the surface of a loaf of bread. Jesus referred to heaven as a treasure like one hidden in a field or like one marvelously treasured pearl of no small sum in price. Jesus said the kingdom of heaven was like a net that gathered fish that was later divided. Jesus had a way of painting a picture of heaven with the common stuff of life.

Jesus' most striking comment about heaven involved talk of angels. He told of "angels always beholding the face of my Father who is in heaven." I wonder what heaven looks like. At least we know where angels look.

Supposedly, Billy Graham once said there would be golf in heaven. He noted that we would enjoy all the pleasures we enjoy on earth in heaven. I am not so sure. C.S. Lewis remarked, "Joy is the serious business of heaven." Joy in heaven, that I can see. The way I play golf, I would not envision golf as joy in heaven or the joy of golf. It is, of course, just a personal opinion, with all apologies to Billy Graham.

The reclusive poet Emily Dickinson contrasted an atom that fell and the heavens that held. She wondered as a child, "Why heaven did not break away-And Tumble-Blue-on me." Like Chicken Little, she feared the blue heavens might fall on her head like a sky. Do you think of heaven as a colorful place, say, hues of blue?

The enigmatic football player Pat Toomay, a once upon a time Dallas Cowboy defensive end from the ghost of Super Bowls past, told of the time he went to play for the Oakland Raiders, and to his shock and surprise, his new coach gave him a day off. He thought, "This never occurred to any coach I ever played for. .... I'd finally found football heaven." Trust me, a tee time on the golf course in heaven, maybe, but football? All I can think of is Pat Toomay sensed that heaven was a wondrous surprise. Truly, heaven must be full of surprise, like a day off from work.

Speaking of surprise, little 4-year-old Jordan stayed at our house the other day. My wife completed chemotherapy recently. She sat in a recliner with no wig and a bald head. "Jordan," my wife said, "where is my hair?" Startled as he studied a bald-headed woman, he shouted four words, child-like words with pizzazz, "It went to heaven!"

Hallelujah! There will be hair in heaven. After all, Jesus said the kingdom of heaven is like a child: "Whoever does not receive the kingdom of heaven as a child will by no means enter into it." Grab your hair and hang on!

Not long ago, Pearlie entered heaven. The octogenarian, sweet with pursed lips, called me and another church staff member to her house on Christmas morning. Throat cancer ravaged her body so that she coughed and talked through a small round tube stuck in her throat. She smiled a sweet smile and unfolded the drama. She whispered, "A big bird came with white wings and hovered over me. It was beautiful!" Did she look into heaven? Was she seeing precious stones and gates with locks, keys, and walls like China's Great Wall? Or did heaven illumine her eyes with tiny mustard seeds, stringed golden pearls, fishing nets, golf balls, or shades of endless blue tumbling like snowflakes on a winter's day? Or did she see a white horse with a rider, maybe a white-winged horse that hovers moments before God's final calling? Did she see angels whose faces with eyes riveted turned toward the Lamb?

I left Pearlie's house that Christmas with thoughts of wonder. What does heaven look like? Several days later, Pearlie begged Jason, her nurse, to come by her side as she sat in her chair. "I am going to bed now, and I am not going to get up. I am being called." She slowly made her way to bed, lay there for a few days, sucked on crushed ice, grabbed the hands of visitors, smiled sweetly, and never got up. The final call came. She slipped silently into heaven's pearly gates, welcomed by angels whose white wings fanned and whose faces shone toward the Lamb.

Heaven staggers my imagination. Staggered himself, C.S. Lewis whispered of heaven, "The apostles themselves, who set foot on the conversion of the Roman Empire, the great men who built up the Middle Ages, the English evangelicals who abolished the slave trade, all left their mark on Earth, precisely because their minds were occupied with heaven. Since Christians have largely ceased to think of the other world, they have become so ineffective in this. Aim at heaven, and you will get Earth 'thrown in': Aim at Earth, and you will get neither."

That C.S. Lewis! Ah, that Pearlie! I am working on not being ineffective in this world. I am aiming at heaven. I look forward to the day I see Pearlie and a host of others, including my Grandmother Ruth, in heaven. I cannot wait to see hair—everywhere! I cannot wait to see the Lamb, "whose head and his hairs were white like wool, as white as snow; and his eyes were as a flame of fire" (Revelation 1:14). Or, in the words of the contemporary band Mercy Me, speaking of heaven, "I can only imagine."

Prospects for the New Year

I'm sitting here under the old oak tree, treasuring the prospects of a new year. My mind pulsates with the pleasures of ministry and a simple goal for a new year—to make more personal visits as a pastor.

My great Uncle John lived in a small town in South Louisiana for over 35 years. He makes his living as a medical doctor. He learned the art of medicine in the Navy. He treated soldiers at Normandy during World War II.

As a child of no more than 6 or 7, I remember riding with him somewhere in the last '60s when he made a house call. Do doctors still make house calls in the 21st century?

I stepped out of the car and walked beside my uncle. Rain fell. The rain fell on huge trees in front of the house, huge South Louisiana bayou trees tangled with vines and drooping limbs bending to kiss the ground.

We walked up the steps, stood on the wooden porch, and a woman greeted us at the screen door. We stepped inside the house, and my physician uncle disappeared carrying his black doctor's kit, stethoscope, and all.

I stood; I waited while leaning against the wall with my hands behind my back next to the screen door in the kitchen. I watched in silence. Minutes later, my great uncle returned. He spoke a few soft words, and we journeyed into the rain under the dripping South Louisiana bayou trees and into the car that felt like an umbrella. That is all I remember.

Do doctors still make house calls in the 21st century? Do preachers still make house calls in the 21st century?

My New Year's resolution is to make more house calls.

The ministry unfolds in the drama of three noble things—a tree, a Person, and people. The tree stands tall, a cross covering us from life's storms like an umbrella. The Person lives as the dynamic Christ who rearranges life's priorities and heals the heart shattered by sin, pain, and unexpected attacks on life. The people march in the mud puddles and daily tasks of life as the saints of God or those whom Christ desires to know him as the Saint of saints.

And that stands as the reason for more pastoral house calls: Storms come; the mud creates a mess of life; rain drips, drips, drips; the cross stands tall like a tree soaking up the storm; Christ makes house calls knocking on the door of the heart, and people need people. The Apostle Paul calls Christ and people needing people, the church. The church is a glorious wonder.

So here I am under the old oak tree. You have heard my new year's resolution.

"For whoever calls on the name of the Lord shall be saved. How then shall they call on him in whom they have not believed? And how shall they believe in him of whom they have not heard? And how shall they hear without a preacher? And how shall they preach unless they are sent? As it is written: 'How beautiful are the feet of those who preach the gospel of peace, who bring glad tidings of good things!'" (Romans 10:13-15)

And how can they hear unless the preacher makes at least one house call?

God and Fishermen

I'm sitting here under the old oak tree, wondering about fishing. Christ loved fishermen.

Last fall, I went fishing in Central Texas on a private pond. The heat of the fall reigned over me and the other fishermen. We ate peanut butter crackers and drank bottled water chilled over ice. Knowing I seldom fished, the teacher instructed me on the ways of baiting the fish and setting the hook.

My teacher placed a rubber worm with glitter on the j-shaped hook and told me to cast my hook upon the waters. The old preacher from Ecclesiastes once wisely instructed his students, "Cast your bread upon the waters, and after many days it will come back." I was casting my hook on the waters in hopes of a fish coming back.

I threw out a fishing line while the sun beat upon my forehead. "Set the hook" kept scrolling through my mind like a message at the bottom of a television screen.

I carefully viewed the surrounding scenery—a rock ledge, a floating tire, seaweed, an upside-down aluminum boat on the sandy shore, a tree waving in the light breeze, a cooler and net in the boat, and fish swimming at the surface of the clear water.

Then it happened. A nibble on the hook sent the line off in a direction opposite the boat.

"Set the hook," scrolled through my brain again.

I jerked the fishing pole—and low and behold; I caught a fish—a gulping fish with jagged teeth and scales and razor-blade fins and speckled skin and a j-shaped hook in the top of his mouth.

My fishing escapade set me to wonder about Jesus' love for fishermen. He called Peter, Andrew, James, and John from their fishing nets. They lived as the sons of Zebedee, fishermen by trade, passionate about gulping fish with jagged teeth and scales and razor-blade fins and speckled skin with meat inside. "Follow me," Jesus invited.

"And they immediately left the ship and their father and followed him" (Matthew 4:22). As they followed Jesus, they became sons of God and so-called sons of thunder. Their faith rattled the earth.

We strung a heavy load of fish that day on the pond. I gloried in the prize of a catch and took digital pictures to prove it. I smelled like fish for the rest of the day.

I find myself thinking about Jesus and the fishermen. He sets the hook in the heart. He glories in fishermen like a prize. He receives them just as they are—stinky fish smell and all. He bids them, "Come, follow me!"

And in the simplicity of his bidding, many follow. After all, the simplicity of following Jesus brings joy, like catching a string of fish.

As Henri Nouwen says, "The loud, boisterous noises of the world make us deaf to the soft, gentle and loving voice of God."

And so here I am under the old oak tree, wondering. On a pond in Central Texas, while setting a hook and catching a fish, I blocked the world's noise out to be reminded of the soft, gentle, and loving voice of God: "Come, follow me!" Will you?

Hope Abounds

I'm sitting here under the old oak tree, pondering the horrors of the devastating tsunami. I find myself grieving at a distance as I observe the pain and misery.

I saw a picture of a girl standing in a crowd of onlookers. She held a sign scribbled with letters: "Looking for lost parents, brothers and sisters." I cannot imagine the pain, the emotion, or, in the poetic words of W.B. Yeats in his poem, "The Second Coming," the loss: "Things fall apart; the centre cannot hold / Mere anarchy is loosed upon the world / The blood-dimmed tide is loosed, and everywhere / The ceremony of innocence is drowned."

I think of a little girl who suddenly has to grow up. Her innocence lost, darkness surrounds her, and life leaps forward with fury. Still, hope abounds in human existence.

We live in historic days. History has been made despite the triviality of Dallas Cowboy losses and paying off Christmas debt. According to a government website, the 2004 tsunami appears to be the deadliest in recorded history. The deadliest tsunami before this resulted from an earthquake near Awa, Japan, in 1703 that killed 100,000. Forty-thousand people were killed in 1782 by a tsunami in the South China Sea, and the tsunami created by the 1883 eruption of Krakatoa is thought to have resulted in 36,000 deaths. The deadliest tsunami between 1900 and 2004 occurred in Messina, Italy, on the Mediterranean Sea, where an earthquake and tsunami killed 70,000 in 1908. The deadliest tsunami in the Atlantic Ocean resulted from the 1755 Lisbon earthquake that, combined with the toll from the earthquake and resulting fires, killed more than 100,000. Still, hope abounds in the center of history.

Nature rampages at times and presents itself as a monster on the march—earthquakes, tsunamis, hurricanes, winds that turn over trucks, rains that drench earth while flooding city streets, and fires that blacken places like Yellowstone National Park.

The poet Gerard Manly Hopkins was right, "Nothing is so beautiful as spring / When weeds, in wheels, shoot long and lovely and lush." But he was also right in declaring in despair that life "yields to the sultry siege of melancholy." Life captures us, takes us prisoner, and instigates a sorrowful sadness not soon satisfied. Nature marches like a monster. Pain arrives like an unwelcome guest. Life hurts. Still, hope shines like a ray of sunlight at the center of nature.

Dietrich Bonhoeffer says, "We must continue to emphasize that Christ is truly the center of human existence, the center of history and now also the center of nature."

Jesus simplified life, "Seek first the kingdom of God and his righteousness and all these things shall be added unto you" (Matthew 6:33).

A new year stands before us. Grief looms, relief efforts unfold, dreams generate in the mind, and God invites us into the center of life. In the midst of human existence in its misery, history in its data, and nature on rampage, the hope of Christ still invites us to find comfort and strength. Make Christ the center of your existence—your existence, your history, and your nature.

Tears Tell Tale of Love

I'm sitting here under the old oak tree, thinking of tears. Tears fall between the ears; they fall amid the years.

Just recently, I watched *CNN* detail a train wreck in Los Angeles. A suicidal man parked his SUV on the railroad track in an apparent suicide attempt. He fled his vehicle at the last minute. The parked vehicle derailed a train.

The story unfolds: Two trains derailed; people died; police officers charged the SUV driver with manslaughter, and a truck driver named Dean Jaeschke rescued a victim from the raging flames. The real-life story possesses the agony and ecstasy of life, the drama of the bizarre, and the tragedy of death.

What captured my attention in the story was the ending. The rescued victim from the raging flames later died in a hospital. The truck driver drove home, received the sad news, and shed tears. "It really shook him up," said his wife, Deborah. "It takes a lot to make that man cry, and when he came home, he was crying." Tears flowed like rainwater dripping from a rock.

The poet Gerard Manley Hopkins says, "Now no matter, childe the name: Sorrows springs are still the same." Fredrick Buechner says he saw his mother cry a few times, not so much when she lost her husband to suicide, but in her late 50s, when she had all her upper teeth pulled. When he lost his wife to cancer, C.S. Lewis walked through the "dark chasm of grief." He adds, "You can't see anything properly while your eyes are blurred with tears." Tears tell a story.

Just the other day, I performed a wedding ceremony. The bride cried while the groom smiled. I witnessed a lady sobbing during a worship service. I watched a 6-year-old cry after falling on a basketball court. I observed a man cry when telling me about his estranged wife. I must confess sometimes I cry: when my daughter went off to college; visits to cancer patients at hospitals; and at the end of emotional movies like The Notebook. Tears reveal the story of life.

This tearful discussion leads me to this: Jesus wept (John 10:35). When tears trickle, it tells us of love. Jesus wept because his friend Lazarus had died. Jesus even wept over the city of Jerusalem because he loved the people so much. Tears reveal Jesus' love.

So here I am under the old oak tree, thinking tears. Dean's story reveals love. Tears speak to the passion, emotion, and even the stress of life. Healthy people cry. Tears cleanse the soul. Dean cried because of love. That's why I sometimes cry and, probably, you, too. Mostly, it's why Jesus wept. He loved. And it's probably why he weeps even now. He loves you.

Now, those kinds of tears aren't so sad after all, are they?

A Priority on Service

I'm sitting here under the old oak tree, thinking in this warm winter of roses, Shakespeare once opined: "What's in a name? That which we call a rose by any other name could smell as sweet." Speaking of sweet, for all University of Texas Longhorn football fans, the hype, the drama, the game is finally over. Texas won the Rose Bowl and the national championship.

What struck me about the game was the intensity, the challenge, and the level of competition. In competition, winners and losers emerge, and Texas wins. The University of Southern California loses. Vince Young, the quarterback for Texas, works his unbelievable magic, and his Texas Longhorns win the championship. Winning brings smiles. Winning means you have gained control. Winning means you have dominated. As legendary Notre Dame football coach Knute Rockne once said. "Show me a good loser, and I'll show you a failure."

The Roman world of the New Testament possessed powerful energy for domination. Roman emperors delivered pax Romana, Roman peace. Never mind that Roman peace meant total destruction and the rebuilding of a city with Roman customs. The Romans did this with a city like Corinth, destroying it and building it anew as a Roman city. If you read the New Testament closely enough, you will find that the political struggle in the days of Jesus between Jews and Romans in Jerusalem centered around the desire of the Romans to dominate and change Jewish culture into Roman culture. Politics defined means that the art and science of government make policy to win control. The Romans were good at it. Jesus wielded powerful words against domination and control, "The greatest among you shall be your servant."

"Where is he going with this column?" you might ask. One thing I ponder here under the old oak tree from day to day is the state of the church. In life, there are winners and losers. Churches rise in the glory of glowing reports—record baptisms, striking numbers for attendance, building campaigns, and sermons served up with style so much that people race home to download a copy on the Internet. Churches also flame out for lack of vision, dissension, poor leadership, fatigue, apathy, or lack of volunteers. It is not that hard to forget the cross and the church's purpose to honor Christ in church life today, whether a church rises or falls. However, what strikes me is the focus today on power, control, and even domination. Reality dictates the necessity of winners and losers. A view of church life necessitates the struggle of churches on the rise and the anguish of churches on the fall. Both pressures can be enormous for pastors, church leaders, and the people who form these churches. What is the answer?

More churches would rise higher, few churches would fall deeper into despair, and more would be done for God's kingdom if power, domination, and control would give way to service.

Fires have burned out of control in our community recently. Wildfires have chewed up land and consumed homes. A local volunteer firefighter was asked, "What makes you want to risk your life as a firefighter fighting these fierce. windswept fires?"

"I just want to help," he replied as the sweat and black soot decorated his face. When the church takes up the banner of risk and gives its all to serve Christ for his kingdom and glory, everyone will win, and no one will lose. If service lessens as a priority in churches, they will die, and everyone will lose.

Here under the old oak tree, it seems like spring, 80 degrees in January. Weather forecasters say change comes soon; a north wind waits to push its way south. May a revolution of change sweep the hearts of Christians and churches. May we voice our words in the spirit of volunteerism like that firefighter. May we heed the words of Jesus, "The greatest among you shall be your servant."

John D. Duncan

Reflection on Tears

I'm sitting here under the old oak tree, thinking of a family from Lake Butler, Fla.—Barbara and Terry, who lost five children and two nieces in a fiery car crash when their car was sandwiched between a school bus and a tractor-trailer. The children's grandfather grieved so hard that he died when he received the horrible news. Friends lit candles, flowers with wreaths decorated the town, and memorial services followed. Residents of the town marched the streets and sang "Amazing Grace." The parents wept and grieved.

Then just recently, here in Texas, a 77-year-old man wandered aimlessly into a deep thicket of woods and could not find his way out for four days. He survived on rainwater and cried out for help for so long that he nearly lost his voice. He said, "Every day, I screamed, hoping somebody would hear me." Tears push out when loneliness surrounds you, and no one hears your cry for help. A police officer found the famished and dehydrated man and rescued him. The man said he did not feel alone because of his faith in God. A blanket of stars comforted him amidst thoughts of death and tears.

Another news story tells us about a baby in Brazil floating in a bag on a lake. Undoubtedly, the baby agonized in trauma and fear somewhere on the journey and wailed dripping tears.

I find myself thinking almost every newscast reverberates with tears—murders, court cases, car wrecks, car bombings, protests, pipe bombs, drug deals, teenage suicide, and athletes in the sadness of defeat sitting on the bench crying because their dream of a championship trophy has died, at least for the moment.

The poets of old often spoke of tears.

- Lord Byron: "We two parted in silence and tears."
- Emily Dickinson: "The soul has bandaged moments."
- John Donne, poet and preacher at Saint Paul's Cathedral in London during the London plague, when funerals were a daily custom: "Drown my world with my weeping earnestly."
- Gerard Manly Hopkins: "Now no matter, child, the name: Sorrows springs are still the same."
- Czeslaw Milosz: "And the sea battering the shore. And ordinary sorrow."
- Alfred Lord Tennyson: "Tears, idle tears, I know not what they mean."

Tears prove healthy, a catharsis, a cleansing like soap and water on the hands. Everyone cries—a skinned knee, a slammed finger, standing at the gravesite of your sweet grandmother, a baby dies before it ever starts living, bad news comes—even tears of joy, celebrating the elation of a goal accomplished or a dream realized. Tears supply life with rain to renew the soul for future days.

I have cried on occasion in my life. The day I took my daughters to college, tears ran down my cheeks, and I was blubbering down the interstate after dropping them off. My 10th anniversary at Lakeside Baptist Church, where I pastor. Every time I took my wife to the doctor the first year after her cancer. Those are just a few.

Sometimes, I lay in bed at night and think of my wife, all she's been through, how much I love her, and Valentine's Day soon coming. And I shed a single, sometimes double, idle tear, the slow drip of a tear that gently slips out of my eye and falls freely on the pillow.

I have talked about tears to say this: Of all the things rarely mentioned about Jesus is this: "Jesus wept" (John 11:35). Preachers often speak of this verse as the shortest verse in the

John D. Duncan

Bible or an easy memory verse. The context is the death of Jesus' good friend, Lazarus, he died. The moment swirled with drama and grief, and Lazarus' sisters said: "Lord, where in the world have you been? Why did you not come sooner?" The Bible succinctly presents Jesus' response: Jesus wept.

Tears mean you are alive. Tears mean you experience love. Tears mean life spits pain. Tears mean that life presents problems and dilemmas. Tears mean that life has joy. Tears mean you remember. Tears mean you wish you could forget. Tears trickle and tickle and flow and go and pour and drip and are salty and real.

The Bible also tells us that Jesus weeps for the city (of Jerusalem). He sees it in its sorrow and sin, and he weeps. He cares.

So here I am under the old oak tree, thinking of that family in Florida, and that man who cried for three days and nearly lost his voice and no one heard, and a crying baby floating on the lake. And I'm wondering if Jesus weeps. I think he does. I know he does. He's alive, and he cares for you!

Grandmother's Simple Faith

I'm sitting here under the old oak tree, anticipating the year to come. On the first of January, I announced to my youngest daughter: "No New Year's resolutions this year! I am not making any New Year's resolutions!" I am not sure why I spoke such words. Maybe because I am weary of resolutions. Maybe because I fear I might break a resolution. Maybe I am bored with the same old resolutions people make—the diet, debt, and discipline resolutions people set as goals every year.

Did you know that 41.3 million Americans belong to health clubs, which increases with the resolve to diet and lose weight in a new year? Did you know the average American has credit card debt of approximately $5,000, and a new year yields a pledge to dig out of debt? Did you know Americans aim for discipline with their new resolutions? They shoot for better education or to stop drinking alcohol or to stop smoking, overeating, or consuming caffeine. All in all, I think all such resolutions are wise and often necessary, especially if the diet, digging out of debt, and adding discipline contribute to a higher quality of life. However, one life coach, whatever that is, noted, "Most people abandon their goals in the first 30 days."

All of this leads to why I am not making any New Year's resolutions this year. I find myself thinking I aim to keep a resolution of old but to keep it fresh and firm. Jesus talked about diets, if you will, when he mentioned fasting. He talked about money, its joys (giving), and dangers (greed) more than any other subject. While telling us to pay our taxes and tithes ("And Jesus answering said unto them, 'Render to Caesar the things that are Caesar's, and to God the things that are God's. And they marveled at him."), Jesus encouraged a discipline of keeping our hands to the plow and not looking back, the discipline of losing your life to find it, and the discipline of sacrifice that leads to service. In a nutshell, I aim to return to the roots of old, the roots of the gospel of Christ in its simplicity and humility.

I am thinking of the year ahead. I make no predictions about disasters in the world. I do not worry about UFOs showing up at airports. I cannot even predict whether the Dallas Cowboys or Dallas Mavericks, or the Granbury High School Pirates will win championships. I can, however, think of the year ahead in simplicity.

My grandmother, Ruth Easter Duncan, lived well into her nineties. Her middle name was Easter because she was born on Easter. Her roots trace back to Scotland, to faith in Christ, in the simplicity of the cross, and to prayer. She lived in the mountains of North Carolina; a town named Spruce Pine that to this day sprinkles the mountain landscape with spruce pine trees. I can tell you she lived a simple life. As far as I know, she rarely left the mountains. She rarely left her home as she aged. She went to church, took care of her family and friends, was good at washing dishes, baking homemade chocolate pie, and was an excellent hanger of clothes on the clothesline. To this day, there is for me no greater smell than that smell of clothes freshly dried in the sunshine and mountain air.

My grandmother also had a garden. I remember visiting her on those summer vacations our family would take. I remember the happiness of playing in the creek behind her white house, the taste of her fresh corn from the garden, the excitement of catching fireflies and putting them in Mason jars with holes punched on the lid, and the exhilaration of sliding down the rail of the stairs in that old house that my grandfather built in the 1930s.

My mind travels back to that garden. My grandmother, bless her heart, would tie a bonnet around her head to protect her from the sun, grab a hoe, and walk through and work the garden slowly, quietly, simply, humbly.

I invited Christ into my life at ten years of age. I remember the circumstances, the moment, the tears, the joy, my baptism in an angelic white baptismal robe at the First Baptist Church of Hurst, Texas, and my first witness about Christ to my friend Matt, who, as it was, turned out to be Catholic, which led to my first real theological discussion. But when I think of yesterday and today and tomorrow and the New Year ahead, I think of that garden my grandmother tilled slowly, quietly, simply, humbly. Her potatoes, green beans that I was forced to eat but did not like, and the sweet corn on the cob that tasted delightful, all which came from her garden, came because she kept her garden daily. She toiled, she weeded, she watered, and she nurtured her crop until the harvest.

When it comes to my relationship with Christ in the year ahead, I resolve to return to the simplicity of faith like a garden. I aim to toil, weed, water, and nurture my faith in Christ daily.

When I visited my grandmother, each night, while a cool mountain breeze wafted through the open window into the room, my grandmother would ease in, sit on the edge of the bed, and whisper in my ear the same prayer ("Now I lay me down to sleep ...") and entrust my life in simplicity to God in Christ by his Holy Spirit.

I aim in a new year to keep to the garden of prayer. Of prayer, George Marshall said, "We must stop setting our sights by the light of each passing ship; instead, we must set our course by the stars." After my grandmother's whispered prayer, I would lie in bed, feel the cool breeze, watch the curtains ruffle in the wind, look through the window on moonlit nights, and stare at the stars. I aim to set my course in the stars in the simplicity of the Maker of the stars.

Simplicity for one in a New Year and humility for two. Peter never dreamed of a basilica named after him or the pomp and circumstance surrounding his final resting place. The rugged fisherman turned fisher of men was brash, bold, boisterous, impulsive, and likely to shop impulsively. If he were waiting in the checkout line at Wal-Mart, he would likely strike up a conversation with the other people waiting in line while handing out his opinions on any subject. As he learned and grew in Christ, his soul nurtured like a garden; he instructed on the importance of humility, "...and be clothed with humility: for God resists the proud and gives grace to the humble" (1 Peter 5:5).

I saw the movie *Rocky Balboa* recently. I like quotes from movies. As I approach a new year, I think of Rocky's words in the struggle of life, in the force of a fight, in the fight for life, or, as a Christian, in the battle for abundant life. Again, I think back to that garden and my grandmother as a young woman living through the Great Depression of the 1930s. I think of humility. Be clothed with humility.

At one point in the movie, Rocky says:

"Let me tell you something you already know. The world ain't all sunshine and rainbows. It is a very mean and nasty place, and it will beat you to your knees and keep you there permanently if you let it. You, me or nobody is gonna hit as hard as life. But it ain't how hard you hit; it's about how hard you can get hit and keep moving forward. How much you can take and keep moving forward."

I can hear my grandmother's prayer, her whisper while the wind sneaks through the window as the mountain breeze waltzes into the room. I can imagine her wrinkled face tilling the garden and how she lived life in simple faith and humility, no neon signs, no me and my, no "Here I am," no song and tune of "It's all about me!" but the simplicity of tilling the garden of her soul in sunshine and rainbows, in clouds and storms, and life punching her in the gut and moving forward for some 90 years and then upward. She died as she lived—slowly, quietly, simply, humbly.

It's a New Year, soulful saint. I have no new year's resolutions. I have no predictions.

I simply aim to till the garden of the soul and learn the sacrifice of service in the soulful song of mountain faith in Christ and put on the clothes of humility.

I aim to pull daily on the rope of grace in the hope of clouds that roll back and bask daily in the sun that shines and wait for the windows of heaven to pour forth showers of blessing in the dark whispers of prayer.

I set my course by the stars.

I pray in the cool breeze of God's grace for grace to keep moving forward.

Maybe that is a New Year's resolution after all. Maybe so. Maybe so.

Happy New Year in simplicity and humility!

John D. Duncan

Unpacking Memory, Nostalgia, and Emotion

I'm sitting here under the old oak tree, thinking about unpacking boxes. The process of moving, transitioning, and changing creates memory, nostalgia, and emotion. As I unpack boxes, the memory, nostalgia, and emotion form tributaries in my mind that flow into the river of change.

First, I think of the memory that moving creates. As I unloaded boxes in our new home in our new town, I stumbled onto a box of baseball trophies. When did I ever play for the Dodgers? I remember the Jets, not New York and Joe Namath of yesterday, but the pee-wee football Jets with red and white jerseys. I remember the spring days of playing baseball in fields of green with bees buzzing, back when I was an expert bunter because I could not hit a fastball from the pitcher. A box of trophies takes up space in a box—the basketball, the football, and the baseball ones, all shiny and dusty and a few with broken pieces, incomplete like a bird with a broken wing. My trophies fill a box, soon to be stashed in the attic.

Second, I recall the nostalgia that moving stirs up. How many pictures have I rediscovered in the process of moving? My daughters' wedding pictures and pictures of places like Hawaii and England and North Carolina and pictures from home and church where people smile around tables stacked with food from potluck dinners? Do churches still have potluck dinners?

One picture stands tall, a chalk sketch of me and a first-grader named Brock standing in front of Lakeside Baptist Church in Granbury, where once upon a time, I served as pastor. The church lay tilted in shades of orange and cream, with Brock and me standing in front of the stained glass in the shadow of the cross, both of us wearing huge smiles like we were licking our chops while waiting for ice cream at the counter or as if we had just seen Jesus riding by on a donkey on Palm Sunday. Come to think of it, standing in the shadow of the cross is not a bad place to stand. Oswald Chambers agrees, "The underlying foundation of the Christian faith is the undeserved, limitless miracle of the love of God that was exhibited on the Cross of Calvary; a love that is not earned and can never be." When I think of Brock and me standing under the stained-glass cross, I can only imagine God's love shining on us like the reflection of stained glass behind a lighted window.

Third, I feel the emotion. Moving is an overwhelming thing. I mean, did our attic hold that much stuff? Do we really need a dozen boxes of stuffed animals and Beanie Babies? And really, does any dear soul place pictures in boxes for future reference in this sophisticated digitized age where people send pictures over waves and wires and where they arrive via the Internet on computer screens? Family pictures and fun pictures like the time you went to Alaska and climbed a glacier and pictures like the first time you rode your bicycle and had no teeth and the pictures when your hair looked bad and pictures of houses with snowflakes in the winter and pictures that make you cry because you remember your deceased grandmother or maybe when life was simple. The digitized world had not taken over, and there was no such thing as a computer or e-mail. Emotion tumbles slowly, like a small rock rolling down a mountainside until it stops when it hits something like, maybe, that ridge in your heart.

Emotion tumbled n my own life in all this moving. My Aunt Mildred died. Life took an expected, but unexpected turn right smack dab in the middle of moving. Expected because she had been in a nursing home for four years; unexpected because, quite frankly, even though she was 83, I thought she had more time on this earth. My aunt Mildred lived in the mountains of

North Carolina. She never married, lived most of her life in the same house, and rarely ventured off the mountain. Life for her was simple things—laughter at the table amid the passing of biscuits, gravy, green beans, and chocolate pie; trips around the mountain on the Blue Ridge Parkway, where often we stopped at a place called Little Switzerland for ice cream; washing clothes in an old-fashioned crank-style machine and hanging them to dry in the sunshine and wind; watching the leaves change an array of colors in autumn; going to get her hair fixed on Friday and catching up on the local news; sitting on the front porch swing and watching fireflies blink in the cool of the evening as the sun set; planting and watering flowers while observing their growth, and attending the red-bricked Pine Branch Baptist Church and singing to the Lord *Amazing Grace* with the gathered saints each Sunday. "These are my people" sounds like a lyric in a country song. Or, as the poet Langston Hughes says, "Beautiful, also, are the souls of my people." Mildred was a simple person who loved simple things in a simple place. And might I add, she possessed a beautiful soul, for beautiful are the souls of my people.

Memory, nostalgia, and emotion form a river that runs deep into my own soul as I unpack boxes. But there are tons of trivia and treasures in those boxes, of junk and stuff. The Apostle Paul, earth wanderer that he was, sojourner who knew how to sew a tent and pack a tent on his missionary travels, referred to stuff as dung: "Yet, indeed, I count all things loss for the excellency of the knowledge of Christ Jesus my Lord, for whom I have suffered the loss of all things, and count them as dung that I may gain Christ." Even Jesus used the word "dung." He told the parable of a farmer who planted a fig tree in his vineyard and found no fruit. The farmer said to the keeper of his vineyard, "What in the world am I finding no figs on this tree?" (my paraphrase). The keeper of the vineyard said, "Leave it alone for a year until I dig around it (to give it air) and dung it (to fertilize it)." So, dung, in essence, is rubbish or refuse or trash, or manure or fertilizer like the kind that turns your yard green when sprinkled in spring.

Dietrich Bonhoeffer adds wisdom, "Earthly possessions dazzle our eyes and delude us into thinking that they can provide security and freedom from anxiety. Yet all the time they are the very source of anxiety." Bonhoeffer is so right. Do you think he wrote that after unpacking boxes?

So, here I am under this old oak tree, thinking and unpacking boxes. I have found memories, nostalgia, and emotion. I have unpacked trash and treasures, junk and stuff, stuff for shelves to behold, and some good for nothing more than making fertilizer to spread on my yard. I have remembered, the past yet anticipate the future because you cannot live in the past. I have reached for the excellency of Christ and yearned for spiritual fruit on my limbs like mouth-watering figs. "My soul," in the words of Langston Hughes, "has grown deep like the rivers," and beautiful are the souls of my people. All told, though, this old oak tree drives deep roots and sprouts green leaves, and so it is with life. And I have concluded one more thing as I stare at unpacked boxes: I have way too much stuff. So, live in his joy and bask in his glory and, every once in a while, give stuff away or at least have a garage sale!

John D. Duncan

Merry Christmas, Ross Wolfe

I'm sitting here under the old oak tree, thinking about Christmas and wondering, in the spirit of the season, about Ross. Where are you, dear brother? Ross, I wish you a Merry Christmas.

You sent me a letter, and I lost it while moving to a new town. You would understand if you had seen the 6,000 pounds of stuff, file cabinets, and hundreds of books and papers stacked high that the movers moved to my new office. I dug deep for your letter, but to no avail. In fact, you have, through the years, sent me letters.

You once sent me a letter that began, "I'm fine, and it's really a blessing in jail." Were you the Apostle Paul writing your epistles from jail and naming them your prison letters? Were you Dietrich Bonhoeffer writing "Letters and Papers from Prison," glorious words like Bonhoeffer's own, "Jesus does not call men to a new religion, but to life"? Or were you in prison because you once stated, "I messed up again"? Ross, I hurt for you and long to see you and thank you for your letters, and I wish you a Merry Christmas.

Your last two letters stated the same thing to me that you aimed to be free again, of alcohol's demon pain, of jail, and of a clouded past to sing again at *Rinky Tinks*, a small ice cream parlor on the square of a small Texas town. Are you writing songs and singing again?

Oh, dear brother, you can sing. I will never forget you once told me you played piano for the opening act for Ray Charles. "For Ray Charles?" I quizzed you as I could think of only one thing: "Georgia On My Mind," which, incidentally, was the name of one of your friends. Your face glowed like an angel as you shared the Ray Charles good news, happiness nipping your nose like you were a child who had unwrapped a toy at Christmas.

I will never forget that twice you gave me CD recordings of your melodic music, *Ross in Memphis* and *Every Day I Praise the Lord*, a CD which has the picture of a beautiful white church with a tall steeple and trees with green leaves and a price tag still on it of $18.48 plus $1.52 tax. How did you arrive at the price? Did I ever pay you the $20.00? Are you attending a tall-steepled church that sings Christmas hymns during this season? Are you still singing *Every Day I Praise the Lord*? Do you know it is almost Christmas, Ross?

Ross, I will never forget your sweet grandmother Opal, the sweetest lady on this side of the Jordan and Brazos Rivers, this side of the moon and the earth. She prayed for you and told me so with a crinkled forehead of concern and prayed that you would walk the narrow road, and she yearned for you to sing the songs of God's amazing grace. She begged God that you would live with the Christ tune of joy vibrating and making rhythm in your heart. She loved you, and how wonderful it is to have people praying for you with hearts pouring out love. She prayed that the devil's hand would not strangle you, but that God's hand would guide you and keep you free.

I will never forget you sent me another letter about your new song, one that I believe you entitled, "Bump it on Down, Devil." In another letter, you stated that you were in "my lowest time" and longed to "Think about COMING HOME." I noted you put "coming home" in capital letters and felt you lived on the edge of despair and hope, on the edge of homelessness and wanting to go home. Despair filtered in your soul, in the words of the Psalmist, "I cried out to God with my voice—to God with my voice; and he gave ear to me. In the day of my trouble I sought the Lord; My hand was stretched out in the night without ceasing; My soul refused to be comforted" (Psalm 77:1-2).

"Despair," Victor Frankl once wrote, "is suffering without meaning." Despair gave way to fear for you because, in your lowest state, maybe you were losing all hope. You feared the devil would strangle your soul, and you wrote a song, "Bump it on Down, Devil," as if to say: Despair cannot win; I long to go home; life has meaning.

Can any place be better than home at Christmas? Can life possess meaning in the Christ of Christmas? Ross, are you writing a song of hope?

Ross, one of your letters stated that you wanted people to see Jesus in you. I know you struggled and maybe still do. We all do from time to time. It's called life, a series of events that add up to the sum of all our parts, the misery and mercy, the mess that imprisons us, the glory that sets us free, and the fear and joy. Ross, I wish you a Merry Christmas and know that what you really long for is joy deep in the fiery depths of my soul and yours. "Joy comes in the morning," the Bible says, and after the pain of childbirth. It is birth I am thinking about now, Mary's birth and the joy of Christmas. Did you know it is almost Christmas?

I love Christmas. While the world seesaws on the edge of great fear in a world of terror and great joy in a world where people long to go home for Christmas, I think of Mary's great fear and her great joy in bringing Jesus into the world; of Mary's great pain and yet the joyful celebration of Christ's birth; of Mary when the devil and Herod tried to do all they could to keep Jesus from living and legions of angels when they showed up time and time again in the Christmas story, like Clarence in *It's a Wonderful Life*, declaring, "You can live again! You can live again!"

I love Christmas! Ross, have you written any songs about Christmas? Hey, did Ray Charles like Christmas? Did he ever write an unpublished song, *Christmas on My Mind*?

When I think of Christmas, I think of hope, for people to be free and full of joy and love and peace on earth that comes from heaven and goodwill towards men. When Saint Matthew announced the birth of Jesus in his Gospel, the encouraging word was one of hope—for God's presence to lead us home; for salvation from sins and when we mess up; for a star that would shine and lead us to Christ who desires to be worshipped. When Luke recorded the message of angels, their wings glistening like glitter, his Gospel proclaimed an angelic announcement of hope that lights up the dark sky. When John philosophically introduced the child born in Bethlehem as the Word becoming flesh and blood among us, his words became a song of hope for all the nations to sing. Hope reigns at Christmas. Hope sings. Hope shines. Hope hums in the heart. Remember, Ross; your grandmother prayed sweet prayers for Christ's hope to hum in your heart.

Ross, it is almost Christmas. I cannot wait. I hope it snows, snowflakes on Christmas Eve trickling out of the sky like cotton balls floating in midair, racing to the ground to see which one gets to earth first to blanket it with a carpet of snow so that boys and girls and men like me can build snowmen in their yards. Yes, I hope it snows, my dear brother Ross. But even if it does not, I think of you this Christmas and am reminded that Jesus washes our sins as white as snow. The prophet Isaiah said that. And this Christmas, I sing the songs of Christmas joy like angels with God's glory, dazzling onlookers to vibrate my soul with peace and love and hope. And this Christmas, I remember that I need not live on the edge of fear because great joy has come, Emmanuel, "God with us." And this Christmas, I guess many people, Ross, will think, like you did that day in prison, of "COMING HOME."

John D. Duncan

Pliny the Elder in this first-century said. "Home is where the heart is." North Carolina writer Thomas Wolfe said, "You can't go home again." But I have found you can go home again, and home fills the heart, and that the heart can make a home for Jesus, Emmanuel, and if it does, despair goes away, peace comes, joy soars, and love flourishes like flowers coloring a mountain and filling the air with a fresh smell.

Love, God's love, Christmas peace, and Christ's joy are what I send to you this Christmas, Ross. Are you in Memphis? Granbury? Georgetown, Texas? Maybe one day I can see you and your bright smile. Maybe, big man that you are, you will give me a teddy bear hug like you did when you got out of jail, and we met with some men from the church at Jack in the Box. You were so happy on that day.

Maybe you will write a Christmas song and send the words to me in a letter. Write a song about Christmas, despair surrendering to hope, fear bowing to joy, and love finding a way in the bitterness of life in the person of Emmanuel.

Oh, Ross, write a song about snow, star-like flakes falling from the sky like glittering stars streaking from the heavens to paint the earth white. I miss your grandmother, Opal. And, Christmas joy, oh boy, I wish I had thought to tell you to say hello to Ray Charles for me before he died.

And to you, Ross, I say, "Peace on Earth, Goodwill to men, Emmanuel, God be with you." I pray you are happy, dear brother; like the day at Jack in the Box, I pray you are free. I pray that Christmas joy hums in your heart, the dazzling glory of God's grace vibrating your heart with the hum of Christ's hope. Ross, I wish you a Merry Christmas. I hope you think of COMING HOME and that you make it home. Christmas joy, oh boy! Merry Christmas!

www.ingramcontent.com/pod-product-compliance
Lightning Source LLC
Chambersburg PA
CBHW071620170426
43195CB00038B/1497